TIPPER

with Stephen Gleeson

www.**HERO**BOOKS.digital

HEROBOOKS

PUBLISHED BY HERO BOOKS
1 WOODVILLE GREEN
LUCAN
CO. DUBLIN
IRELAND

Hero Books is an imprint of Umbrella Publishing
First Published 2020
Copyright © Stephen Gleeson 2020
All rights reserved

A CIP record for this book is available from the British Library

ISBN 9781910827185

Cover design and formatting: jessica@viitaladesign.com
Ebook formatting: www.ebooklaunch.com
Photographs: Inpho and Tipperary family collections

★ DEDICATION ★

To my daughters Lilly-May and Nora.
And Tipperary supporters worldwide.

★ CONTENTS ★

★ ACKNOWLEDGEMENTS ★

THE FIRST BIG Tipperary match I remember was the drawn Munster final in Thurles in 1987 when Nicky English kicked the ball into the Cork net. I recall being on my father's shoulders behind the goal, and grasping his hair for dear life as the terrace erupted for that goal and, then again, for Pat Fox's late equalising point. This memory came flooding back to me in the process of writing this book.

We hit Killarney after that and the rest is history. It's probably part of the reason I love following Tipp hurling to this day. It amazes me that a ball passing a post can control the behaviour of thousands of people and can decide the mood of a county; until the next game at least.

Tipperary hurling is a passion, something alive within our hearts and minds. All of us have our own standout memories of when sport and life rhymed and flowed. We carry it with us in the slipstreams of our mind and for supporters it has an expression every summer when championship beckons and those clad in blue and gold take the field.

We are blessed in Tipp because we can recall such wonderful moments in our own unique way and share such a love for sport. Hurling is our language.

With this book, I hope to bring you, the reader, back to revisit some of the most memorable moments and matches from the past 70 years, through the stories and memories recalled by hurling legends of Tipperary.

First and foremost, I would like to say a sincere 'thanks for your time' to the 35 brilliant Tipp hurlers who are part of this book. Since 1950, the legendary names within these pages filled Tipperary supporters with joy and hope. My wish is that this 'leabhar' holds, in some way, the majesty of the hurling games that Tipp were involved in across the decades.

Since writing this book, two of the heroes who feature have passed on to their eternal reward. In November 2020, Tommy Butler was buried on the same day as the Tipp hurlers took the field in the championship against Cork. I paid my respects at The Ragg that day, and drove to Limerick for match commentary - and though there was no crowd at the game, you could almost feel his presence in the ether.

Tommy picked a game against the same opponents from 1976 for this book. I was so glad he got a copy of Game of my Life and it was read to him before he died.

A week later was the last time I spoke to Theo English, dropping him an early copy and chatting about life and Tipp's upcoming game against Galway. Theo's chosen game was the 1958 meeting of the same counties. When he passed away early this January 2021, Tipperary hurling lost another icon. I'm so glad I got to know Tommy and Theo and that they are part of this book.

To my publisher, Liam Hayes, sincere thanks for believing that I had the ability to create this book. The support, positivity and encouragement has been so reassuring that I hope this is the first of many!

My thanks to Liam O'Shea and all at *Tipp FM* who shaped me into a hurling commentator and gave me the opportunity to learn on my feet with a game in front of me. It was, and is, a real privilege to commentate on county, Munster and All-Ireland finals.

Thanks too to journalist, Trudy Waters, who I learned so much about communications and reporting from – she urged me to seek perfection in my reporting and find the true story in sport.

Over the years, the buzz of playing hurling has been magnificent and has helped me relate to and develop the stories contained herein. I've learned so much through victory and defeat whilst playing for Upperchurch since the age of 10 and I'm grateful to all who keep the club so vibrant. I continue playing because of the excitement and camaraderie that comes from living in the moment and sensing the magic that the game brings to villages, towns and counties.

To my uncle, PJ Ryan, thanks for the advice and help in getting the ball moving on this book when we visited and sat down with Jimmy Finn at his home in Borris Ileigh.

To my parents, Joan and Anthony, thanks for usually saying yes and supporting me in whatever crazy dream I came up with! Your lifelong support is wonderful. Similarly, the encouragement from my sister, Antoinette, my extended family and friends does not go unnoticed.

I can honestly say too that without my wife, Petra, this book would not have been possible. Her input has been invaluable. I trusted her instinct and professionalism and took her advice too when needed. In the course of writing this book, Petra has been my rock.

I sincerely hope you enjoy this book. It's about the glory of the blue and gold jersey.

Tiobraid Árann Abú!

Stephen Gleeson
February, 2021

JIMMY FINN

TIPPERARY 1-9, KILKENNY 1-8
All-Ireland SHC Final
Croke Park
SEPTEMBER 3, 1950

Jimmy Finn (third from left) and his teammates training for the 1951 All-Ireland final

★ **TIPPERARY:** A. Reddin; M. Byrne, A. Brennan, J. Doyle; **J. Finn**, P. Stakelum, T. Doyle; S.Bannon (0-2), P. Shanahan; E. Ryan, M. Ryan (0-1), S. Kenny (0-2); P. Kenny (1-2), M. Maher, J. Kennedy (0-2). Sub: T. Ryan for Maher

★ **KILKENNY:** R. Dowling; J. Hogan, P. Hayden, M. Marnell; J. Kelly (1-0), P. Prendergast, W. Walshe; D. Kennedy (0-1), M. Kenny; D. Costigan, S. Downey, J. Langton (0-6); J. Heffernan (0-1), J. Mulcahy, L. Reidy. Sub: P. Buggy for Costigan.

THE ACTION

TIPPERARY'S 15TH ALL-IRELAND crown was secured at Croke Park after a dramatic ending to this battle of the giants before the eyes of 68,529 attendees at a game which yielded gate receipts of £6,103-14-2.

This game was like a firework, slow to get going but quite the bang at the end.

Two minutes from time, Paddy Kenny beat Hayden to the sliotar and let fly goalward much to the delight of Tipperary hearts which soared at the thoughts of victory. Four down, Kilkenny stubbornly refused to surrender.

Within seconds the Kilkenny puckout went long to Carrickshock stylist, Jimmy Kelly. Quick as a dart, the ball sailed into the Tipperary goalmouth from 70 yards out and as Mulcahy charged down the Tipperary goalkeeper, Tony Reddin the sliotar dropped until the net shook. Despite protests about an assault on Reddin, the goal stood.

Kilkenny cheering was short-lived and as Reddin sent the puckout skyward Con Murphy raised the whistle to his lips, signalling back-to-back titles for Tipperary.

The champions showed their mettle in the second-half. Kilkenny led by 0-7 to 0-5 at the interval and while the Marble County folk had previously won five All-Irelands by a single point, they couldn't best their superior neighbours who displayed smartness and courage in equal measure.

Tipperary switched Kennedy to left half-forward, Ryan to the left-corner berth and Sean Kenny roamed after the restart which resulted in Sean and Paddy Kenny adding points before a beauty from Seamus Bannon. As the sliotar dropped from the heavens it was met with an overhead shot of the ash stick for a score much to the delight of their supporters. By contrast, the Kilkenny forwards couldn't break down a resolute Tipperary defence, with youngsters, Jimmy Finn and John Doyle both hurling with steel and composure.

Shortly after Tipperary had edged clear in the second-half through that sublime overhead shot from Bannon, a frustrated Langton struck a 21-yard free towards goal but the sliotar flew an inch above the left upright. Then, Buggy attacked again but was denied by Byrne, Finn, Doyle and Tony Brennan as a goal bound shot was deflected out for a '70'.

Such moments decide destinies.

The difference in the end was the leadership of Sean Kenny in the forwards mixed with the steely play of Jimmy Finn, Pat Stakelum and Tommy Doyle on the Tipperary half-back line. That solid line must be commended for thwarting the Noresiders onslaught. The dividend was on the scoreboard at the end.

★★★★★

66

MY FIRST CHAMPIONSHIP game for Tipperary was the 1950 All-Ireland final against Kilkenny. It stands out among all the matches. I was brought onto the team for the final because Seamus Bannon was moved from the backs to the forwards to strengthen them.

That left a space in defence, so I was put in to start at wing back.

I had only played for a quarter of an hour in one league game before then; when I was put in for Pat Stakelum, who got knocked out! 'Twas big at the time to be called in to start the All-Ireland final, more so because I was on Jimmy Langton, and he was *the man* for Kilkenny during that period.

But I wasn't intimidated, it just came ordinary!

Paddy Kenny scored a goal in the last minute to put us four points up. It had been close until then. All of a sudden, Kilkenny scored a goal with a long ball dropping in from near 80 yards!

When that goal went in, Pat Stakelum said to the referee, 'Con… there were two men in the square… and Tony Reddin was taken out of it!'

Con Murphy was the referee, and he became president of the GAA later in life. That day he answered Pat Stakelum with some good words.

'I know that Pat, but don't worry… the match is over when the ball is pucked out!'

He blew it up and we won by a point.

It was a big thing to be on Jimmy Langton but it worked out well because we became great friends after. Friendships can come from playing a game. The Langtons were well known all over; they had the popular pub down the town in Kilkenny where we used to go after the hurling days finished.

Jimmy had relations in the Ragg, near Thurles and there was a sister of his married there so they often visited later in life. We got very friendly with all the Langton family and other Kilkenny fellas too over the years.

There were friendships with those we hurled against from other counties after the hurling days ended, but with Jimmy Langton above others it was special. He introduced me to GAA people all over Ireland, because he knew everybody!

Back then we trained three times a week.

I was farming in those days, and one time I forked 50 trams of hay from 12 o'clock until six and then went training after it. I always remember that day!

Going training I was usually picked up by an organised taxi from Nenagh to Thurles, and after training we'd go down the town for a bite to eat. Phil Purcell trained us and was secretary as well at the time. He organised nearly everything.

His wife, Josie looked after the jerseys and Jimmy Doyle's father was a 'runner' which meant that he was taking in and out hurleys, as well as looking after the team. Purcell always gave a speech before we went out on match days and he had an impediment but there'd be no impediment when he was giving a speech!

Tony Reddin was in goals and his hearing was bad.

In the early stages, Tony Brennan, the full-back, used to tell him when to puck out the ball as Reddin wouldn't hear the whistle. When we went to America in 1950 he got hearing aids and they turned him inside out.

It was great for him; it changed his life for the better.

He hurled with Lorrha, but came from Mullagh in Galway. He was the biggest loss Galway hurling ever had. Seanie Duggan was a great forward for Galway at the time and he was also their second choice goalie. If Reddin stayed in Galway, Seanie would have been full-forward but they had to bring Seanie back to play in goals.

They lost a great forward to the goals and a great goalie to Tipperary!

I watch hurling to this day.

And I was thinking, wasn't Brendan Maher lucky that his knee came right after a bad injury. I was very glad he got to hurl for Borris Ileigh and for Tipperary in 2019.

I got a belt of the ball in the eye in 1959 and I never saw with it since. I got the bang while hurling in a club match against Roscrea and was in terrible pain with it. Lar Ryan, the Lord have mercy on him, drove me down to the hospital.

A couple of hours went by with no doctor, and then this nun came around but there was no rosary said! They got me the doctor then, and took me to the theatre. I had a deep cut into the corner and he stitched it with five or six stitches.

'You're alright now,' he told me. 'You can go home.'

'I can't see,' I told him, before I started to haemorrhage.

They got real worried and got the ambulance right away and sent me to Limerick. I was two weeks in Limerick and I will never forget the pain on the face of anybody who came in the door and gave a look at it.

A doctor came and held up numbers in front of me, like you'd do for an eye test, and that's when I realised I couldn't see with it.

Then I fell back in the bed.

I tried to hurl afterwards with sight in just one eye. We were playing Roscrea in Nenagh and I tried to play that day. I had a great friend, Dick Fogarty who was a doctor in Nenagh at the time, and at half-time he came to me.

'I want to see you afterwards down at the hotel,' he told me.

I went down to meet him anyway and we were having a drink, when he said, 'I want you to do something for me… never hurl again, Jimmy. You were looking for the ball today'.

So I never did.

That was the only game after the accident. My last game.

When we went to America after, I went to an eye specialist who was meant to be the top man in the world, but he could do nothing.

'The back of the eye is injured!' he told me.

But still, I had great sight in the other one.

After all these years, the friendships stand out as much as the games do. In 1950 a writer in one newspaper, John D. Hickey, spoke about *"The Two Babies"* and the way they got on so well. It was John Doyle and myself he was writing about.

Doyle was a year and a half older than me and was a county minor in 1947 when Paddy Kenny captained the minors to the All-Ireland. Doyle made corner-back on the senior team by 1949 when they won the senior All-Ireland. I was on the minors that same year and we won the All-Ireland as well, so winning both in the one year was a fierce big thing.

"The Two Babies" were both playing in Croke Park then for the 1950 final.

Christy Ring was another great friend.

I played against him but I was never really marking him. Back in the 1950s there was a show one day where the dog track is now in Thurles, and I met Christy there. We shook hands and the first thing he said to me was, 'Have you a hurley? Will we go over to the field and have a few pucks?'

So we went over to where Semple Stadium is now, and hurled for the day. The two of us just hurling on the field and talking.

I remember him saying that day, 'You know, you couldn't practice enough… especially as a forward'.

I hurled alongside Christy for Munster in the Railway Cup which was a big thing that time. In 1956, on St Patrick's Day, I buried a grand-aunt of mine and had to go to the funeral mass that morning, and then get to Croke Park to play in the Railway Cup final that afternoon.

I organised a lift, and when we got near Croke Park I jumped out of the car and into the crowds until I got by the Cusack Stand side. They let me in past the first entrance and as far as the dressing-room, where I knocked and waited.

Who opened the dressing-room door, only Ring who says, 'Oh come on quick… come on! We didn't know if you were coming!'

You see, there were no telephones in those days!

Hurling had a huge effect on my life. It was always there as my two uncles, Jack and Ben Finn, played with Tipperary and they had great stories to tell. My uncle Jack played in 1910 and went to Brussels in Belgium for some exhibition games against Cork, called the Tailteann Games.

They won the first game; Cork won the second one on the battleground of Fontenoy. And for the third one the Union Jack was put up in the field they were to play on. They didn't agree with it and there was a kick-up that they wouldn't play until that was taken down, so it was nearly dark when the final was played.

There was a bit of roguery going on!

Jack was the first to bring an All-Ireland medal to Borris in 1913, when junior and senior were the same. He was butchering in Borris and trained all the younger crowd growing up… the Priors, the Kennys and Stapletons. They all turned out good hurlers and the finish of them turned up in 1949 and '50 when we got to county finals and won them.

Back then, the hurley and ball would nearly always be in your hands wherever you went. Borris Ileigh were strong at the time and when we won that county final in 1949 it followed that Sean Kenny captained Tipperary for 1950, because the county champions picked the captain back then.

The next year, 1951, Sean Kenny got injured which meant Ned Ryan and myself were the only two from Borris Ileigh on the Tipp team. Neither of us wanted to win the toss but I happened to win, and so I became the captain which was a fierce big thing for me. There was a bit of luck attached to it all but at the same time, it was almost too much as I was only 19 years-old at the time and a lot of that team had hurled with Tipp for years and were going for three All-Irelands in-a-row!

But it all turned out well, as we beat Wexford in the All-Ireland final. Big crowds gathered in Thurles for the homecoming and Bishop Kinane was there to receive us. Then we had a great night out in Borris after that too.

Ah sure, I had a great hurling career really. I suppose we have memories and records that will never be broken.

THEO ENGLISH

TIPPERARY 4-9, GALWAY 2-5
All-Ireland SHC Final
Croke Park
SEPTEMBER 7, 1958

Theo English and Christy Ring wait for the ball to be thrown in

★ **TIPPERARY:** J. O'Grady; M. Byrne, M. Maher, K. Carey; J. Finn, T. Wall (1-0), John Doyle; **T. English**, J. Hough; D. Nealon (1-2), T. Larkin (0-2), Jimmy Doyle (0-3); L. Keane (1-1), L. Devaney (1-0), L. Connelly (0-1).

★ **GALWAY:** M. Sweeney; F. Spillane, P. Burke, S. Cullinane; J. Duggan, J. Fives (0-2), F. Benson; J. Salmon, PJ Lally; T. Sweeney (0-1), J. Young, T. Kelly (0-2); PJ Lawless (1-0), W. O'Neill, T. Conway (1-0). Subs: E. Derrivan (for Spillane), M. Fox (for Young)

THE ACTION

TIPPERARY SECURED THEIR 17th All-Ireland in impressive fashion seeing off a Galway side that were coming in cold. A bloodless victory for Tipp in this contest will raise questions among hurling folk as to why the westerners were allowed straight passage to the All-Ireland final while Tony Wall's battle-hardened side had to beat the pick of Munster and Leinster en route. A bye into the final, as GAA congress approved, did Galway no favours as two swift and early goals left no doubt about the stronger team.

On a blustery but sunny day for hurling, 47,276 attended which is a far cry from the 84,856 that showed up in 1954. Those that did get to this year's final saw a brief contest. Tipperary struck first blood with a goal coming in under two minutes. The goal was a typical 'Tipperary style' one.

The puckout went to Theo English in midfield. Swiftly it was moved to Donie Nealon, who directed the ball into the pathway of Jimmy Doyle. Cleverly evading his marker, the 'Boy Wonder' lobbed the ball into the square. Appearing in a flash, Larry Keane belted it first time, and the roar went up.

The marvellous teamwork was to be admired. Many sensed it was *game over* as the westerners were jittery and error prone after the early goal. Tipp sensed it and shortly after Wall's long-range effort sailed to the net. Galway, playing with the wind and into the Railway End in the first-half, were under pressure.

Goals were piled on as the champions-elect led 4-4 to 1-3 at the break. Salmon, Galway's best player, was picked up by Theo English in centrefield and that duel was one to feast upon. Time and again English moved quick ball into the forwards as Devaney, Nealon and Jimmy Doyle thrived on it, showing skills close to perfection.

Tony Wall, the outstanding centre-back in the country, once more played a captain's part. Flanked by John Doyle and Jimmy Finn, the trio set the platform for success. In attack Donie Nealon of UCD shined alongside Devaney and Larkin while young Jimmy Doyle is a livewire. Duggan kept as close as he could to him but Doyle's clever pass set Nealon up for the goal that broke Galway hearts before half-time.

★★★★★

"

OF ALL THE games, the first senior All-Ireland win in 1958 is the one I really cherished, because it was my first and at 28 years of age I was wondering was it ever coming. The game against Galway itself doesn't stand out as much as the feeling of victory just after.

There was a lot of quality in that '58 team with the likes of John Doyle hitting his prime, Jimmy Finn, Mickey 'The Rattler' Byrne and Noel Larkin, so it was a right good team. Not having won since 1951 was too long, and if we didn't win it in '58 we could have been moved on and new players brought in.

That's just the way it is in a county used to success.

I watched winning teams growing up.

I can remember being 13 or 14 years-old and cycling to Thurles to see the Tipp team of the 1940s. It was a fair spin from near Clonmel, but was worth it to be watching players like Sweeper Ryan. I had great time for Sean Kenny, as well as Mick Mackey and Christy Ring from that era.

'Ringy' was the best hurler of all time.

Fellas would cycle all over the country to see him play the game. Hurlers are born, not made and with all the training in the world people couldn't do what Christy could, but I did get to hurl alongside two of the all-time greats, in Tony Wall and Jimmy Doyle.

Coming from a football area around Clonmel, my father and others around there never saw much hurling, but the sport was for me. At home I trained by myself most of the time, mostly with the hurley in my hand.

I'd head to a big field four or five nights a week, striking the ball and doing all kinds of sprinting or longer running. I was never in a gym in my life and didn't need to be! Players back then had a natural fitness from physical labour as they were on the go all the time. Most of us were doing physical work daily. I worked with my father cutting timber from a young age until I went working elsewhere.

Going back to 1950, my club, Marlfield did well in the junior championship and I made the Tipp juniors, coming on as a sub against Kilkenny at Carrick. That was the start of it for the county.

I played football for the county too, but loved hurling and after a junior hurling All-Ireland win in 1953 I got the call onto the senior team. By 1958 we had won 3 National League titles but we couldn't get out of Munster and it was hard to take.

We had to do it the hard way in '58, beating a Limerick team called 'Mackeys Greyhounds' before we met Cork. Christy Ring had a broken rib going into that game but that didn't stop him, as he was everywhere!

It was a fierce hard match and we were carried shoulder high after winning it. We had a big following after that. We met Waterford then in the final at Thurles. They had won Munster the year before with the likes of Tom Cheasty who was a big strong player, but we won it well.

Croke Park was packed for the semi-final against Kilkenny; it had the feeling of a final about it. That Kilkenny team had won the All-Ireland the year before. You have to win it one game at a time.

John O'Grady, who took over in goals from Tony Reddin, brought off a great save from Dick Rockett and we pulled away after that. John Doyle and Tony Wall were great in defence, tearing through hurleys; never a bother on them!

Jimmy Doyle went to town. He gave an exhibition, scoring 1-8 out of 1-13. You can check the record books, he scored the same as the entire Kilkenny team that day!

Galway and Tipp met in the first ever final in 1887 and only once after that so it was a rare final pairing and they threw everything at us. They had got a bye to the final but we were sharp and never let them settle. I operated around the middle and kept it moving.

I wasn't letting anyone by me.

We hurled well and tore into it with Liam Devaney, Donie Nealon and Larry Keane getting first-half goals. They had no way back after three goals were scored.

Tony Wall scored one from a '70' that dropped all the way into the goals. We kept going and didn't want to let them back into it, as it was hard enough just getting there!

When it was over I was taking it all in. I played for the honour and glory of days like that, and I cherish those few minutes after the game the most.

Tony Wall and Jimmy Doyle would grace any team before or since. Tony Wall was captain and was great in the backs and ended up Hurler of the Year. As for Jimmy Doyle? You could put him down for 10 points before a game started; the

GAME OF MY LIFE

scores were guaranteed when he played. He was minor hurling captain when he started playing with the senior team the year before. He was slight of build but had fast feet, like a boxer and very few before or since had the skill he had with a hurley and ball. Jimmy trained every day and was the top scorer in the championship that year.

We had a great reception back in Thurles with bonfires lit. It didn't go on for six months though, we were all back at work reasonably soon after. Hurling was for enjoyment and you had to keep your feet on the ground.

When Pat Stakelum was captain in 1949 he took the cup home that night on the bar of the bike!

We had a great man in charge of us. Paddy Leahy was what is now called 'the manager'. They all still say he is the greatest of all time; certainly he is the best ever from Tipp.

Paddy was very popular and was very fair.

If you did what was asked of you and were good enough, you'd be on. It didn't matter what club you were from once you could hurl. He was born in Tubberadora, near Boherlahan, over the road from John Doyle's place. Paddy Leahy was there across decades of Tipperary hurling. He won All-Irelands as a player as far back as 1916, and was a selector too in the 1940s when I was a chap cycling to matches.

Then he was the boss for the All-Irelands from the 1949-51 three in-a row win until the second double in 1964 and '65. His influence is there for decades since. Every manager since is just doing what he started.

Sean Ryan, Jimmy Hennessy and Jim Stapleton from Solohead were selectors too but they wouldn't make a change unless Leahy was there as he was the chairman of the selection committee that picked the team. For training sessions, Ossie Bennett took charge.

Jimmy Doyle's father, Jerry would do the running and organised training matches and then, after, I'd practice the sideline cuts and other lads would take frees. Sometimes we'd have the Blakes from Coolcroo Athletic Club in Thurles doing running with us too.

We were the fittest around and were prepared, but when you went outside that dressing-room on the big day you were on your own. There was no selectors running on to the field having to tell you what to do.

You did your own thing, that's why you were there.

Back in those times I made all my own hurleys.

I made them for other hurlers or whoever wanted them. Ten bob each or six pounds for a dozen! I made them at home and cut the butts as well. I would have an eye on a tree for a while until it was time. We knew when the ash would be ready, be it months or years. Everyone knew where the timber for their hurley came from back then.

Often a few fellas would go together to cut a butt, get it planked out and make the hurleys together. Ash grows best by the river banks they say, and if the soil and climate is right you get better hurleys.

We knew the location of all the ash trees for miles and miles around.

It's different nowadays as a lot of players don't know where the ash in their hurleys has come from, as a lot of the timber is imported or even made from plastic! The ash tree and the hurley maker had a different meaning before.

I always made sure my hurleys were tapered off a certain way for sideline pucks. Every night coming up to a big game I'd go to the field by the house to practice driving the ball down the field so I'd have it right for the sideline pucks. I hurled in All-Ireland finals with sticks I made myself and would often break one or two in a match!

It was common, even in club matches, that there would be five or six hurleys broken in a game. It took longer to make them than break them!

The hurley shape and the ball used in matches changed as time went by. There's not the same type of 'Clash of the Ash' or challenging for the ball now in hurling. A lot of the physical stuff and skills like overhead pulling are gone.

It's an easier game to master now.

That toughness isn't there anymore. There was less and less toughness in it as time went on, and now, same as in a lot of other sports, the ball is hit to the fella with no one near him!

Looking back now at near 90 years of age, the record books will tell you that the best Tipp team was that team in the early 60s. That team set new records and took hurling to a new level. We should have won five in-a row but we didn't, we lost one year in the middle between 1961 and '65.

It was a team that made history. Tony Wall, Jimmy Doyle, Liam Devaney and a few more were giants. Take John Doyle, for example, he won 10 Munster senior medals as well as eight All-Irelands, and 11 leagues. Now wasn't that some going in a time when it was knockout hurling!

It was a great joy getting to hurl for 17 years for Tipperary, playing at centrefield most of the time. That's where I wanted to be until I finished up in 1967. I won five All-Irelands at senior level but after my first one in 1958 the monkey was off the back. That first win, against Galway, is the one I cherish most.

TONY WALL

WATERFORD 9-3, TIPPERARY 3-4
Munster SHC Semi-Final
Cork Athletic Grounds
JULY 12, 1959

Tony Wall, one of Tipperary's greatest leaders on the field, receives the Liam MacCarthy Cup

★ **WATERFORD:** N. Power; J. Harney, A Flynn, J. Barron; M. Lacey, M. Morrissey, J. Condon; P. Grimes, S. Power (1-1); L. Guinan (3-0), T. Cheasty, F. Walsh (1-2); C. Ware (2-0), D. Whelan (1-0), J. Kiely (1-0). Subs: M. Flannelly for Morrissey, M. Morrissey for Power, S. Power for Ware.

★ **TIPPERARY:** T. Moloney; M. Byrne, M. Maher, K. Carey; M. Burns, **T. Wall (1-0)**, John Doyle; T. English, D. Nealon (1-2); Jimmy Doyle (1-2), L. Devaney, G. MacCarthy; M. Maher, J. McDonnell, W. Moloughney. Subs: R. Mousney for Moloney, P. Stakelum for McDonnell.

THE ACTION

IT WAS A day that no witness will ever forget.

This game was out of this world. A stunning display of galactic hurling before an attendance of 27,236 saw Waterford record their first championship win over Tipp since 1943 and teach them a lesson too. A red hot first-half at Cork Athletic Grounds saw eight goals scored, yes eight goals!

Tony Wall, the Tipperary captain who lifted the Liam MacCarthy Cup last September, amazingly opted to play against the storm force wind. A call he will no doubt reflect on for the rest of the long summer and probably for years to come. The team mentors had advised to play with the wind but decided to leave the final say to the players and, after that call, Tipp hurled into two storms - the elements and the opposition.

Fifteen minutes later a startled Tipperary were 5-1 to nil in arrears. Bear in mind Tipperary had beaten Waterford by more than double scores in a massive league game just before and, with the quality of player the Premier County possessed, no one believed this was possible. But Waterford hurled like an elemental force. Playing with the near hurricane force wind, they immediately set about the business of scoring goals. Frank Walsh led the attack for a rampant Waterford as he took advantage of his marker, Mick Burns who hurled with a shin gash. The Waterford forwards kept going for goals and getting them too. By half-time Waterford led 8-3 to 0-0 and it was game over.

After that shell-shocking, Stakelum came on and Mousney went into goals for Tipp but the horse had already bolted. Barron and Cheasty shone for Waterford while Tipp had just one who hurled majestically no matter how much the storm went on around him. Tony Wall stood defiant and prevented a whitewash in the first-half, while leading the retaliation in the second.

First at centre-back and then, with his head swathed in bandages, Wall moved to centre-forward and hurled on there in valiant fashion. He was assisted by Byrne and the Doyle duo, Jimmy and John, who kept going despite the tornado.

Previous to this game, Waterford had beaten Galway in the first round after they accepted the invite to join the 1959 Munster championship. Who in their right minds would have thought that Waterford could beat both of the 1958 All-Ireland finalists with such ease?

The winning of it against Tipp was eight goals in 22 minutes which beat their return against Galway which was five goals in 20 minutes. Buoyed up by results to date, the Deise will have their eyes on a Munster crown, and who knows, perhaps an All-Ireland too.

★★★★★

66

He traced and talked of matches lost and won,
the greats he met,
the friendship and the fun.

THAT LINE IS from a poem by the late Br Perkins about Tommy Treacy, a Tipperary hurler of olden times. The poem often comes to mind when talking hurling.

It always stayed with me.

It could be about anyone who ever played the game. Like all hurling careers, mine had both victories and defeats. Of all the All-Irelands or other games we played, it's a defeat in 1959 that made the greatest impression on me.

The most extraordinary game was against Waterford in the semi-final of the Munster championship. We were the reigning Munster, All-Ireland and league champions at the time. Being captain, I chose to play against the strong gale in the first-half but a driven Waterford, with fluent hurling, fired in eight goals by the end of the half!

After beating us they went on to win the All-Ireland final that year.

They haven't won it since. In my time playing, there were all sorts of wins and losses, and there was never any great surprises. But 1959... well, that was the great surprise.

All the other games were tight, and I was good or mediocre or bad, and sure you win some and you lose some. But that particular game stands out as the most exceptional, the most memorable... and the most stupid even!

I had the bug for hurling since I started at Thurles CBS.

The game was everywhere. The hurlers from the early years of the GAA were still alive when I was young. There is still the remembrance of Paddy Brolan, and also of Jim Stapleton, who was the winning captain in the first All-Ireland in 1887.

They were old men then, like I am now!

Tom Semple, whom Semple Stadium is called after, lived four doors down from me, but I rarely saw him. He died in the early 1940s, when I was a child.

As a young fella I would have just known about them, I wouldn't meet them but I'd see them or hear about them a little bit. My father came from county Meath and my mother from Clonmel, so my family wasn't a hurling one, but ya pick it up… it rubs off on ya!

When I started playing the game I was just getting my place as a corner-back, barely. And I was never sure of my place until I was about 16 and played in the Harty Cup, and then subsequently the 1950 Tipp minor team. From there, until I made the senior team, it took time to become established but I was always training on my own and getting strong.

I had the drive to get on the Tipp team and win an All-Ireland eventually. That came in 1958 and you couldn't have a better year than '58. But then we had this incredible match in 1959 against Waterford which shattered all our All-Ireland dreams that summer! When I talk about matches, that match stands out.

Believe it or not, the others fade into a blur!

The background to it all was that Tipperary had won three in-a-row at senior in 1949, '50 and '51, and I came on at the end of that era. I was a Tipp minor in 1950, '51 and '52, winning the All-Ireland in 1952 and subsequently getting onto the senior team in '53 at centre-forward. I didn't make a great success of it.

However, I survived evidently at corner-back in '54 and then I was centre-forward in '55 against Clare, but we got beaten again.

My recollection is that after that win in 1951, until '58, Tipperary never won a championship game! We won the league alright, but every year we were beaten by Clare or Cork by a point or two, and there was always disputed goals or extraordinary happenings. But we just couldn't win!

At the beginning of 1958 no one expected much from us in the championship. Nearly all the players from the three in-a-row team were gone, bar Mickey Burns, John Doyle and Jimmy Finn. But Jimmy had been in America and got injured so he hadn't played in the league which we were beaten in.

We were starting '58 with a new look team and I was captain.

Things were bleak.

A lot of the old stalwarts were gone and there was controversy over the selection committee as well! My own club, Thurles Sarsfields led by John Lanigan decided seven was too many selectors and after much controversy, decided to withdraw the two Sarsfields' representatives.

Paddy Leahy was our boss and took control.

'We'll be fine,' he told me. 'We will get Jimmy Finn back and I will talk to John Doyle about playing in the half-back line.'

That solved a lot of issues.

Then Kieran Carey from Roscrea, a newcomer, had played well in the league and slotted into the full-back line. We played Limerick, known as 'Mackeys greyhounds' at that time as they were trained by Mick Mackey, in the first round of the championship. They were expected to run rings around us, but we beat them and went on to play Cork.

I started centre-back against Cork, with John Doyle on one wing and Jimmy Finn on the other, and winning that game put us into the Munster final against Waterford. They had won Munster in 1957 and were beaten in the All-Ireland final, and they were a hard team to beat. But we did, finally bridging the gap in Munster.

Jimmy Doyle shone in the All-Ireland semi-final against Kilkenny, scoring 1-8, and then we played Galway in the final. We won it and the title was secured for the first time in seven years. I was delighted to collect the Hurler of the Year award, the Caltax Trophy, which was awarded for the first time. Everyone was on a high.

Everything was going well at the start of 1959.

I was captain again. We beat Waterford in the league final in Kilkenny in May. People were highly confident of more success as the attention turned to the championship. We played Waterford again in the semi-final of the championship.

Thousands travelled that day to Cork expecting us to win.

It was a long journey then, but a big championship game like that always drew the crowds. That day there was a gale blowing in from the sea, a wind as strong as I ever remember. Two years before, with serious wind as well, we had played Wexford in a league final in Croke Park. That time we played *with the wind* and hit 15 points in the first-half, but they came back and beat us!

That memory was in my head when the time came to toss the coin with the other captain to decide which way to play. The captain makes the call. To this day I can remember deciding to play against the wind when I won the toss!

I was quite confident we'd hold them against the wind. But all of a sudden we were overcome by a storm, the likes of which I have never seen at any match ever!

We had to face both Waterford and the wind.

The timing of it was hard to believe.

The wind was so strong you had to turn away from it to catch your breath! In the first-half Waterford scored 8 goals and 2 points, and we scored nothing! No one there could believe it when we went in 8-2 to 0-0 down at half-time!

Waterford gave the greatest exhibition of fluent and unstoppable hurling I ever saw before or since.

8-2 in one half against the reigning Munster, league and All-Ireland champions in the first round of the championship!

The funny thing is, no one on our team was playing badly or seemed to be beaten by their man. Our goalie, Terry Moloney never made a mistake. He didn't even get a chance to make a mistake!

The balls were flying past him like bullets!

We scored 3-4 in the second-half but we were well beaten. It was the most resounding defeat possible. Some of the most decorated Tipperary hurlers of all time played that day and a lot of them went on to win four All-Irelands in five years in the early 60s. But 1959 was Waterford's time!

They beat Kilkenny after a replay to win that year's All-Ireland. Looking back, that first-half of hurling by Waterford against us in 1959 was the greatest exhibition I have ever seen. That is the game, at 86 years of age, that has made the biggest impression on me in my life and it's the one that stays with me!

It was the first big Tipp match my wife, Betty was at, and what an introduction to Munster hurling it was! She was a Dub and we met after the All-Ireland in 1958. We got married that summer of '59; we couldn't have got married at that time if Tipp were still hurling!

I was one of the first of that team to get married and from then on Betty was welcomed into the hurling family and made feel at home. The same as now, hurling is a way of life and there was great socialising and camaraderie with both club and county.

With Thurles Sarsfields, we won 10 county finals in 11 years. One of the first championships I won was in 1952 when I played in the All-Ireland minor final on the first Sunday in September and the county final the following Sunday. I was playing centrefield against Borris Ileigh, marking Sean Kenny, who was the big man at the time, the driving force for the county team.

He had captained Tipp to an All-Ireland in 1950. It was a big ordeal but we won it and then we kept on winning. The team changed slightly but we were a solid team and then we had Jimmy Doyle coming on in the late 1950s and he drove it on further still.

Teamwork was down to a fine art.

The ball was being passed so fast. One of the Holycross fellas told me one time they thought they'd horse us out of it, but they couldn't catch us. They'd go for a bit of toughness but the ball would be gone! The Holycross fellas were big strong fellas, a lot of farmers, but the speed of play and skill of the Sarsfields team at that time was unmatched.

There was a lot going on those years. Back in 1964, after Tipp won the All-Ireland, I met Mickey Joe Costello who was a General from the Irish army that had taken over a sugar company. He came to me at the homecoming celebrations.

'Tony… you should write a book,' he told me. 'There's no book on coaching and you're the one to write it.'

I was living in Cork at the time and went back after the All-Ireland to think about it. I was digging in the garden one day, and I thought… *Maybe I'll start it now!* After that I went into the house, got some paper and a pen and started writing!

After that I would give it to Betty who typed it up, and I kept writing.

Lo and behold, after a few months, I had a book written! We got some support and then published *"Hurling"*. It was ready for the All-Ireland of 1965 and sold like hotcakes.

Those days were great.

Those All-Ireland wins were fantastic, but the losses are often more intense, so the Waterford game in 1959 stands out.

That poem by Brother Perkins about the old Tipperary hurler is one I cut out from the newspaper and held onto. He had a column called 'Tales of the Gaels' in the *Tipperary Star*. Sometime in the 1980s he visited Tommy Treacy, who was a famous Tipp player from the 1930s but by then he was living in Phibsboro in Dublin.

When Brother Perkins went back home he composed a poem about the visit. But the poem could be about any old hurler.

He sits there resting on his chair,
the once strong, well known, well-built player.
The kingly head, the shoulders just the same
as when we saw him play his last great game.

The hands that often held the stout caman
are still the same but the strength has gone.
He still retains the spirit and the soul
that urged him on to score the winning goal!

'How's Tipp?' he said, 'Are they still the same
as when we played that grand old hurling game?
Have they got that same old spirit of old,
would they die to wear the county's blue and gold?'

He traced and talked of matches lost and won,
the greats he met, the friendship and the fun,
I said, 'Soon again we'll see Tipperary play,
for the MacCarthy Cup, upon All-Ireland final day!'

I bade goodbye and left him sitting there,
the old Tipperary hurler in his upright chair.
He's happy now for youthful days well spent,
a simple smile a symbol of content;

Though old and grey and full of years at last,
his thoughts are those of youthful days now past.

MATT HASSETT

TIPPERARY 3-6, CORK 0-7
Munster SHC Final
Ennis Road, Limerick
JULY 30, 1961

Matt Hassett with all the trophies in 1961 and (right) welcoming Tommy Dunne home

★ **TIPPERARY:** D. O'Brien; **M. Hassett**, M. Maher, K. Carey; M. O'Gara, John Doyle, M. Burns; T. English, L. Devaney (0-1); Jimmy Doyle (1-4), D. Nealon (2-1), T. Ryan; T. Moloughney, W. Moloughney, J. McLoughlin. Sub: J. McKenna for T. Moloughney.

★ **CORK:** M. Cashman; J. Brohan, D. Brennan, D. Murphy; J. Sullivan (0-2), D. Riordan, J. O'Connor; P. Duggan, T. Walsh; P. Fitzgerald, P. Barry (0-1), T. Kelly; R. Browne, M. Quane, C. Ring (0-4). Subs: W. Walsh for T. Walsh; N. Gallagher for P. Duggan; JJ Browne for R. Browne.

THE ACTION

THE HAY IS saved and Cork are 'bet' as the 60s are starting to look mighty sweet for Tipperary.

A record 60,177 supporters, and very likely a few thousand more not counted in that number, were packed in like baked beans in a cramped tin can long before this match started. The atmosphere was turbocharged but when the ball went in Tipperary meant business with Liam Devaney and the ageless Theo English in the thick of things and relishing it.

The key to success was three goals in 18 minutes that ensured a solid 3-3 to 0-1 lead by half-time. Nealon's dropper from 50 yards was the first goal, then the same fellow let fly from a rebound, while the pick of them was Jimmy Doyle's goal, a 'solo and strike' bullet.

Tipp's defence was magnificent. John Doyle, who is a modern day 'Matt the Thresher', held Pat Barry while Cork's other dangerman, Christy Ring was well marshalled by Matt Hassett who gave Ring no room to wave his magic wand. Ring, sensing the game going away from Cork, got caught up fist fighting with John Doyle and in the fracas, Tom Moloughney received a nasty eye injury that required stitching.

No Cork team went down without a fight and, even with Tipperary's huge lead, one sensed Ring was still capable of magic in the misty rain. Ring fired goalward a couple of times but the defence held Cork in a tense game that never opened up into a free-flowing contest. Perhaps there was too much at stake for both sides.

Cork were so determined and accurate against a fancied Waterford in the semi-final but they weren't allowed have the ball to play with in the final as a 'Lion like' Tipperary team pounced on breaking ball and used it intelligently when they had it in possession. Kings of Munster and rightly so.

As well as the seniors, the minor and intermediate teams are in the mix for All-Ireland honours and the signs are there that Tipperary hurling is sailing away from the rest of the pack and taking the hurling silverware with them. This collective of hurling giants that claimed Tipperary's 25th Munster hurling title will now face Dublin in the All-Ireland final and will be the popular pick to win the grand slam of hurling titles.

★ ★ ★ ★ ★

66

IN SOME WAYS, having people everywhere you looked on the day made it more memorable than the All-Ireland win. The crowds were dangerous in Limerick that day though; you'd think they were nearly going to tumble onto the field.

I'd say there were 60,000 at it, and another 20,000 that went home.

It was frightening for a lot of people.

The gates were opened eventually but they couldn't get in or out. Thousands were turned away outside too and didn't get to see it at all. Rules and regulations came in since! The Munster final in Limerick in '61 is the game I always go back to and it became known as… 'The day of the big crowd!'

I had a lucky innings as it was most unusual that I even got to play with Tipperary. My club, Toomevara weren't challenging for county titles in the 1950s and it was only when a couple of us played for Tipp in a challenge match against Cork in Mallow in '58 that we were put in the shop window so to speak. That was early March, and then on St. Patrick's Day the club played Faugh's of Dublin in Borrisoleigh. I broke my finger that day and it had to be reset so I didn't get back in with Tipp until 1960!

Toome won the county final of '60 and the year after, so in my late twenties I became Tipperary captain. The winning team picked the captain, but there wasn't much made of it at the time. Things were easy going.

After the county final win the first round of the league took place in October and, as I was running out onto the field, Tommy Barrett called me over and said, 'You better be captain today!' And he handed me the team list!

Playing against Cork in 1961 was hard to top.

Everyone that I talked to a week or two before was going to the match. I lived at my home place on the main Dublin to Limerick road, between Toomevara and Moneygall.

That morning I cycled into Moneygall mass for nine o'clock and there was a continuous line of cars coming against me. One car even pulled up to talk to me!

Kieran Carey was to pick me up at 12 o'clock to go to Limerick, but by that time the road was deserted.

They were all in Limerick!

We drove to the Ardhu Hotel on the Ennis Road which was where the team met up, and the team walked from there to the field. There was nearly as many people coming up against us as were going down to the match. A lot couldn't get in. It was frightening because there was pushing and there was too many people.

There was no speech beforehand, as it took us an age to make it from the hotel to the dressing-room so there was hardly time to tog out and get out on the field.

It was a roasting hot day.

Sweltering.

The dust was rising.

I was playing on Ring that day. I had played on him the year before when we beat them in Thurles, and when he started to talk I ignored him and walked out in front of him! If you ever want to find out something about somebody you talk to them.

I never talked on the hurling field.

You'd lose concentration!

Ring got no score from play that day. I had a habit of trying to get first to the ball when it was coming in. That was the only way to play Ring; not from behind, because if he had the ball you could be sure they would score very soon after.

But if you missed the ball there was no chance. He was deadly. At that stage he was coming near the end of his career, as his peak would have been in the 1940s and 50s. Even by 1961 though Ring was still the main attraction.

Ring was different class and he made millions for the GAA.

I wasn't able to get up on the stand after the match to get the cup because of the crowd! I don't know who brought the cup back to us, but it was handed to me in the dressing-room a good while after the match was finished. By the following week the talk had moved on from the Munster final to the All-Ireland.

We beat Dublin in the All-Ireland final by a point.

On the Monday evening, a lorry took us around Thurles, and down to meet Archbishop Morris as was the custom at the time. Borrisoleigh, where Liam Devaney hailed from, was our next stop, and from there to Nenagh.

After midnight, we arrived in Toome and it was crammed.

They were waiting all night for us. That was a late finish now!

We had a Toomevara captain again 40 years later when Tommy Dunne was the Tipp captain. There were great celebrations then as well.

After our win in 1961 I kept the cup at home for the year.

People would come from all over to see it, but there would be no school visits and all the going there is today. The cup sat on the table in what we called the parlour… now called the sitting-room! My aunt was very proud and used to say to people, 'I have an uncle and nephew that won All-Irelands!'

My background in hurling is that on my mother's side my granduncle was Jim O'Dwyer and he was on the first team to win the All-Ireland in 1887. Very few knew that. In that final, Thurles had a selection from across the county but they were mainly locals. He was from Cloughjordan which was a long ways away, so how he came to be selected for Thurles I have never found out.

On the other side of the family was the famous 'Wedger' Meagher, a first cousin of my father and a noted hurler in the 1920s. Tipp won the All-Ireland in 1925 and they sailed across the Atlantic and toured for months playing matches in New York, Boston, Chicago and San Francisco. Wedger went with that team, who were the first county team to tour like that.

They were well looked after and drew huge crowds.

It made the sport international and, because it was a big success, it led the way for other teams to go. The GAA asked him to go back to promote hurling and set it up so he went back to America, but he never came home again.

I never captained a losing Tipp team as in 1961 we won the league, the Munster championship, the All-Ireland and the Oireachtas tournament. That was another big tournament that time, that was played after the All-Ireland.

We did draw once, with Wexford in the Oireachtas with a crowd of 40,000. I have a lovely photograph with the four cups outside our home.

Our team that time had a mix of the 1958 winning team and the team that dominated in the 1960s. Waterford had given Tipp a hiding in 1959 and I recall that day as I was in Knock with my mother.

I had promised to take her and we were on the street when I met someone we knew, and I asked him if he had heard how the Waterford game was going?

'I did,' he replied. 'But it can't be true that Tipp are several goals behind at half time!'

It was an unbelievable scoreline.

The team bounced back in 1960, beating Cork in Munster before losing the All-Ireland to Wexford. I came onto the team that summer, after Mickey Byrne, known as 'The Rattler', retired after the league finished. I went into his corner-back spot for the championship in 1960, and was there too for '61.

Moving on, in the first round in 1962, we played Limerick and it ended in a draw. I made bits of a finger the same day. It was so badly injured they weren't able to set it in the hospital at the time and sent me home.

Later I went to a great surgeon, Ferghal O'Donnell who looked after it and he had to break it and reset it again. It was 10 weeks before I could hit a ball so I had lost my place on the team and never got it back. When I got injured, John Doyle went into the corner-back position again and I dropped off the team. The full-back line then became known as 'Hell's Kitchen' … which was Doyle, Maher and Carey.

I got married after that and was training to be a solicitor and as I was on the road to Dublin every week I finished hurling. I spent two years going up and down to the Law Society and UCD.

They wanted me to hurl in the college in Dublin but I didn't because I was coming home at weekends, and then we had two kids at the time. I qualified as a solicitor and took over the business later on and was still going in to the office every morning until the Coronavirus lockdown of 2020 came around in the Spring!

I never stopped going to hurling matches and hope to stay going! I had the honour of presenting the current Tipperary team with their medals when they won in 2019.

We have a lot of top class players with Tipp at the moment but hurling is totally different now. If I was young today, I don't think I'd stick the training they are doing now. The culture was different back then.

I lived on the main road but there'd only be a car every half an hour in the evenings. We lived at a crossroads and people would meet, and some would play pitch and toss and others skittles. The rest of us would be hurling.

There was a bond between the hurler and the hurley.

It meant something to players to know the history of their hurley. It was a time a lot of players liked to make their own, or at least get the ash for their own hurleys. A few on our Toome team would go off to a farmer at night and cut a tree with the makings of hurleys and then we'd bring it home in the dark with a flash-lamp between us.

It was a social thing; we used to go off to a farm in the evening for a suitable ash tree. We'd bring the butts to Spike Nolan in Moneygall. Spike was treasurer of the county board and the Tipperary supporters club for many years and he made great hurleys.

Three generations of the Nolans made them for me.

Spike, his father and his grandfather!

I had the same hurley all the time playing with Tipperary. I had it for six years. It was from a glorious ash tree near Toomevara.

A teammate and I cut it on St Stephen's Day.

The hurley is that connection with the soil and the game then is an extension of it. It runs deep. You'd remember where the tree grew, when you cut it and what games you hurled with it.

There was a special connection there.

I got two hurleys from that tree we cut on St Stephen's Day. One I had in the Munster final in 1961 and other games. The other one was a spare.

For the All-Ireland in 1961 I gave a fella the spare to mind, so he was instructed to run in with it if the one I was using broke. Dublin were well in the game and it was a close ending, and didn't he get so excited during the game that he left it on the field afterwards!

The hurley I had for six years is now in the Nenagh Heritage Centre.

I have a great grá for the hurley and the game.

LEN GAYNOR

TIPPERARY 5-7, KILKENNY 4-8
Oireachtas Final
Croke Park
OCTOBER 18, 1964

It all started for the amazing Len Gaynor against the brilliant Eddie Keher

★ **TIPPERARY**: J. O'Donoghue; John Doyle, M. Maher, K. Carey; **L. Gaynor (1-0)**, T. Wall, M. Murphy; T. English, M. Roche; Jimmy Doyle (1-5), D. Nealon, M. Keating (2-1); L. Devaney, J. McKenna (0-1), S. McLoughlin (1-0).

★ **KILKENNY**: K. Purcell; P. Henderson, P. Dillon, J. Treacy; S. Cleere, T. Carroll, M. Coogan; S. Buckley (0-1), P. Moran; E. Keher (1-1), J. Teehan (0-2), T. Forrestal; J. Dunphy (1-0), J. Lynch (2-0), T. Walsh (0-4). Subs: F. Larkin for Coogan; D. Heaslip for Larkin.

THE ACTION

TWO BEATINGS BY Tipperary within weeks of each other is hard to take for Kilkenny. Even harder when it's in an All-Ireland and an Oireachtas final. The kingpins proved their worth once more against a determined Kilkenny team. Taking it all in their stride, the hurling kings of Ireland added the Oireachtas title to the league, Munster and All-Ireland won earlier this year.

It's difficult to say if Tipperary dropped their performance levels from the heights of the All-Ireland final or if Kilkenny upped their level dramatically. Whichever, Tipp won again. This same Kilkenny side went down 5-13 to 2-8 in the All-Ireland final but, fired up, they built a 3-5 to 1-2 lead after 25 minutes.

Nine points down Tipp found their rhythm. In defence, Tony Wall was outstanding once more. Mick Murphy followed Wall's example. So too did Len Gaynor, a youngster new to the big stage, who proved his worth as he grew into the game and kept a tight rein on Eddie Keher as the game wore on.

Paddy Leahy and the other Tipp mentors wasted no time shaking things up when they were nine down and fearing sinking. Michael 'Babs' Keating and McKenna were moved before the tireless Theo English worked the ball into Keating who fired the ball past Purcell in the goals. The 'Tipp Ship' was back afloat and gathering wind in its sails as the impressive Gaynor sent in a beautiful goal-bound sideline from out near midfield and, as it dropped from the sky, Sean McLoughlin and the defence tussled. Eyes were off the ball as it ended up in the net. The golden goal roused Tipp with Kilkenny leading 3-5 to 3-2 at the break.

Right on the restart scores came in waves as Jimmy Doyle put the ball in the Kilkenny net and pointed twice before McKenna and Keating added scores. The peerless Tony Wall and young Gaynor kept the ball moving but when it looked like it was game over for Kilkenny their sharpest duo, Forrestal and Walsh, combined in the 14th minute of the half to set up Eddie Keher for a beauty of a goal, giving them a lifeline.

Tipp rallied. Keating buried another goal and that was that. The younger players, following their recent win in the inaugural All-Ireland under-21 hurling championship, really shined for Tipp. The duo of Gaynor and Keating both look like they have great futures.

What an era for this Tipp team; many believe them to be the greatest of all time. This year they have won everything going and in 1965 they will go in search of a fourth All-Ireland title in five years.

★★★★★

66

SEAN MCLOUGHLIN CAME over and pinned me up in the corner of the dressing-room.

'You know you're going to be marking Eddie Keher?

'If you stop him scoring, we're going to win this match!'

It had just been announced that Mick Burns of Nenagh Eire Og was unable to play and that I'd be playing instead of him.

I was togging out when I heard this and thought… *Not so bad…. I'll get a few shots at it now anyway!*

Then Sean McLoughlin pinned me.

Sean McLoughlin was a great competitor. We all wanted to win the championship but he had a great attitude and wanted to win absolutely everything. Out we went then and marched in the parade behind the Artane Boys Band.

It was a big day, so no pressure!

That was the day my Tipperary hurling career started. We were playing Kilkenny in the Oireachtas final but there had been a lot of hurling done already that year; 1964 was the first year of the inter-county under 21 championship and I must have played well enough in some of those games to be called onto the senior panel during that summer.

I was a sub on the senior team when they won the Munster final and got to the All-Ireland final. Croke Park sent out word before the final that there was only 20 players allowed on the panel, the starting team and five subs, so I was one of those.

Tipp beat Kilkenny fairly well in that All-Ireland and there were great celebrations after it. Four weeks later then, the Oireachtas final was between the same teams.

The tournament was huge at the time but eventually the Oireachtas competition went the same way as the Railway Cup and it was abandoned by the year 2000. But back in the 1960s it was big news.

I was delighted to be on but was very excitable at that stage and when it started, I was swiping at the ball. It was a time where hurling was changing from ground hurling to much more rising of the ball.

Tony Wall was beside me.

'Take your time. Pick it up and get the ball in your hand,' he told me.

I don't know how I played but we were being slaughtered by Kilkenny in the first-half and they went 11 points up.

Coming straight onto the Tipp team from club hurling, I got a rude awakening from Eddie Keher. The minute he saw the ball on the opposite wing he took off and raced into the square, and went for the far goal post from where we were. If the ball broke to him, he would have scored a goal but it didn't and I caught up to him then.

I was never caught off guard after that.

He was a very clever player, well able to lose his marker and he was one of those good players that would have you lost before the ball would come. He was way ahead in his thinking and movement.

I went out around midfield to take a line ball at one stage. No one else went near it so I went over and took it. I got a great shot at it and it went all the way up in the air and into the square, and it hopped on the ground and into the net!

It wouldn't have gone in only Sean McLoughlin did a war dance in front of the goalie! He told me after he never touched it, but the papers the next day gave it to McLoughlin.

In fairness, it wouldn't have gone in only for him but it gave me a great boost.

Whether I was good or bad I don't know, but that gave me a bit of a lift. The great manager and trainer of Tipperary that time, Paddy Leahy, said after, 'Good man young Gaynor. That was a great goal!'

That was my introduction to it and I was on the team after that.

It was unexpected, but I was delighted to get the chance.

We got the medals immediately after the match. It was a lovely gold medal and it was a lovely way to start.

First day in Croke Park.

First medal, and away you go!

I was on the team from that day on. After that, Mick Burns came back in on that wing and I switched to the other. There weren't many places to be got on that team because every place was nailed down by an experienced player but Mick Murphy, who captained Tipp in 1964 to the All-Ireland, injured his knee in a club game.

He was never able to play after which was unfortunate for him but it was a lucky break for me, as I got his place at left wing back.

Every day in the championship was a great day.

The Munster finals were hard won. Generally, it was ourselves and Cork in the final with Limerick or Clare an odd time. Mostly they were played in Limerick and everyone that paid at the stile got in; it didn't matter what the numbers were.

If there was a big crowd, they'd spill onto the sideline and lie down there. You'd be hurling away with them beside you. Going to take a line-ball they'd just move back and let you take the line ball and then move back in again.

No one would interfere, but they'd be cheering and roaring alright. It was a great atmosphere to have the crowd so close to you. Electric at times. I remember one hot day there were fellas getting water from the tap, selling it and making a lot of money!

People would be there for hours waiting for the game. The team always left it until late to go but the spectators would be leaving home early after morning mass. Cars used to be parked from Barringtons Hospital and all the way in along.

Parked facing for home.

On the morning of one of the big games in Limerick I went for a walk. There's a laneway near me that goes down to Kilruane Cemetery and I walked down there. Next thing this man came along on his bike with his hedge clippers heading down to the graveyard and he said, 'Why aren't you gone Len?'

I told him not to worry that we'd get there, and said, 'Sure the match isn't on until three o' clock!'

Everyone would be gone bar the team.

It was always a great day out as a supporter, people taking a load of sandwiches and if you got separated you might not get any sandwiches!

I loved the big days.

The Munster finals in particular. I never felt intimidated going out. I knew I'd have to be at my best to try and hold a forward but I'd never be overawed or anything like that. I had great men around me with John Doyle at corner-back and Kieran Carey in the other corner. Mick Maher full-back.

Sure, they were like armoured cars beside me!

Mick Burns, Sean McLoughlin, Mackey McKenna, Donie Nealon… they were all phenomenal players. Theo English was a great leader in the centre of the field. I'd rate them all very highly.

Tony Wall was a leader and was ahead of his time in many ways.

He would have two or three hurleys and would have them weighed so that each one would be exactly the same as the other. That was back in the 1960s. A lot of us didn't understand that because we'd have a light hurley today and a heavy one tomorrow.

I used a 37-inch and would have a different stick from time to time. Hurleys then were for ground hurling, whereas today they are for rising the ball and getting it into your hand. Players use one hand to rise it nowadays; before if you used one hand you could be taken off because we were always told to use two hands to rise the ball!

Tony Wall always said we were the best. People look at it now and say the hurling was slower and we weren't as skilful but there's a lot of reasons for that. We weren't doing the same training as they are doing nowadays and the ball was completely different. It was a handmade ball, and no two balls would be the same.

I remember doing a coaching course up in Gormanston College in 1970, with Fr Tommy Maher from Kilkenny giving the course. He said, 'You never know which way the ball is going to land,' and he threw a ball against a wall which came back into his hand.

He did it two or three times and it came back; then he threw it again and it skewed off sideways.

'Now, do you see what I'm talking about?' he said.

There was an uneven lump in the ball and if it hit your hurley you wouldn't have control of it. That was one reason, and of course it was a much heavier ball as well so it wouldn't travel as far as the type of ball used today. The present-day players are so skilful and tremendous to watch. People say the ball is too light but I don't think so; they have a uniform ball now, machine made, and they can drive it a mile.

Being on the senior Tipp panel was an honour, but it was great craic as well. Mackey MacKenna was a great character, as well as a great hurler.

I travelled with him in his car as whoever was farthest away would bring the car and would get an allowance. Mackey would pick me up, then Donie Nealon and then we'd go into Nenagh for Mick Burns and maybe Liam Devaney in Borrisoleigh.

That was the load and we'd have right craic going and coming home.

It was great times but when the match would start you'd see the change in our attitude. No one would be late for training coming up to a big game.

Every second year there was a trip to New York to be played for! We won it in '65 and had just won the All-Ireland that year as well. You had to be inoculated two weeks before going to New York that time.

We were due to travel just after the All-Ireland final and the team had been inoculated except me and it was coming up near the final.

They had a dilemma, as I was on the team at this stage and they were afraid to give me the needle in case I'd get sick for the All-Ireland. The needle would leave a mark on the shoulder, so they put the marks on me anyway; but there was nothing in the needle so there was no fear of me getting sick!

We'd be put up in Hotel Manhattan.

It was mostly Tipperary people out there that would look after us and show us around the place. I remember my first time going out on the plane the county secretary, Tommy Barrett stood up.

'I'm going to tell ye now what's going on tonight in New York… there's a banquet in Gaelic Park for you all,' he announced.

Being New York, I imagined that Gaelic Park was way ahead of what we'd have in Ireland. John 'Kerry' O'Donnell, a Kerryman, had a bar in Gaelic Park and the idea was to get the crowd in to make a bit of money. I saw Theo English and Doyle picking up rolls on plates and eating them.

'Why aren't you waiting for the banquet?' I asked Theo.

'Hey,' he says. 'This is the banquet, take what you can as quick as you can!'

It was no more a banquet than the man in the moon!

In 1968 we won a trip again. Bobby Kennedy had just been shot so on account of that there were no matches played that weekend. Kennedy was lying in state so we went as a team to pay our respects.

With the crowds, it was going to take hours to get in but Babs Keating went over to a policeman. 'We're over from Ireland,' Babs said, as he chatted to the policeman.

'Oh my God, come over here you guys, get up here!' said the policeman, so we by-passed the crowds and went straight in! It was sad to see Bobby Kennedy lying there, a great man.

The following weekend we hurled on rock hard ground without a blade of grass but there was a good atmosphere.

Finishing up playing the game was a huge change and it felt like one part of my life was gone forever. I found it hard.

It was a huge part of my life but you have to live life alongside it as well. Do a day's work, maybe get married and have kids... to be able to co-ordinate all parts of life is the thing, and to enjoy them all.

Staying involved with my club Kilruane MacDonaghs was important to me and I had coached the club's minor team in 1970 and then at under-21. I kept at the coaching and it kept me involved up until the present day, where I still do a few small bits with kids starting off.

DINNY RYAN
(& TADHG O'CONNOR)

TIPPERARY 4-16, LIMERICK 3-18
Munster SHC Final
Fitzgerald Stadium, Killarney
JULY 25, 1971

Dinny Ryan breaks through the Limerick defence in the 1971 Munster final

★ **TIPPERARY:** P. O'Sullivan; N. Lane, J. Kelly, J. Gleeson; **T. O'Connor**, M. Roche, L. Gaynor (0-2); S. Hogan, PJ Ryan (1-0); F. Loughnane (0-3), N. O'Dwyer (0-1), J. Flanagan (0-5); Jimmy Doyle (0-1), M 'Babs' Keating (3-4), **D. Ryan**. Subs: L. King for Lane; R. Ryan for Doyle; P. Byrne for O'Dwyer.

★ **LIMERICK:** J. Hogan; T. O'Brien (capt), P. Hartigan, J. O'Brien; C. Campbell, J. O'Donnell, P. Bennis; S. Foley, B. Hartigan (0-1); R. Bennis (0-12), P. Graham (0-2), E. Grimes (1-1); D. Flynn (1-0), M. Cregan, E. Cregan (1-2). Subs: E. Prenderville for P. Bennis; W. Moore for Flynn; C. Shanahan for Foley.

THE ACTION

THIS WAS ONE of those epic Munster finals. The quality and mystique of this Killarney final won't ever be forgotten. There's something epic and ancient about hurling in such splendorous surroundings and far from the driving rain dampening spirits, the setting seemed to add to the fairytale, from a Tipperary point of view at least.

Captain Tadhg O'Connor, who hurled full of spirit, is the first Roscrea player to lead Tipp to glory and what a day to do it.

For wanton abandon, speed and drama this final is hard to be topped. It moved score by score until John Flanagan's late puck separated the teams to uproar. The fair haired Moycarkey native's winner ensured the Munster crown returned to Tipp after a three-year absence. Despite the torrential downpour there was a cracking atmosphere in Killarney all weekend. Once it started it was fast and furious. The heavy ball and greasy conditions merely added to the skill levels on show where character, craft and spirit were in abundance.

Being an 80-minute game Tipp were well prepared for a marathon but Limerick took off in a sprint. The Treaty County had two goals 'in the bag' within 10 minutes. Donal Flynn directed the opener from a Richie Bennis line-ball into the goal and then Eamonn Cregan added one. Limerick could have been out of sight were it not for the brilliance of Mick Roche and his wing backs, Len Gaynor and Tadhg O'Connor who held firm. Tipp emerged for the second-half with a new set of jerseys and a new attitude. Dinny Ryan, who was having a storming game, took up the running around the middle and sent smart, accurate ball to the inside forwards. Liam King came on and shined in the mist.

Tipp were going well, however midway through the half one of their top players, Noel O'Dwyer, was struck and went off with a facial injury. It transpired to be minor enough, merely needing two stitches below the eye but in his absence others showed leadership. Dinny Ryan, returning from his long suspension, was a 'tour de force' around the middle while Gaynor, O'Connor and Roche were in startling form.

The gifted Michael 'Babs' Keating... what else can we say?

He withdrew the statement he made to the media in the aftermath about the 'new sliotar' he used for a free which caused all the controversy. Suffice to say his scores and influence were central to the win. His first goal was the pick as it whizzed across the goalmouth and into the net. He tormented the Limerick defence for every single minute and shook the net from a free, which was the controversial one, as the Limerick players maintained afterwards that he had used a new ball which was completely dry and destined for the net.

Limerick, for their due, didn't go meekly as Richie Bennis pointed and Eamonn Grimes swept a lengthy Pat Hartigan clearance to the net. Then Flanagan stepped up and decided proceedings. An epic ending to a classic.

★★★★★

66

PLAYING AGAINST THE neighbours in the Munster final in Killarney in 1971, without a doubt or hesitation, is the game of my life because I had been suspended for a full year... and the suspension ended at the stroke of midnight on the night before the game!

I had been playing in a tournament game in my neighbouring parish of Doon, in Limerick, and I got a 12-month suspension.

They gave me six months for 'Suspected Striking' and a further six months on top of that for 'Refusing to leave the field of play'.

So my first game back was against the next door neighbours!

County Limerick is a puck of the ball from where I grew up in Curreeny, Kilcommon so there was always great rivalry there. And friendship too.

Two of the Limerick lads, Jim Allis and Willie Moore played with Doon just over the road from my own club, Sean Treacys and the three of us were great friends. Jim had got put off and been suspended along with me the year before in the tournament game.

Jim was back and available for the Munster final too. I was great pals with Jim O'Donnell, the Limerick centre-back, as well.

Back then, I used to cycle three or four miles to meet a car to go to training. We were fit as fiddles, no one got hamstring strains in those days!

Noel Lane drove from Inagh in Clare and passed by the cross where I'd meet him. Being suspended at the time, I wasn't meant to be training but that wasn't going to stop me... sure I trained away!

It was a different Ireland.

I was smoking back then, and I remember Donie Nealon saying a few words to the team on the week of the game in Killarney.

'Lads, if you usually have three drinks... cut it back to one drink... PLEASE and, if you're smoking 10... cut it back to five... RIGHT NOW!'

But no one would be smoking 10 a day because we wouldn't have the price of it!

I was working in the Silvermines, down underground.

I was on the explosive end.

We were mining lead and zinc. Other lads would make holes underground, then we'd come along in the evening, wire it up, go back up to the surface and press a button to let it off. Dealing with explosives was good money but it was dangerous.

You'd need your wits about you.

After that, I worked with Eircom for years but when I was hurling, that's where I was and I always enjoyed great banter in the mines leading up to the big games… and Killarney was as big as they came. It was novel playing in Kerry.

Travel plans were made and on Saturday I headed to Killarney with Tommy Doyle and John Flanagan. We went down early but got little sleep that night.

I can clearly recall John Flanagan and I looking out the window at four o'clock in the morning on streets thronged with Tipp and Limerick people!

There was singing and dancing with a few banjos going. Little sleep was got with all the shouting and roaring on the streets!

The morning of the game we went to the cathedral, and then just waited for the throw in. The atmosphere in the town and in the stadium was unbelievable.

The rivalry with Limerick at the time was fantastic, in a way that only the knockout Munster championship could be. It lashed rain all day and everyone was drowned to the skin but they didn't even know it, they were so into the game!

For years after, when that game came up in conversation, people talked about the 'dry ball'. It was a new ball that Donie Nealon brought in for a 21-yard free and it was something that wouldn't have been done before.

We were playing the game with a rain soaked one until then.

It was a completely different ball back then to the light ones they use today, so a dry ball would travel twice as fast as a wet one.

Babs had some strike.

I can still see the rain going off the netting in Killarney with the shot he hit. A sheet of rain just fell off the net as the bullet struck.

It was silent for a small fraction of a second and then, a roar went up just after the net shook!

It was an honest game, hip to hip and hard but fair.

You'd give it and take it but there was no going down pretending to be injured and trying to get someone put off.

Limerick had a great team with players like Eamonn Cregan that would shine in any decade. He was exceptionally skilful. I was marking Jim O'Brien and started corner-forward. During the game we moved about so John Flanagan went into the corner and I went wing forward, and stayed moving.

I'd say it was my best game for Tipp, but I didn't score.

I was small compared to some of them but I remember catching three or four balls in the middle of the field with Bernie Hartigan on me. He was throwing weights for Ireland at the time but my timing was just spot on, and I fed them the ball inside in the full-forward line. Babs and John Flanagan did the rest. The last quarter of an hour I was on Phil Bennis, who was a brother of Richie.

At the final whistle Phil shook hands with me and I saw a Limerick man run in from the sideline. He ran up and hit Phil a punch right into the jaw!

I presume he had a few bob on the game!

I thought it was me he was going for but the supporter hit the player from his own county! Every county has that, people get hot headed and dealing with it is part of the game. It was knockout hurling, so it was a full year until the next chance to win. It is different now with a league-type championship.

I loved that day in Killarney because it brought great joy to those around me. A game like that is always big for the family and friends of a player. They all have an involvement in the spectacle.

My family went to every match back then; my mother used be praying at them all, Lord have mercy on her. My father had died in 1963 so she was left with six boys and she went to all the matches we played.

It wasn't easy on our farm rearing so many, she was a great woman.

I had an aunt home from Texas and she decided she'd go to Killarney too. She prayed all through the match. After living in the heat in Texas since she was 18 she was dying with the cold in the downpour!

Next up was the All-Ireland semi-final.

We were lucky to beat Galway in a high scoring game at Birr and wouldn't have only for Mick Roche switching to midfield on John Connolly. That was the winning of it. Mick was an all-time great, with very few I've seen play even near as good.

Some of the players I hurled with that time would get on any team of any era. The skills Babs Keating had were a joy, and add in Noel O'Dwyer, John Flanagan, Francis Loughnane, Jimmy Doyle... and that's only in the forwards!

Croke Park was next.

They were powerful times.

To be playing Kilkenny in the final with over 60,000 people looking on and scoring the winning goal was great. There were 10 goals scored in it, yet there was two right good goalies with the famed Ollie Welsh in one goal and Peter O'Sullivan in the other.

It was the first senior medal coming to Sean Treacys.

I adored my club. I was delighted for my family, cousins and friends too. Everyone has their own band of supporters they think about after a big game.

Babs Keating used to always say to me, 'Stay watching Dinny… if I can't shoot I'll hit it across. Be ready to go'.

He was saying that to me all the time, so I always went looking for the ball when I was near the goals. I'd find the space to take a pass if I could.

Scoring the winning goal was about being in the right place at the right time. For that goal it came back out off Ollie's hurley, and I tapped it in. The joy and the roar was like that day against Limerick in Killarney all over again.

You'd be remembered by many for scoring the winning goal against Kilkenny in an All-Ireland final but Lar Corbett's goals in 2010 against the same opponents were better than mine!

Credit where it's due. Lar was brilliant.

I don't think he got the credit he deserved at all; I loved watching him play.

There's character in every winning team.

You just can't compare eras fairly, as everything is of its time. Players are fitter now but it's looser and more like a seven-a-side at times than a 15-a-side game.

Players look to find room and get the ball with no one near them. Very seldom now do you see two lads going to a ball and pulling at the same time. It's moved now through the lines from full-back to half-back to midfield, but it was more direct in the 1960s and 70s.

I would love to see it go back that way but I don't think it will.

Players are fitter now but a lot of the skills that supporters loved are gone from the game. The linesman placed the ball for sideline cuts back when I was playing whereas now you can tee it up and take it in a foot, and players get away with it sometimes yet not at other times.

Growing up, Philip Kenny in Borrisoleigh made my hurleys; then as time moved on he slowed down making them. I changed to Denis O'Brien in Cahir who made a lovely stick. But even the hurleys have changed shape since.

The lighter ball changed the game too. Players are putting over sidelines from half-way. I'd love to see the ball going back to the same weight it was in those days because a lot of the hip to hip battling in the midfield area is gone on account of the ball being so light and moving so fast.

Having said that, I still love hurling and love the matches.

Tipp have had great players like Padraic and Brendan Maher and Seamus Callanan leading them for the past decade. Padraic was in hard luck in his two years as a captain. He is a player I admired since he came on the scene in 2009.

In some ways, Padraic Maher and Mick Roche are alike, in that they were the standout players in their generation. They are very similar. Both of them captained Tipp for two years and they were close to winning but in the end didn't win the All-Ireland.

I made some great friends from that game. I often talk on the phone or meet old friends or foes from hurling days. As well as with Tipp, I had great days with the club as we won seven West titles.

They were great years for the 'Treacys'.

When we were knocked out early I'd head over to the States and play in New York for the weekend. You'd get a phone call and pack your bag.

I remember going and there was a return ticket left for me in Shannon then; I was picked up at the airport over there and had a great few days. We'd play the match and be well looked after. I loved those trips.

I met people from all over the world there and I remember meeting some of the Offaly footballers on one trip. They were one of the top teams back then, and I've been great friends with Tony McTague and Seamus Darby ever since.

There were a lot of perks that went with hurling, like getting to play in Wembley Stadium twice. I recall Peter O'Sullivan pucking a ball from one sideline to the other in Wembley! There was a swimming pool between the dressing-rooms in Wembley when we were there and, Lord have mercy on him, John Flanagan, threw me into the swimming pool but I couldn't swim so they had to come in after me to pull me out!

After the All-Ireland in 1971, I remember the county chairman, Seamus O'Riain got in touch to say the Tipp team would be going on tour to San Francisco the following April and all players were advised to get their passports in order. Trips like that were fantastic, you got to see the world through hurling in a time when travelling like that was rare and very expensive.

Tipp teams went on big trips going back as far as the 1920s.

There was always a bit of glamour and prestige to wearing the blue and gold jersey. To play in big stadiums over there and meet the Irish abroad meant a lot to us and to them. On that trip to San Francisco I met a very good friend of mine, Fr. John Ryan Giant from Upperchurch. We had hurled together with the Treacys before he got ordained in 1970.

To come face-to-face again and see what life was like for him over there was wonderful. That's the power of hurling. We stayed with Irish families in America when we went in the Spring of 1972. It was much more personal than staying in hotels.

I think we got £200 off the county board, with a shirt and blazer saying, 'Tiobraid Arann' on it. Trips like that were treasured.

It's hard to say exactly why, but Tipp faded in the 1970s. There were different selectors every year and players got a game and then were dropped.

Things became unsettled. The golden era was in the past and panic grew year-on-year which made it harder to win. The county champions always had a selector and the captaincy but the players were chopped and changed too much.

I was told I was a 'veteran' one year and I was 25 years of age!

The turnover of players was too great and the consistency that was there in the 1960s was gone. For the Tipperary supporters, 1971 proved to be the sole highlight of the decade.

Of all the days, I never again experienced another day like Killarney in '71.

It was great for a small club like Sean Treacys to have a player at senior level and I was very proud to be the first to go on to win an All-Ireland at senior level."

99

TADHG O'CONNOR

Tadhg O'Connor and GAA president, Nicky Brennan on the 35th anniversary of the All Stars

❝

THERE WAS SOMETHING magical about Killarney in 1971.

It seemed so far away. I think it was a special weekend for everyone there and I still hear new stories about it. It's hard to know where to start, as so much happened that year.

So many milestones.

On a personal level, I got married and my first child was born; club-wise, we won the club All-Ireland final as well as two Munster club titles and, last but not least, I had the privilege of captaining Tipperary in an incredible year.

The Munster final in Killarney was in the middle of it.

And that was the game of all games.

Limerick were our biggest rivals as we met four times that year. They won all

54

three league games, beating us in the final with a last second free from Richie Bennis.

In the Munster championship we beat Clare to set up another final with Limerick. Everyone knew it would be close again. Neither of the county boards would give an inch, and they couldn't agree on a home or away venue so we all got ready for a trip to Killarney.

Between 1968 and '82 the Tipperary team only stayed in a hotel twice for big games. That trip to Kerry for the Munster final was the first, and the second was for the All-Ireland later that year when we stayed in Barry's Hotel in Dublin!

People made their way from near and far to Killarney. A huge Tipp following from North Tipp made their way down the same road as the Limerick supporters that weekend, so I heard stories afterwards that supporters had great banter.

Travelling was huge compared to today.

It was easily a five or six-hour road trip without stopping.

Cars were scarce then so they were all packed going to games. Often bonnets were open at the side of the road; cars were boiling, fan belts were off, and people would be out waving flags at the side of the road.

It was a different life and the journey was an experience in itself.

The team arrived early by car on the Saturday and we had a meal. We broke into groups after, the backs would chat amongst themselves and likewise the forwards. The team probably picked itself after the league final, with Jimmy Doyle back from injury beside Babs Keating in the full-forward line.

The trainer, Ossie Bennett had us fit and with Donie Nealon coaching us we felt ready. The senior players like Babs, Mick Roche and Len Gaynor always talked a small bit the night before or on match days.

Roscrea won a number of county finals in those years, so Francis Loughnane was captain one year and in 1971 it was my turn to captain Tipp. Overall, it was a great honour for the club that I was captain but for me playing well on the field was always my focus.

I was quite young and my role as captain was to have the team list for the ref which I always stuck down my sock! You'd give the list to the ref then, and give the opponents team list back to Tommy Barrett, our county secretary. I'd be in for the coin toss to pick a direction to play in, and with the experience within the team no words were needed from me. All I needed was to play as best I could!

That match day was dream-like.

Killarney just had that effect, there was something mystical about it. We got a garda escort up to the field through the crowds. It was spilling but it was atmospheric.

Before the game there was no shouting or ranting in the dressing-room. One or two players would get excited, but most were very relaxed and I've often wondered afterwards why that was?

I think it was that the guys over the team and the players that had experienced so much success in the 60s just took it all in their stride.

They had a calming influence and knew the right time to turn the switch on. When we left the dressing-room, the noise from the crowd hit me right away.

The ground was like being in a big basin… or a goldfish bowl.

It was like the crowd were on the field with us, we could almost feel them in the rain. Marching behind the band, I just took in the surroundings… and I can still picture it.

We had only four sliotars for the warm-up so everyone did their own drills.

While those moments flew by, the parade seemed to take ages. I just wanted the game to start. I was right half-back on Eamon Grimes, and knew his style of play.

He'd run all day. I'd stay with him. On our line Mick Roche controlled the middle, with Len Gaynor strong under the dropping ball on the other wing.

It was a physical game in the heavy rain and there was a bite in tackles as most lads had marked each other in the three earlier games that year.

The game became a struggle in the conditions.

No one missed a second. The ball seemed to be always dropping on top of us in the half-back line. We were struggling early on before we came into it near half-time. At the break the team were told to 'UP IT'… more was demanded of us.

Limerick came back at the start of the second-half with Eamonn Cregan to the fore, but Babs was motoring and then John Flanagan got a lovely point from way out on the sideline. Everyone there knew it was one of those moments.

The game is often recalled for Babs' famous score from the free. He lined up to take a vital free when Donie Nealon, our coach, came in with a towel to dry his hurley and the Limerick players claimed they saw a new ball being brought in under it.

The argy-bargy started.

You see, the ball then was very different to the ball now. There used to be a big leather rim on it and it was like a sponge in the rain.

There was a huge difference between a soggy ball and a new ball. It was innovative and no one expected it! Donie and Babs were ahead of their time. Babs was cute enough, he just ignored all that was going on around him and struck it well. Babs was just a superb player and picked up the Hurler of the Year award later that year.

We saw it out.

Barely.

Mick Roche was the outstanding player for us throughout, influencing the game from centre-back. He was a superb athlete and at the end of the day was probably the difference between the teams. Mick wore a hair-net when he was hurling to keep his long hair out of his eyes and opponents often tried to curb his influence by trying to take the net off, or pulling at it.

In one match we played against Cork I remember when one player took Mick's hair-net off to upset him, but Mick taught him a hurling lesson. He was too clever to let it bother him. Limerick tried everything to stop him but he was unstoppable.

There were very few speeches made after the final, but Roscrea was packed that night on our return. We made the All-Ireland final against Kilkenny.

I needed to have the cupla focal prepared for that day!

I had my speech ready for it well in advance. At that time I was studying accountancy and took the time to sit down with my boss, who was a fluent Irish speaker. We practiced getting it right and worked on it line by line until it was ready for the big day when I got to deliver it!

Like winning in Killarney, winning in Croke Park was unforgettable.

To collect the cup and be hoisted up shoulder-high afterwards was a huge honour. Incredible stuff.

Monday evening, we arrived back to fantastic scenes in Thurles and then on to Roscrea where 20,000 or so were waiting. There was a lorry also waiting for us on the Templemore Road and that was a night I will never forget. It meant so much to so many people, like John Joe Maher who was our secretary for 34 years.

It was a superb night.

The cup was brought up to John Joe's pub across from the barracks and there were plenty of speeches made from the back of a lorry! 1971 was such a huge year.

Sporting-wise and family-wise too.

Mary and I got married in February, and when we got back from the honeymoon in Spain the matches were non-stop.

Tipp and Limerick played the league final around April, and Roscrea won the delayed 1969 Munster club final where we beat Glen Rovers on Easter Sunday. I never added up how many games I played in that year but I loved it!

We won a second provincial club title against Clarecastle in August; that was the Munster club final of 1970. It was a whirlwind of club and county games. It was busy but I was delighted to continue playing, and we kept winning!

The club games continued until winter.

We played our All-Ireland club semi-final against Loughiel Shamrocks up in the north. Mary was due that November, so I wasn't supposed to go. But one of our key players, Francis Loughnane couldn't travel and a couple of others were missing too, so Mick Minogue who was in charge of the Roscrea team asked me, 'What are you going to do Tadhg?'

'Of course I will travel Mick,' I replied. 'But, you see, Mary is expecting our first child the day after the game.'

Straight away, Mick made arrangements to look after Mary so I could travel to the game. Doctor Hanley, who was a great GAA man, was contacted and a plan was put in place. Sure enough, on the Saturday in question my wife went into labour and Mick Minogue's wife, Maisie contacted the doctor right away to be sure that Mary had the best care.

We were half-way up to the north at that stage on the Saturday.

We stayed overnight in Dundalk before travelling on for the game the next day. On Sunday morning in Dundalk I went down for breakfast and was met by my father-in-law, Luke who was a selector with Roscrea. He had got word from home.

I can still remember where I was when Mary's father told me that I had a new baby daughter! Fiona had arrived as we were en route to the match!

There was no such thing as turning around, so we travelled on and played the

All-Ireland club semi-final against Loughiel that Sunday afternoon. Only in the last 10 minutes of the game did we pull away.

Having captained Tipp to the All-Ireland there were a lot of functions to attend and two very immediate events. When we came back from the north that Sunday night I was under pressure to bring the MacCarthy Cup to a function in a hotel in Roscrea. Tony McTague, who played football with the All-Ireland champions Offaly, was bringing the Sam Maguire Cup to the same event.

There was so much happening and as if that wasn't enough, Fr Cuddy a local priest from Toomevara, had arranged that I would travel to England early the next morning to bring the cup to the Irish community over there!

All that time Mary and our new baby, Fiona were still in the hospital.

That was November, 1971 and then in December we played the first modern day All-Ireland club final. The first ever was held in Birr; it was fixed as the venue for us against Offaly champions, Banagher.

We won it well, making history.

To cap a memorable year, four of the Tipp team picked up a new hurling award called the All Stars It was a great night when Francis Loughnane, Mick Roche, Babs and myself collected our awards.

Now that was some year, not much could top that!

That's the story of 1971.

BABS KEATING

TIPPERARY 5-17, KILKENNY 5-14
All-Ireland SHC Final
Croke Park
SEPTEMBER 5, 1971

The inspirational Babs Keating led Tipperary back onto the All-Ireland stage

★ **TIPPERARY:** P. O'Sullivan; L. King, J. Kelly, J. Gleeson; T. O'Connor, M. Roche, L. Gaynor; PJ Ryan (0-2), S. Hogan; F. Loughnane (0-4), N. O'Dwyer (1-0), D Ryan (1-1); J. Flanagan (1-2), R. Ryan (2-0), **M. Keating (0-7)**. Subs: J. Doyle for Hogan, P. Byrne (0-1) for Flanagan.

★ **KILKENNY:** O. Walsh; P. Larkin, P. Dillon, J. Treacy; W. Murphy, P. Henderson, M. Coogan; F. Cummins (0-2), P. Lawlor; M. Murphy (1-1), P. Delaney, E. Keher (2-11); M. Brennan, K. Purcell (1-0), N. Byrne (1-0). Subs: P. Moran for W. Murphy, P. Cullen for Brennan, T. Carroll for Larkin.

THE ACTION

PERHAPS BECAUSE THE All-Ireland final was being televised in colour for the first time, the 1971 meeting of Tipperary and Kilkenny saw the smallest crowd in Croke Park on the first Sunday in September for the first time since 1958. The attendance totalled 61,393, and those sitting at home did not get to fully savour a game for the ages.

Tipperary had scored 3-26 against Galway in the semi-final, but never hit their top form on the day and needed Michael 'Babs' Keating to run riot on the field with a personal total of 2-12. Kilkenny had struck 6-16 against Wexford in the Leinster final, and had an easy passage through London in their semi-final.

It was the first 80-minute All-Ireland final, and the opening half was typically as tense and hard fought as the previous 12 meetings of the counties in the championship decider. Tipp defended the Railway end. They had a strong breeze at their backs. Nineteen minutes in, Noel O'Dwyer scored the first goal of the day but within 60 seconds Eddie Keher, who would finish the afternoon with a personal tally of 2-11, blasted to the net from the 21-yard line.

The game was finally 'on'.

Tipp led by 2-10 to 2-4 at half-time. Kilkenny surged into the game on the restart and brought the margin back to a single point, and although Tipp fought back to go three up, a Kieran Purcell goal left The Cats level on 4-11 to 3-14. There was over 60 minutes played when Frank Cummins put Kilkenny one up.

Tipperary now had to fight for their lives and for one more precious All-Ireland title.

★★★★★

66

COMING FROM WHERE I came from, an area with no hurling tradition, getting to be the first from the parish to wear the blue and gold in an inter-county match, and then going on to march behind the Artane Boys Band on All-Ireland final day and bring that medal to the parish... that was life changing.

My first All-Ireland win in 1964 was incredible. But I think I got more satisfaction from the 1971 All-Ireland final against Kilkenny than any other win because Mick Roche, Len Gaynor, John O'Donoghue and I were the only four left from the early 60s. Being on the 1964 team I didn't carry any responsibility.

But being 27 years-old on the 1971 team, the four of us felt that extra burden as the county had lost All-Ireland finals in 1967 and '68. There were no minors breaking through in the 60s so there was a general feeling that if we didn't win in '71 it was the end of the road for the four of us.

That All-Ireland final day at Croke Park in '71 was the destination for a journey that began when I was very young

My father was an out-and-out Tipperary fanatic.

Hurling was always a topic of conversation throughout my juvenile years and there was no Sunday that we weren't at a match. We came from a middle-sized farm and were all educated reasonably well. My mother and father both worked hard, but there were no luxuries.

I was particularly lucky that hurling coaching had started in the schools and I had a teacher from Kerry who sparked the match in the school. From there, hurling and football became part of the parish and we grew up with it. I dreamed of playing with Tipperary and was lucky as I had a home-grown hero living near the banks of the Suir.

When I think back to my childhood, I looked up to Theo English.

Cycling to the High School in Clonmel if I met him on the road, or anywhere, my day was made. I often went out of my way to meet him. He'd encourage me to be a hurler and make hurling my number one sport. Theo's influence was of huge importance.

He set the tune for the rest of South Tipperary. We were basically the poor hurling relation, both south and west, but the west had the tradition of having more inter-county hurlers than the south to some degree, particularly in that era with the Cashel fellas and Willie O'Donnell from Golden.

Theo was the only one from South Tipperary that hurled with the county at that time.

Making the Tipp senior hurling team changed my life. To be mixing with players I admired so much and sharing the same dressing-room as John Doyle, Tony Wall, Nealon, Devaney and the likes, was just a great place to be.

John Doyle was an amazing leader.

Everything about his approach to the game was about making yourself be the right person for Tipperary hurling and doing whatever you had to do to be the best you could be. Doyle ploughed fields in his bare feet to build up his ankles and legs. Mick Maher was of a similar philosophy but the likes of Tony Wall was unique and saw the world differently.

The chemistry for success was there. John O'Donoghue, Mick Roche and myself started the same day and joined a group of leaders. To top it off, we got to train in Semple Stadium which was just marvellous!

The first big county game I played was a league final and there was a trip to New York at stake. The winning team would get to travel with an allowance which was a huge reward for the likes of Mick Roche and myself. In those days flying anywhere was much less frequent than now.

There were so many people from Tipperary that had to leave Ireland at the time of Independence and the Civil War that never got to come back. We brought Ireland to them Stateside and loved singing songs with them as well as living it up.

Donie Nealon, Liam Devaney, Roche, Theo and myself all got on great together so we ensured we played our part in pubs and house parties that were often organised for us. That was the scene with Tipp that I entered into. There was glamour and privilege both here and abroad.

Being a county hurler put you on a pedestal and it would carry you around the world.

It was a special year in 1971 for me as I missed out on a lot of the '70 campaign due to a football injury. I spent the winter getting myself fit and ready for the '71 championship.

I was living in Limerick back then, near Thomond Park, and I had a colleague at work who was a member of Young Munster rugby club and I spent the winter training with the rugby team! When the hurling got going I was ready to came back for a league semi-final against Cork, where I scored about 1-13 on Pat McDonnell who was the previous year's Hurler of the Year.

Limerick beat us in the league final, but I was up and running.

Time rolled on until we met Limerick again in the Munster final. They threw everything at us that day as Limerick hadn't won a Munster final since the peak of Mick Mackey in the 1940s. It was a tense game.

A key moment arrived when we were eight down, and got a '21'.

There was no such thing as a penalty back then so I took all 21-yard frees. The hurling balls in those days were much heavier than now and were hand-made. Donie Nealon brought in a dry ball for the free, which added to my chances against the packed defence.

I hit the net.

I hit 3-5 that day in Killarney and it's often recalled for that famous story of the 'dry ball'.

Some even nicknamed me 'dry balls'!

I'd say one of the best games I ever had was against Galway in the All-Ireland semi-final. I got scores that day that I'll always remember. For one point I was at the corner flag and played it over the bar.

The final against Kilkenny didn't stand out from a performance point of view, as much as Killarney or the semi-final against Galway because I had an exceptional day against Galway and we needed it. Winning the final stood out but, overall, it was the year that stands out.

The 1971 final against Kilkenny was a cautious affair.

It was an 80-minute final and a typical age-old Tipp and Kilkenny type of test with Frank Murphy from Cork in as the referee. Throughout the 60s there was bitterness between the teams.

Very few were on speaking terms.

I couldn't find the words to describe the bitterness and, thankfully, a lot of it is water under the bridge now decades later. I think Eddie Keher of Kilkenny best described it when he told the story about the time both county teams went to New York. Both counties travelled on the same plane and stayed in the same hotel in Manhattan. We were staying on the 15th or 16 floor, one floor above the

Kilkenny players.

They were waiting for the lift and the lift stopped on their floor.

There was four of us from Tipp already in it so the doors just opened and closed without acknowledgement, and they let the lift go.

They preferred to wait.

Or walk all those floors rather than join us in the lift!

Croke Park was no place for the faint-hearted on the day of the final. We hurled with the wind in the first-half but there was no room there at all. I was on Fan Larkin, who was a ferocious marker; he had me in a vice-like grip but I played the ball every chance I got. I took the frees, moved the ball and made things happen for others.

They were hardy backs, the likes of Fan, as well as Jim Treacy, Pa Dillon and Pat Henderson. They were as tough as it gets.

I took my boots off in that final but it's never been explained properly why I took them off. In the lead in to the game I was at a conference in London for my employer Esso, and I went shopping and bought the most expensive pair of boots. They were beautiful.

No one in Ireland had a pair like them at the time I'd say, because in Ireland you were restricted to buying a pair of Irish Blackthorn boots. After our last training session before the final I threw my gear bag, with the boots in it, inside the door of the local hotel.

That was the last I saw of the new boots.

So I went back to my old pair and took them to the shoemaker in Clonmel before the final to be fixed up. A nail came up through them shortly after half-time in the final. When a nail comes up through the boot in Croke Park you take the boot off.

Then you realise you have to take off the second one! It was a wet, misty second-half and the socks were coming off over my toes, so then I had to take off the socks as well!

The commentator Micheal O'Hehir made a hero of me for taking them off, if that is the proper word. But I think now it was utter stupidity on my behalf!

It sounded great for those listening and after too, but I will tell you now, for someone taking the frees in maybe the most important game of their life, it was a stupid thing to do. When I became manager in the 1980s I made sure everyone in my squad had two pairs of boots each and it's a big part of the reason the Tipperary Supporters Club was set up.

The satisfaction I felt winning that day was immense.

The 1971 team was a real team, and it will be until the very last whistle sounds for us all. There was no such thing as individualism in that squad. That would have been despised.

There was a golden rule… 'If a fella is in a better position, give him that ball'.

The on-field positioning and movement in Tipp hurling for decades before and since was based on that mantra.

When it comes to great players you can't compare backs, centrefield and forwards but I've no doubt that Mick Roche was the best player I ever saw. He won his first two All-Irelands at centrefield and he played centre and left half-forward for his club.

The rest of them one might mention as the greats – be it Keher, Doyle, Mackey, Shefflin, DJ Carey or Christy Ring – were all confined to one position on the field.

Tony Wall was magnificent too. I didn't see enough of our 1949 winning captain, Pat Stakelum to compare to the others as he was before my time. Of all I did see though, Mick Roche had the ability to excel anywhere on the field; if you asked him to play in goal or full-back he could do so without a problem. Again though, you can't compare. Roche was versatile, but didn't play corner-forward… and Ring won eight All-Ireland finals.

Seeing my old friend Christy Ring play, all my generation will say that he was the best. He was Maradona and Messi rolled into one. And such confidence! I loved meeting him for lunch when I was playing and after; he would have you thinking about something new in the game for days afterwards.

It was the first year of the All Stars and Mick Roche, Tadhg O'Connor, Francis Loughnane and I collected awards, and I was glad to get the Hurler of the Year award. It had been a big 10 years for Tipp hurling, from the glorious early 60s to the disappointments after.

We lost the 1967 final to Kilkenny.

We lost too after leading Wexford by eight points at half-time in the 1968 final. It felt like a puck around in a church field but they stormed back and we couldn't withstand the pressure in the second-half. We had a bad year in 1970 and the clock kept on ticking, so that's why winning in '71 was so sweet.

After that Tipp hit the rocks. Limerick beat us in 1973 in a close game when Richie Bennis got that controversial point in Thurles and they won it out after. That game against Limerick should have been the end for me. I played in 1974, but I shouldn't have.

Time beat me. I knew well it was over for me but I wouldn't accept it. I played every game in hurling and football I could from my first minor All-Ireland in 1960 to that last match in '74.

Becoming manager of Tipperary in 1986 was defining after my playing days ended. Tipp were gone for 15 years at that stage.

Those who were children when we won the All-Ireland in 1971 were hitting 30 years of age, but had never seen a Tipp victory. There were grown men crying when we won the Munster final in 1987 beating Cork in Killarney after extra-time.

That time is cherished too. I remember John Doyle said once, 'There is an in-built something in Tipperary people that demands success, and I think that will continue.

All any of us do is build on the tradition of Tipperary hurling, and there's very few things that have the glamour and colour of a Tipperary team in full flight with the county behind it. Down all the days, to get to line out in the golden era of the 60s with players I admired so much was marvellous, but that All-Ireland win in 1971 brings a satisfaction that makes it stand apart from all the others.

TOMMY BUTLER

CORK 4-10, TIPPERARY 2-15
Munster SHC Semi-Final
Páirc na nGael, Limerick
JUNE 13, 1976

Tommy Butler and son, Micheál enjoy Tipperary's 2013 All-Ireland intermediate victory

★ **TIPPERARY:** S. Shinnors; B. Fanning, J. Kehoe, J. Dunlea; T. O'Connor, M. Coen, N. O'Dwyer; J. Kehoe, S. Hogan (0-1); F. Loughnane (0-1), **T. Butler (1-3)**, P. Quigley (0-1); S. Power (0-1), J. Grogan (1-8), J. Flanagan. Subs: P. Fitzelle for O'Connor; J. Ryan for Quigley.

★ **CORK:** M. Coleman; B. Murphy, P. McDonnell, M. Doherty; J. Crowley, J. Horgan, D. Coughlan (0-1); G. McCarthy, P. Moylan; B. Og Murphy, M. Malone (0-1), J. Fenton (1-2); C. McCarthy (1-3), R. Cummins (capt) (1-1), S. O'Leary (1-1). Subs: J. Barry Murphy (0-1) for Murphy; B. Cummins for Moylan; J. Allen for Fenton.

THE ACTION

DESTINIES CAN BE furnished by the width of a post and when Seamus Power was denied by the upright the Russian roulette wheel turned in the direction of Seanie O'Leary, who hit the winning point and danced away in jubilation after breaking Tipperary hearts. The ferocity of the exchanges left pulses running high. The post, breaking ball and some harsh refereeing calls went against Tipp. Lady luck shined upon Cork.

The underdogs struck first four minutes in when Jim Kehoe took off on a solo and sent it goal-bound where John Flanagan let fly before Tommy Butler shook the net. Tipp dictated the play. Mick Coen had the better of Mick Malone by then as Tipp led 1-8 to 0-4 after 27 minutes. Cork hung in there though as Charlie McCarthy buried an opportunist goal before the break to leave Tipp just 1-8 to 1-5 up despite their industrious hurling.

After the break John Fenton sent a low flying bullet beyond a helpless Seamus Shinnors. The decibel level was turned up fully when raspers from Tommy Butler and Seamus Power were somehow deflected away by Cork keeper, Coleman. Had these gone in the story might be so different but Cork weathered the storm. The combination of Tadhg O'Connor's injury and Jimmy Barry Murphy's ascendency suited the blood and bandages as Ray Cummins goaled on 52 minutes giving Cork oxygen. John Allen then entered the fray as Cork subs brought a new wind.

Showing leadership, John Grogan buried a rocket. Level for the fourth time and looking like a draw. Then Seamus Power held the ball that would decide the game and perhaps the hurling year. Everyone held their breath as the bullet whizzed. The rattle off the post will haunt Tipperary.

Such moments decide players' legacies. Those watching knew it instantly. The underdogs had their moment but it slipped away. The ball zoomed to the other side where a Tipp hurley went to rise the ball but a moment of hesitancy grasping it gave the hunter, Seanie O'Leary an opportunity and that was that.

Tipp will feel hard done by, that protests about steps before O'Leary's goal were unheard. Similarly, that Sean O'Grady awarded Cork a free out when Francis Loughnane's hurley was held with seconds left. Tipp arguably deserve more than to be cast on a scrap heap for the rest of the year and left to rue refereeing calls and half-forgotten chances. Messrs Doyle, Ryan and Kenny's team epitomised 'the spirit of Knocknagow' as best they could.

★★★★★

66

WHEN I WAS a young fella at home in the Ragg, I was mad into hurling, as were my brothers, sisters and parents. We were reared on stories of great feats on the hurling field. I recall listening to an All-Ireland on the radio and the battery running low, and I was dispatched off to the shop to get a new one to finish the match.

I reckon now it was the Tipp and Galway 1958 final.

A couple of years later, the hurling final was on telly and my father had found a house we could go to and watch the match – it was Nicky Callanan's in Dovea.

It was packed to the rafters but old Ned insisted that no one come between his armchair and the telly. I 'snooked' in right beside him, he was kind to me. The result wasn't favourable but I enjoyed my first match on television.

A year later, Tipp brought home the MacCarthy cup and Liam Devaney was named Caltex Hurler of the Year. I remember being at home one night, a few months later, and a fellow stuck his jaw in the door.

He may have knocked, but no one heard him and he wasn't shy.

'Oh Jesus Delia, how are you? You have the place full of children!'

'Billy! Your welcome!' she said.

We were gobsmacked that my mother and our hero were on such friendly terms. He had no bother selling a few loads of lime in that house that night!

A couple of years later my brother, Eamonn and I set out for a Munster final in Limerick on a Honda 50. It was barely able to pull us up the hills as we went through Upperchurch, Kilcommon and down past the white walls of Newport, but not too long later we safely made it to a parking spot in Limerick.

Our Honda 50 didn't take up too much space.

Excitement was building and we bumped into other neighbours and picked our spot about the '21' at the Town End.

Soon enough, the blue and gold brigade came onto the field and it was a great sight mixed up with the red. The game wasn't on long and our No 15, the one and only Liam (Billy) Devaney, was popping over a point.

And better was to follow.

He snapped a ball with lightning speed, realised what was on and sure enough, the net was bulging! There were no hills on the way home.

I knew it was time to get a new hurley, so the wheels were put in motion. My mother's brother was the principal in Templemore CBS, so a favour was called in. It was a big deal but the hurley was delivered.

The follow-up was to get it hooped with a Tommy Doyle hoop. I managed a half crown from my grand-uncle who got his pension every Friday worth three half-crowns. Off with me, my hurley and my half-crown to town on my bike, up past the Cathedral in Thurles. I found the shoe mending shop.

Tommy was very nice, dropped whatever he was doing and put on two 'specials'. I parted with my money and came home a very happy young man.

The county final of 1965 was much talked up and our neighbour, Con Broderick was playing with Carrick Davins. A huge crowd descended on Clonmel but the great memory I have was the display of Mick Roche and, looking back, I now feel that hurling was getting to a new level of skill, enjoyment and entertainment.

Tipp and the 'Yellow Bellies' were playing in 1968 and my Uncle Toby brought a crowd of us on the train. As we were walking up the quays he steered us into a church for mass. Every place was thronging with people. Inside the chapel people were going out and others coming in. There were three masses on at the same time.

One at each side of the altar, and one in the centre!

After about five minutes, Toby blessed himself and started to head for the door. Any protests about mass not being over were dismissed, as he showed us the priest leaving one altar!

Out on the streets with us and up into the Canal End.

Somebody asked me after if there was the great colour there and my answer was that there may have been fifty shades of grey but when the hurling started there were no grey areas. We were familiar now with Tipperary's style of fast ground hurling, mixed with some super players. I remember that the first-half flew and Tipp were having the best of things. Supporters were chatting at half-time and someone asked Toby what did he think. He said, 'I never saw hurling like that before'.

He was talking about Mick Roche more than the match.

I remember well being filled with ambition to make the county minor team. Tom Everard took me to loads of trials and there was also the question of the Leaving Cert. I didn't make the cut for the first game, and Tipp went onto a Munster final. I got a further trial without success.

Such stupid selectors!

A bit of a setback to a fella's hopes but I enjoyed a good year at club level and came back into the minds of the under-21 mentors for the following year. A couple of decent games, but we lost to Cork after a competitive outing. My club, Drom Inch started making ripples with a young team and this gave us a window to show our worth.

Before that time, I would say there was a lack of confidence and a fear of losing that I expect may not have been in bigger clubs. It took a while to build up a bit of momentum and get that inner belief that is necessary.

Templemore CBS was a big help to me because I saw and played with very good players who moved through the ranks with ease, like Timmy Delaney and Noel O'Dwyer. Winning trophies was very satisfying and were part of the building blocks for the big challenges that might lie ahead. One was always hopeful of being selected on Tipp teams and a word of encouragement along was always welcome and helpful.

I recall a few times when those encouraging words were a great boost to a flagging confidence. On the other hand, it was no bother to hear the criticism.

They had no mufflers at that time. I just carried on playing and a good game or two were hugely beneficial. The county championship was opened up to all clubs, previously it was divisional first and if you weren't successful there, your year was over. That could not be helpful for the development of young players or emerging clubs.

One game on a straight knockout basis was very harsh. The inter-county scene was also on such a system and we – Tipp – suffered at this hurdle one year after another.

My debut on the Tipp senior panel came as a result of my club winning the Mid championship for the first time, and so I was thrown in at the deep end in a league tie against Limerick at the Gaelic Grounds. I survived and played the rest of the league reaching the final where we lost to Galway.

Another one that got away.

After a forgettable league there were a few months till the championship date. This was not unusual at the time so plans were laid on how training would be best implemented. Very little collective training would happen during the league, unless you reached the knockout stages. The long evenings arrived and so the intensity was moved up several notches.

Any injured players were getting physiotherapy with a view to being ready for championship action. A few recently retired players were being chatted up; not a great sign of confidence in the panel who were putting in the hard yards.

Babs and Roche didn't return, but Flanagan did.

Little by little, a good level of fitness was appearing and a definite focus was emerging. We had enough strong leaders in the panel to face the task ahead. Many of them were All-Ireland winners from '71. There was no lack of motivation and definitely no fear of the opposition.

Cork were favourites, not because of anything major they had done but because they had a lot of potential from recent under 21-successes. I believe our preparation was first class, it was of its time – An Modh Díreach.

Our main driving force was John Doyle. Much the same as he was as a player, which was successful for him and was still a tried and tested method, Doyle believed in Plan A, which was to take them on at every opportunity. Make life difficult for them, especially their fancy hurlers; and they had some very accomplished players.

We were in no doubt what was expected from us and that we were able to deliver on the big stage of a Munster championship before a big crowd on the Ennis Road grounds. If it didn't happen on the day it was a long time again before you could atone, if at all.

No place to hide then.

After the pep talks there was serious noise in the dressing-room. You'd be fired up, alright. But you need to get over the nerves and on with the game. Tipp had a very bright opening half which could have been better with some luck but still we led by three points at the break. A softish goal conceded took some of the gloss off our endeavours but there was still nothing wrong with the commitment.

I can still recall as we were preparing to leave the dressing-room, John Doyle jumped up on a stool and by God did he give it wellie about 'Knocknagow' and the great heroes of the past, and doing our bit to further Tipperary's cause!

A few unlucky breaks and goals against us were our undoing.

Cork went onto win three in-a-row of All-Irelands and it would be fair to say we were about six points a better team than them. Whether we could have gone on and achieved more is only speculation.

In the early 70s Tipperary hurling was as competitive as any other and the county was in contention every year. They had taken part in competitive games against Limerick, like the Munster final of '71 and the 'never to be forgotten' Munster final in '73. They also made the transition from that successful 1960's team and a new squad emerged.

Looking back, one blip that could be identified was that not much was happening at minor and under-21 level. We had won a Munster under-21 in '72 but gaps emerged. That was an indication that the conveyor belt was running thin.

We didn't think we were behind anyone in quality or expectation, but that defeat to Cork in '76 proved a body blow we didn't recover from. We can have no regrets, but Lady Luck and a costly refereeing decision towards the end of the game were decisive. Such are the vagaries of life.

Hurling has always been an enormous part of my life and it gives me great satisfaction to see the huge involvement in games at all levels today. Every youngster in every parish is proud to play and wear the colours of club and county.

Drom and Inch players are able to represent their club at all grades at county level and who would have believed that one of ours would achieve Hurler of the Year and lift the Liam MacCarthy cup in the Hogan Stand in 2019.

The greatest Tipperary captain ever is Seamus Callanan.

Tiobraid Árann Abú!

99

EAMON O'SHEA

TIPPERARY 1-13, CORK 2-7
Munster Under-21 HC Final
Semple Stadium
JULY 25, 1979

Eamon O'Shea offered everything he learned as a young man to a new breed of Tipp hurlers

★ **TIPPERARY:** V. Mullins; P. Loughnane, J. Ryan, E. Hogan; T. Slattery (0-1), G. Stapleton, B. Heffernan; P. Ryan, G O'Connor; **E. O'Shea (0-1)**, M. Doyle (1-1); T. Grogan (0-8); M. Murphy, P. Looby (0-1), P. Power (0-1).

★ **CORK:** F. Sheehan; P. Murphy, M. Murphy, S. O'Brien; N. Kinnerfick, P. Horgan (0-1), T. McCarthy; W. Ashman, M. Carroll (1-1); J. O'Sullivan (0-2), J. Buckley (0-1), J. Cremin (0-1); R O'Connor (1-0), S. O'Gorman (0-1), L. Mulcahy. Subs: D. O'Donovan for Mulcahy.

THE ACTION

CORK WERE LOOKING for a hurling grand slam in Munster but were denied by a Tipp team that realised their power in the second-half. Watched by 6,000-plus spectators, with a large number of 'home' supporters eager for vengeance after the senior side's eclipse in Páirc Uí Chaoimh, Tipp rolled up the sleeves and got on with grinding out a win.

Cork led 1-5 to 0-5 at the break but such has been the rarity of blue and gold successes over Cork in recent years that many felt history would repeat itself, however confidence and keen endeavour are attributes of this Tipp team.

The second-half saw the kind of performance we grew accustomed to seeing from these players since the minor success of 1976. Their revival was swift. The score of the match arrived just after the break when Ger O'Connor, brother of senior star Tadhg, gathered in midfield and moved the ball quickly on to Michael Doyle who slipped to ball to Eamon O'Shea. His cleanly struck shot left a point between the teams. The combination by the latter two established county seniors roused the partisan following who sensed Tipp were only getting going.

O'Shea then set up the unmarked Pat Power for a score before a long ranger from Tommy Grogan. Supporters breathed a sigh of relief when Mulcahy's shot 14 minutes in skidded away. Tipp kept digging. Pat Power laid off to O'Shea who fired at goal but it was cleared as far as the captain, Doyle who hit a bullet, but somehow Finbarr Sheehan saved with eight minutes to go. Anxiety grew as Cork were still in the hunt.

Tipp rallied and when another opportunity presented, Doyle made no mistake from close range; 1-11 to 1-7 and the Cork fight was weakening. Another point, then O'Connor fed O'Shea on the wing who worked the ball into Doyle again, and a gutsy roar rang around Thurles as Tipp went six up. A last-minute goal by Carroll wasn't enough to trouble the victors who claimed badly needed honours.

For Tipperary the 70s are bleak when compared to the glorious 60s. An All-Ireland senior in 1971 and a minor in '76 was the height of it. This under-21 side will now do all they can to finish the 1970s with a third hurling title across the grades. It's Antrim up next as Tipperary look to atone for last year's final loss. Michael Doyle, O'Shea, Vincent Mullins, Purdy Loughnane, Joe O'Dwyer, Gerry Stapleton and Tommy Grogan all started last year against Galway in a disappointing final replay defeat. This time around they're doubly ambitious for honours.

★★★★★

66

LIFE WAS SO free. Untouchable in a sense.

In a way that youth brings. Those glorious nights of under-21 hurling. Although I can't remember exactly how I played or how much I scored or anything like that, I do remember an incredible sense of immortality and a sense of it being a big occasion.

In fact, I remember more about what went on before the game, than the game itself! I remember my parents parking up two hours before the game, and I can remember travelling down from Dublin on the train and being in Hayes' Hotel in Thurles for a team meeting beforehand and rocking up to the field.

During that summer, we were allowed one Sunday to train in the stadium after a senior championship match and I remember that evening I had that sense that the ball was hopping the right way all the time.

There was a flow to everything.

It was the time of my life and it was linked to the game. Linked to a time when almost all the stars were aligned. It seemed like it at the time!

It was at the end of a period of Kilruane MacDonaghs' dominance at club level as well so there was a lot going on, combined with the touch of exuberance that youth brings.

In 1976, a lot of our team had won Tipp's first minor final in 17 years. We played Cork then at under-21 and all those games blend in together in a way now. The Cork games really caught people's imagination.

We beat them after a replay in '78 but Galway beat us in the All-Ireland final after a replay. In '79 we beat Cork and went on to beat Galway to win the All-Ireland. There was a hope that those under-21 teams of '78 and '79 would go on and begin the process of Tipperary winning senior All-Irelands again.

The feeling was that after winning a minor in '76 and then an under-21, that there were better things to come. I remember it as a very enjoyable time.

There were some big personalities there. Michael O'Grady was the coach and Mick Minogue was around the place and they kind of led the way. But it was left to each player to man their position in the game. The under-21 game was played on a Wednesday night and we wouldn't know the opposition in the way players at that age group do now through college or seeing them play. The Cork players were new to us, bar Dermot McCurtain and Tom Cashman, who were playing at senior level as well.

On our team, it was great being in the forwards alongside the likes of Michael Doyle, who was such an intelligent player. We all got to know how each other hurled.

As I was in UCD at the time I wouldn't see many of them, but sometimes those of us living in Dublin would travel down to training sessions and matches together by car. Other times I'd get the train to Thurles.

There was no communication in the way that there's 'WhatsApp' groups today, but it was a different and very easy way of being.

I don't remember the games so much as the camaraderie and the joy of playing. It was all a bit 'off the cuff' and that's still there today in the under-21 or under-20 grades. I see it now in young players.

It's brilliant that they aren't impacted by any feeling that things aren't going to work out; you feel you're going to be the superstar! Even though things didn't work out like that as a player, it actually didn't matter.

I still remember that feeling that you could do anything.

Everyone should have that. It's not that I was the top player on the team or anything, but it was a time when you felt life was opening up a bit. I had left home and moved away, but a lot of the lads I was playing with were really good friends. It's a really interesting period because even though I wouldn't have seen a lot of those guys for a long time, if I met them again today, there would be a very easy kind of relationship there.

Even after 40 years or so.

They were bonds that didn't need constant work on.

Funnily enough, I don't think I won anything with Tipperary after 1979.

Not that I consider winning the be-all and end-all, but by the end of '79 I had won nearly all I was going to win as a player. A national league with the seniors in '79, an All-Ireland in minor and under-21, three county championships and I never realised it was about to unfold. Granted, with the club we won the All-Ireland final in 1986 but it was a surprise as Kilruane MacDonaghs had won their three in-a-row of county finals in the 70s and then to win an All-Ireland club final seven years later, with a team that was seven years older, was a surprise.

1979 was a beginning in one sense and it was an end in another but it is timeless in my memory.

But there is no 'one moment'.

If you were to ask me about particular years, I'd have to look them up. At the same time, I do know there was a kind of flow of engagement, and I recognise the importance of it. Not just for me but for others.

My story would mirror thousands then and right up to now in terms of the excitement of playing for Tipperary, and of dreaming about it. The dreams I had are much more vivid than the disappointment of subsequently not achieving. This kind of anticipation is so important as it gives us an attachment and meaning.

From my point of view, even though you would be distanced from it physically, the attachment is still strong and maybe even stronger because of the distance. Not in any kind of lonesome way. It's about the memory of the game, and not necessarily just the 60 or 70 minutes, but also what went on before and how you felt about it.

It can be feelings of disappointments, but it brings you back to feeling... *I'm really at home here and happy at this.* These emotional feelings are related to home, to the club and to Tipperary.

It's the ties that bind us through the distance of the years.

Our senses are still alive to what we felt back then. The sense of anticipation about whether some of these players would go on to play with Tipperary and the sense that you knew some of them wouldn't. The way people came in early to Thurles to watch those games, and the talk around those matches.

All of that is part of the game itself. The constant narrative, the constant engagement with the game and the people. One of the things I still get at under-20 games is that sense of absolute freedom that's there. I think that's related to the age group itself, to the possibility and naivety that's associated with that time in your life when you don't see all the problems that lie ahead... Thank God!

You're just there.

Living the moment. And for me, the game is all about living the moment.

In a sense there's a thread going back through time. I can talk about players before my time. We've all seen snatches of videos of players like Christy Ring and think...

Wow… what he brought to the game! I can talk about the 1968 All-Ireland with Tipp playing Wexford that I saw on television during lockdown in 2020.

Those players were my heroes.

I'm 62 years of age now and I'm telling my own kids, who are adult children, about my childhood heroes, like Jimmy Doyle and Liam Devaney. I could tell my kids things about other players that I hadn't thought about in 40 years.

I could even tell them what Mick Burns worked at! All those things that I hadn't thought about in so long. So there's a constant element that connect generations. I always thought they were Gods of the game. People you hoped to emulate but never really could because they were so good.

That's a connection through time. I often meet people in their thirties or forties who say things like, 'I took my dad to see Tipp play Cork and it was almost like we were completing the circle. Instead of him driving me, I drove him'.

There's a continuity through that relationship which the game allows to happen. Something that can be quickly evoked in a memory which is to do with the game, family or community, or it might be just a fleeting time with a group, like the group my age that played with Tipperary between 1976 and '79. You can appreciate the time you had together in a different way as time goes by.

As a group we just had really good fun. Later on, I played senior with some of them or they marked me in a club game later on. Some of them I haven't seen for years. Time moves on and yet there's a continuation with the game connecting us even though times have changed. It's a totally different world now in terms of technology, communication, socially and economically. Hurling is a very different game now too.

Growing up in Cloughjordan, I saw the deep engagement that hurling gave to people. The natural thing for me was to eat, sleep and drink hurling.

It was, and still is, deeply important to people. When you see the old games on television during the lockdown people realised there's almost a timelessness to it. You're looking at something that's gone but it's so real, it's almost surreal!

It still seems a part of you. A natural part.

There is a rhythm and a soul to the game and I often reinforce that to players I coach. Hurling and camogie have even been given a UNESCO affirmation which is so apt when you think about all the UNESCO sites around the world which define countries and civilisations. Hurling can move you to another plain when you let it, and when it is played as it should be played.

For me, there's an elegance to it. Sometimes the possibilities seem endless. And for me, 1979 was when those possibilities seemed endless.

99

JOHN SHEEDY

TIPPERARY 2-11, CLARE 1-11
Munster SHC First Round
Páirc na nGael, Limerick
MAY 29, 1983

John Sheedy watched it all unfold as Tipperary ended a decade of misery

★ **TIPPERARY: J. Sheedy**; Eddie Hogan, J Ryan, Enda Hogan; P. Fitzelle, J. McIntyre, B. Ryan; L. Bergin (0-1), R. Callahan; Michael Doyle, L. Maher (0-1), P. Dooley (0-2); N. English (0-1), J. Grogan (1-6), T. Waters (1-0). Subs: Cormac Bonnar for Callahan; D. Cahill for McIntyre; S. Bourke for Bonnar.

★ **CLARE:** S. Durack; J. Minogue, S. Hehir (0-1), T. Keane; G. Loughnane, S. Stack, M. Meehan; T. Nugent (0-1), D. Coote; J. Callanan (0-1), J. Shanahan (0-1), M. Quaine; E. O'Connor (1-0), C. Lyons, G. McInerney (0-3). Subs: P. Morey (0-1) for Quaine; C. Honan (0-3) for Lyons; S. Fitzpatrick for Shanahan.

The Action

THE WAIT IS over. Since 1973 the Tipperary hurlers have waited for a championship victory. Afterwards Tipp manager, Len Gaynor who played against Cork way back in 1973 when Tipperary had last won a championship match, said his side's 'edge in keenness' played a vital part. Though unexpected, this win was greeted with unbridled scenes of joy among the 16,500 attendance.

A ferocious appetite for the ball and a willingness to harass and tackle were the defining features of this victory. Debutant goalkeeper, John Sheedy was the personification of the honesty and ambition this group possess. Sharp saves and good organisation from the defence up gave a solid base for a side that featured 10 players making their debuts. Sheedy, who hails from junior club Portroe, earned the Man of the Match title for his cool, calm and collected display across the 70 minutes.

John Grogan, who was Tipp's best forward, fired in a speculative shot that ended up in the net after 10 minutes. It lifted the Tipp supporters, and the 10 debutants hurled sharper afterwards. Psychologically the score had great value and despite a Gerry McInerney point Tipp edged 1-3 to 0-3 ahead after 20 minutes. Clare fought back to level it at 1-4 to 0-7 by half-time.

It remained tit for tat after the break, though Clare drove on with inspired play from Ger Loughnane and Sean Stack. The last 10 years must have crept into Tipp heads but they held firm. Changes in defence, in particular the moving of Pat Fitzelle to centre-back, steadied up Len Gaynor's side. The steadiness of goalkeeper, Sheedy kept Tipp in the game during a lull for them before the key moment arrived on 58 minutes.

Substitute Cormac Bonnar made an important block on a Clare stick and Michael Doyle gathered. Tom Waters gratefully took the pass and soloed away before unleashing 10 years of hurt past Seamus Durack. It was manna from heaven for the Tipperary supporters who sensed magic in the air.

In rejoicing, the inexperienced Tipp side allowed O'Connor to slip in for a late goal which made for a nail-biting finish. Tipp shoved off the weight of history. Grogan pointed to put Tipp three up and the nerves turned to joy.

When Cork's Frank Murphy blew for full-time there was a release of pent-up emotion after a decade of disappointment. A golden day, more intense perhaps due to the absence of the winning feeling for so long. Such is the power of Tipperary hurling; all the old rivals from those hazy days of glory will sit up and take notice because this is a new dawn.

★★★★★

"

IF HURLING GETS into your blood, it never leaves you.

It stays 'til the day you die.

Hurling is something else. There's nothing like it. That championship game against Clare in 1983 stands out. I was just after getting married too! My wedding was in April, then I went back training, and then the championship started!

When I think of it now, there was so much going on in a few short months! My brother, Liam would only have been a young fella at the time and I remember himself and our mother, Biddy were very excited after we won that day against Clare.

I have to say, in my hurling career, my mother had a huge influence on me. Daddy died when we were very young. Liam was only a year and a half old at the time. Our mother guided us along and once you could hurl in our house you were made!

Anything else didn't really matter, you had to be able to hurl though! That day in 1983 she certainly enjoyed it and she got good mileage out of it. It was a great time and it's one I will always look back on fondly.

I know a lot of Tipperary people will hardly believe this, but at the time we hadn't won a game for 10 years! Richie Bennis scored a point for Limerick in 1973 to beat Tipp in the Munster final, and in the next 10 years Tipperary failed to win a Munster senior hurling championship match.

Not one game.

There was real doom and gloom around the place.

It's hard to believe now but we were gone after one game in 1974, '75, '76, '77, '78, '79, '80, '81, and '82. All those years spent without getting past the first round!

A lot of good hurlers played for Tipperary in those days but it was Cork that dominated back then and won three All-Irelands in-a-row with a great team. Clare came with a strong side and won two National Leagues too.

There was heartache in hurling circles around our county.

Every year we were just bet by a point or two in the first round, and the team that had beaten us often won the All-Ireland after.

So there wasn't much expectation for success when we arrived in Limerick that day in 1983. I think 10 fellas made their championship debut. Can you imagine looking for the first win in all those years?

I was very nervous in the build-up, as 'twas my first time playing senior championship with Tipperary. Even though you'd be very nervous, you still had to play and be right on the day. We had some great players at the time.

Bobby Ryan and Pat Fitzelle were there with Nicky English, and the likes of John Grogan too. We weren't overconfident but we were confident enough to know that we were going to be competitive. Over the winter we trained hard and while the league didn't go well we trusted ourselves that we would come right, but we didn't win a game until the last round of the league when we beat Offaly.

That win gave us a little spark of confidence going into the championship. There was an invisible weight on our shoulders though. The weight had gotten bigger and stronger for every year that we lost and as a county we were feeling that pressure.

We needed to get a win.

It was nip and tuck the whole way through that day. There was never more than three points between us from start to finish.

We got a soft enough goal in the first-half and we were really up for the battle. Tom Waters, a big strong man from Carrick, got a goal in the second-half to see us home.

We were busy enough at the back.

I always liked to be vocal inside in the goals. I was always either calling the backs or telling them what to do. In turn, they used to give out to me, saying that I was doing too much talking inside in the goals!

In the second-half, a late surge came from Clare and there was some tense moments. It was a nerve-wracking finish as they were coming back at us and I can still see the ball coming in late on. That would focus the mind quickly!

Clare were on the attack with one of the O'Connor brothers from Tubber coming in towards me with a ball, and it looked like he was going to score but we kept it out somehow. I can still see him in my mind heading for me in the goals; it was a great moment to fend off an attack like that.

Near the end, when we were ahead, the game just seemed to go on and on. All we wanted was the final whistle!

When it comes into those last few minutes and the bounce of a ball can decide it, everything gets frantic. The Tipp crowd were really anxious for that victory.

Then the whistle sounded.

The joy of that moment is a stand out highlight. There wasn't a huge crowd in Limerick, I think about 15,000 people were there but the real, true diehard Tipp supporters were there. That time crowds were let onto the field after a match and there was great joy among the Tipperary supporters.

It's intense going from concentrating on the game with all you have, to the feeling of winning at the final whistle and then all the supporters racing in to you! It was something new. I can remember it like it was yesterday.

I think the heading on the *Irish Independent* the following day was *"Sheedy's saves keep Clare at Bay!"*

Mick Dunne from *The Sunday Game*, may he rest in peace, interviewed me after the match. It was a big deal back then to be on television! It felt like Tipp hurling had sparked into life again.

After 10 years in Tipperary without winning a match.

You can only imagine it now! We had so much heartbreak that all the genuine Tipperary people were absolutely thrilled that we could win a championship match!

There was a great sense of relief afterwards that we had finally won a championship game and it lifted the weight off our shoulders. The management did their best to keep our feet on the ground. We had great time for the backroom team, the manager was the great Len Gaynor. Pat Stakelum, Ray Reidy and John Kelly of Cappawhite were there too.

They were great hurling men. Pat Stakelum, may the Lord have mercy on him, I remember him saying to us after the game, 'This is only one day... but we will have a bright future!'

He was right, but it took time.

Waterford beat us in the next round in Páirc Uí Chaoimh, a match we should never have lost but at least we had taken the first step back.

The following year was a big one as the 'Centenary' All-Ireland final was to be held in Thurles. We wanted so much to be in it. In the summer of 1984 we played Clare in the Munster semi-final in Thurles and we were lucky to come out of there alive. The ref had his whistle in his mouth and we were two points down, and Nicky English got a goal so we qualified for the final even though no one expected it.

In that Munster final it was Cork we were up against. We were in the eye of the storm that day. Late on in the game the ball was going over the bar and I brought it down and back into play.

But in came Seanie O'Leary and got a goal with nearly the last puck of the ball.

I'd say if Hawkeye was there it was gone over the bar before I brought that ball down! It all comes down to choices and you have a split second to make them. If I had not brought the ball down and they won by a point, I would have said to myself that I should have brought it down.

So it's a game of choices.

One of my heroes growing up was Noel Skehan who was a Kilkenny goalkeeper. He was deadly for controlling it and bringing the ball down. If he thought he could save it at all from going over the bar he'd save it. He'd have brought it down, and so did I that day.

It didn't work out for us on a number of levels. Pat Fitzelle, Dinny Cahill and Bobby Ryan were all playing in defence, and the three of them all had to go off that day.

Being the centenary of the GAA, the hunger for success was overwhelming in 1984. I'm involved in hurling all my life and I never felt an atmosphere like it.

The Tipp crowd were really vociferous, they wanted to win the match. The loss was tough to take for us players and the supporters were also deflated afterwards. Cork won the All-Ireland final in Thurles that September.

Sport can be cruel. But that's hurling and I'm in it long enough to know that there's ups and downs to it.

Moving on, it took time to come right.

Babs arrived in and brought a freshness with him. There were a lot of people behind the scenes that were coaching and building silently for the day Tipp would emerge into the sunshine again.

Paddy Meara was one of the selectors in the 80s and I'd have to say Paddy, Mick Minogue and Mick Ryan from Holycross all deserve huge credit for developing players through to senior level. Beating Clare in 1983 gave us a boost at the right time and as a county we found a bit of oxygen and began to grow.

Small things can make big things and that was one of the small steps along the way.

The years aren't long flying by, I keep telling the younger hurlers that. Build the memories and live the here and now.

Being part of the backroom team for the Tipp minors and under-21s that won All-Irelands in recent years, I always told them, 'You get a window of opportunity and it can pass very quickly'.

Some of those under-21s were part of the senior team that won the All-Ireland in 2019 and it's the same story.

Enjoy it and make the most you can of it… it goes fast.

99

KEN HOGAN

TIPPERARY 1-18, CORK 1-18
Munster SHC Final
Semple Stadium
JULY 12, 1987

Ken Hogan arrived in the nick of time to serve Babs Keating and Tipperary in the 80s

★ **TIPPERARY: K. Hogan**; J. Heffernan, C. O'Donovan, S. Gibson; R. Stakelum (0-1), J. Kennedy, P. Delaney; J. Hayes, C. Bonnar; J. McGrath (0-1), D. O'Connell (0-4), A. Ryan (0-2) ; P. Fox (0-9), B. Ryan, N. English (1-1). Subs: L. Stokes for McGrath; P. Kenny for Hayes.

★ **CORK:** G. Cunningham; D. Mulcahy, R. Browne, J. Crowley; D. MacCurtain, P. Hartnett, D. Walsh; J. Fenton (0-12), J. Cashman; T. MacCarthy (0-1), T. Mulcahy, T. O'Sullivan (0-4); J. Fitzgibbon, K. Hennessy (0-1), K. Kingston (1-0). Subs: M. Mullins for T. Mulcahy; P. O'Connor for MacCurtain; G. Fitzgerald for Fitzgibbon.

THE ACTION

PAT FOX, THE scorer in chief for Tipperary, held his nerve and sent two difficult frees over the bar in the last 90 seconds to earn his county a share of the spoils in this absolutely pulsating Munster final. A match that Tipperary dominated for 55 minutes changed utterly as Cork came back like a boomerang. With the thoughts of the crushing fade out of 1984 still fresh in their minds, Tipp must have feared the worst but Fox ensured they live to fight another day.

This game held all spellbound. 56, 006 was the official attendance but the unofficial attendance was higher. So it began. John Fenton hit Cork's first point but thereafter Colm Bonnar dominated the engine room and curtailed the Midleton man's effectiveness. Alongside Bonnar the impressive Joe Hayes had the better of Jim Cashman. Tipp forwards made use of the ammo provided. With Fox reliable on frees, Donie O'Connell and Aiden Ryan scores pushed Tipp 0-11 to 0-7 clear at the break.

Twenty seconds after the restart Ken Hogan, who was in the form of his life, produced an outstanding full-length diving save to deny Kieran Kingston. The Lorrha net minder, who hails from the same club as former legend Tony Reddin, made another vital save on 42nd minutes, this time from John Fitzgibbon. The 'Goal a game Man' slipped silently away from defenders with the ball at his feet but Hogan judged the moment perfectly and denied the Glen Rovers' attacker.

Things were going Tipperary's way. Fox added a point in the 12th minute before a spectacular goal two minutes later. Hayes lobbed a hopping ball towards goal. Nicholas English lost a grip of his hurley getting past Richard Browne but followed the flight of the ball, dribbling for a yard with a slight touch, before side-footing past the advancing Ger Cunningham. Supporters went wild as Tipp moved 1-14 to 0-10 clear.

Frankenstein-like though, Cork just wouldn't go away. Whatever bullets Tipp sent towards them, Cork simply got on with it. The confidence from years of success oozed through and they clutched to thoughts of a record six in-a-row of Munster crowns. Tony O'Sullivan and Teddy MacCarthy raised flags before the excellent Fox steadied Tipp nerves to leave it 1-16 to 0-16 with six left. Hauntingly for Tipp, Fenton pointed before Kieran Kingston rattled the net.

It was left to scorer-in-chief Fox to save the day. A remarkable climax. Despite how well they played the Tipperary dressing-room resembled a morgue afterwards. 'Cheer up for God's sake' were the words of advice dished out by selector, Donie Nealon to the team. 'This team showed what it can do,' manager Babs Keating told reporters before adding, 'We will play even better in the replay'.

★★★★★

66

RICHARD STAKELUM, OUR captain, led us out that day into the sea of noise. They reckon there were about 65,000 people packed into Thurles for that Munster final. The hunger and passion in the Tipperary people was something else, they just wanted something tangible to hold onto.

There were many highlights and many lowlights in my time hurling, but the game of my life was the 1987 Munster hurling final.

The leadership and the example that Richard gave us is something I will always remember. Now in my time – and I've been involved in coaching, management and as a player – Richard was just the most inspirational captain. A brilliant leader.

The best I've seen.

He hurled his way into that team even though he hadn't played minor for Tipperary. He was Dublin-based, as were John Kennedy and I.

The three of us played in an old inter-county 'Sevens' hurling competition in Islandbridge in Dublin. Babs was also Dublin-based and was up there managing at the tournament, and he trusted what he saw on the pitch. So on the back of that 'Sevens' competition the three of us were lucky enough to be called in to the Tipp squad for the 1987 season.

We made the Tipp team that summer.

On Munster final day Richie was wing back, John was centre-back and I was in the goals.

It had been 16 long years without championship silverware. The belief that we were invincible had gone from Tipperary hurling.

I had made my debut against Roscommon in Athleague and knew we were coming from a very low point. We were playing Division 2 hurling against Roscommon, Meath and Down, so it was a long way from the teams challenging for All-Irelands.

We were in the doldrums.

Babs took over in the autumn the year before and brought in Donie Nealon and Theo English to work alongside him when things weren't going well. It was the famine period for Tipperary hurling, and a lot of people didn't see that changing after Clare beat us again in the 1987 National League semi-final in Cork.

The Munster Championship that summer began with a tentative victory over Kerry at Killarney. We had a huge game then against Clare, also in Killarney.

That match finished level with Gerry McInerney of Clare scoring a last minute goal to draw it. I remember Donie Nealon coming in to the dressing-room, and he was absolutely irate. With all the underage success people were expecting more from us, so that last minute goal was a huge jolt.

I suppose there was great frustration at the time because Tipperary hurling just wasn't able to get going again. We got a lifeline that day.

Thankfully, in the replay we had a comprehensive win over them which was Ger Loughnane's last inter-county game. He had the tough task of marking Pat Fox, who had transformed his game, going from a corner-back to a corner-forward.

Next up was Cork in Thurles.

They were the reigning All-Ireland champions and we were the underdogs. It was a huge game as our hearts had been broken by Seanie O'Leary in the Centenary final in 1984. Those memories were flooding back for people, so in 1987 we were all out for revenge. As the match time came close, the management were strong in referencing 1984 by saying, 'What is lost is lost... and what's gone is gone forever. This is now... we have to make a statement today'.

Before the game we went to St Patrick's College where Fr Tom Fogarty, a future Tipp manager himself, said mass for us. It was a very quiet place to be.

We were humbled by Fr Tom's oration.

He talked about trust. About having belief in each other, and about having faith. He made us conscious of the fact that our blue and gold jersey meant everything.

It was a scorching day, and the town was thronged with supporters.

Nowadays, teams have two coach buses going to matches but we actually travelled up through the crowds from St Patrick's College near the Cathedral, up through the town and in as far as Semple Stadium on a small mini bus!

It was something akin to the pope going through the Phoenix Park!

We were starting to sweat and a few of us were standing on the bus. We were really nervous but it turned into something like *The D'Unbelievables* and we all had a laugh when Joe Hayes lightened the mood.

'Oh lads, I'm going to get sick,' he shouted. 'Let me off the bus!

'NOW!

'QUICK!'

We entered the stadium then and made our way through the crowds.

We were a hugely close bunch. The trust Fr. Tom had spoken about was in my mind.

I had lost my father in 1983.

He saw me win a minor All-Ireland but he wasn't alive to see that day in 1987. Under the stand I met the great Tony Reddin and he said to me, 'Your daddy's with you'. Tony was a famed Tipperary goalkeeper who played with Lorrha and for a man of Tony Reddin's stature to say that to me before the game gave me a huge lift.

His words were a huge inspiration. I firmly believe that my father was with me and was behind me all the way.

I remember hitting the pitch.

There was an overspill of people on to the field. The stands were all-ticketed but the terraces weren't, so health and safety measures went out the window! The pre-match warm-up was brief. I pucked the ball with the sub-keeper, Tony Sheppard. On the field I said to Bobby Ryan, 'This is our day Bobby!'

'I just hope it is Ken!' he replied to me.

Most of us on the team were young and hungry to win but it was harder for the older lads. They were hurting and those previous defeats were driving them. Donie O'Connell, Bobby Ryan and Nicky English were the elder statesmen.

Bobby was our only All Star the previous year, but he hadn't come back to training in the best of shape after the All Stars trip. Babs called the shots and wasn't impressed at Bobby's level of fitness at the time so, despite being an All Star half-back at the time, Bobby ended up at full-forward, beside Nicky and Pat Fox.

Our centre-forward, Donie, had given me strict instructions to land puck-outs in on top of him in the half-forward line. He took on Cork's Pat Hartnett in a key battle. Ball after ball landed on him as he led the charge.

There were hurleys broken and blood was spilt, but Donie didn't relent.

The first ball that came in was something similar to 'Hawkeye' incidents of recent years in that John Fenton cut a ball across the square.

It was close to the crossbar, and I felt I had the height and reach.

At that moment you have to make up your mind quickly so I decided to risk putting my hand to it rather than putting my hurley to it.

I caught the ball and cleared it.

That was a huge source of confidence to me because the first ball is very important for a goalkeeper. The crowd was behind me. I was in the game. The puck-outs were going well, we were playing well and Cork were fairly rattled by us.

At the start of the second-half, Cork went for the jugular.

Kieran Kingston struck to my right hand side for a goal bound shot but I was fortunate that I got my hurley to it and turned it around the post outside for a '65'. I think that gave the team a big lift. Richard Stakelum came storming into me, caught my jersey and lifted me up!

'This is it Ken, this is it, we are going to do it!'

After that John Fitzgibbon took a shot at me and I managed to divert it; another one hit me in the Adam's apple! Then came a huge moment in the game.

Joe Hayes made a long clearance. Nicky lost his hurley but he was held on to by Denis Mulcahy. He got through.

He had no hurley but got his balance right and side-footed the ball past Ger Cunningham for a famous goal. The place erupted.

It was one of those sweet days!

We went a couple of points up but Cork being Cork, came back into it.

They inched ahead as Fenton scored a great point, as did Tomas Mulcahy and we were two behind with time near up. It felt like everyone was saying, 'Here we go again, déjà vu… Tipp are in trouble'.

We hung in there though, we had discussed all that beforehand.

We kept going and Colm Bonnar won a free and up stepped Pat Fox, and slotted it between the posts. We won another free 40 or 45 yards out and people might say it's easy score a free from there but the ball was different then, it was the All Star ball with the big rims, and Foxy showed huge calmness; just ice cool, and slotted it over for the equalising score!

The whistle sounded.

Pat Fox would have had a huge say for all the classic games between Tipp and Cork in my opinion. He was the key player and he slotted that valuable score.

It made us believe.

We knew we could wear them down. In a way it was a moral victory for us in the fact that we didn't relinquish, we didn't surrender as some people expected.

We were delighted to get out of it and head to Killarney again! Our fourth game there that summer! The replay was seven days later.

We stayed over the night before in the Aghadoe Heights which was a fine 5-star hotel. Babs wouldn't do it any differently, of course! That day we went to mass down in the cathedral and there was huge goodwill behind us, the people of Kerry were willing us on to victory.

Such a scenic setting, a real saga in that Cork were a point up again.

Time was very near up.

A ball went wide beside me. The Cork crowd were whistling.

I let it go wide but once it went over the line I controlled it. I caught the ball on the hop because I was afraid the referee was going to blow the full-time whistle.

I didn't dare hesitate.

In the one movement I handled it and pucked it out as I didn't want to wait for him because he could have spread his arms for full-time; so I just launched it as far as I could. It landed 30 yards from goal.

There was a clash of hurleys.

Nicky ran onto the ball and he could have gone for a goal, but he was clever. That time you could drop the hurley so thankfully he was smart enough to hand pass the ball over the bar and set up extra-time. I think his brain even surpassed his genius as a hurler.

Taking a point was the best option.

It's amazing how things can differ in a week. The day of the draw, a Tipp supporter by the name of Martin McGrath watched from the terrace in Thurles. In the couple of days after that game Babs got in touch with him.

Martin got the call-up to the panel and ended up being brought on in extra-time!

He hit three points in the game in Killarney!

The brilliance of the three wise men – Donie, Theo and Babs – came into play that day. There was the history of Tipp playing in Killarney.

Tipp were there in 1949 against Cork in Killarney, and there was the belief that Tipp would win an extra-time game against Cork. We trusted ourselves and did it in style in extra-time.

That week between the Thurles game and the Killarney one was the greatest week of our lives.

They were two of the greatest, if you include the week after Killarney!

What a summer!

99

COLM BONNAR

TIPPERARY 4-22, CORK 1-22 (AET)
Munster SHC Final Replay
Fitzgerald Stadium, Killarney
JULY 19, 1987

Colm Bonnar became an amazing force of energy for Tipperary in the middle of the field

★ **TIPPERARY:** K. Hogan; J. Heffernan, C. O'Donovan, S. Gibson; R. Stakelum (0-1), J. Kennedy, P. Delaney (0-2); **Colm Bonnar**, P. Fitzelle (0-1); G. Williams, D. O'Connell (1-1), A. Ryan (0-3) ; P. Fox (0-11), N. English (1-1), B. Ryan. Subs: M. McGrath (0-2) for Williams; M. Doyle (2-0) for Delaney; G. Stapleton for O'Donovan.

★ **CORK:** G. Cunningham; D. Mulcahy, R. Browne, J. Crowley; J. Cashman, P. Hartnett, D. Walsh; J. Fenton (0-13), T. Cashman; M. Mullins, T. McCarthy (0-3), T. O'Sullivan (0-3); K. Kingston, K. Hennessy, T. Mulcahy (1-2). Subs: G. Fitzgerald (0-1) for Mullins; J. Fitzgibbon for Kingston; S. O'Gorman for J. Cashman; D. McCurtain for Crowley.

THE ACTION

'THE FAMINE IS Over' were the words the 24 year-old Richard Stakelum uttered as he raised aloft the cup that signalled that a proud hurling county once more had found their voice. Sixteen years of hurt were wiped away in an emotionally charged day. An occasion to savour for a whole generation of Tipperary supporters who had heard the stories about the great days but just hadn't experienced success. They know what it means now having lived through this glorious chapter.

How satisfying too for the three wise men – Babs Keating, Theo English and Donie Nealon – who shared in the last distant success at the same venue in 1971. To go further back it's all of 36 years since another famous Borrisoleigh captain, Jimmy Finn brought the Munster cup back to his native village. The crowd in Killarney for this feast of hurling was estimated to be in excess of 45,000 but was closer to 50,000 with the match worth over £220,000 in takings for the Munster Council, but for Tipperary people, this day was priceless. It took over 170 minutes of hurling to break the Cork stranglehold on the cup.

It took Michael Doyle, whose father, John had been a key part of the great Tipp side of the 60s, to slay the team in red as the sub scored two goals in extra-time. Three stunning goals in extra-time made the day a glorious one for Tipperary.

The young guns from Tipperary, who experienced much success over recent years, played key roles here. They trailed 1-10 to 1-5 by half-time but stormed back into the game with under-21 All-Ireland medallists John Kennedy, Colm Bonnar, Aiden Ryan and Paul Delaney all making key contributions. In the second-half Bonnar took over the Commander-in-Chief role in midfield while the half-back line, especially Paul Delaney, controlled proceedings there. Throughout the game Donie O'Connell and Pat Fox were the two forwards most consistently challenging the Cork backs and, through their work rate and industry, a six-point deficit was levelled up by full-time. Cork were tiring, their race was nearly run, but Tipp were only getting going.

Cork left John Fenton on the field for extra-time but by then, like the two Cashmans, he could barely run. Tipp were sprinting to the mountain top. Fox and O'Connell earned the lead again for Tipp before a great solo run from midfield by Bonnar set up an attack for super sub Doyle who put the ball in the net.

The pain of losing to Cork in 1984 was fading away for Doyle as once more he rattled the net after a good ball in from midfield. By now the three wise men were celebrating and hugging as they knew the famine was over.

★★★★★

"

KILLARNEY WAS MAGICAL.

Just crazy stuff. The satisfaction I got out of that game surpassed any other. It meant more to me than any other game which is incredible to think of today because it was a Munster final.

A whole generation had never seen a Tipp team win a provincial title.

Until that day.

Cork were going for 'six in-a-row' in Munster, which hadn't been done before but we knew we could match them.

The Thurles drawn game had energised us.

Killarney was starting to feel like home after playing there against Kerry and then twice against Clare. We were happy enough to travel because we won a replay in the semi-final there. Babs harnessed the spirit of the place too, as Tipp won the county's last Munster final, in 1971, at the same venue and he had played a pivotal role that day.

There had been a home-and-away arrangement with Cork previously but not at that time, and Babs didn't want to travel to Cork. It wouldn't have suited us to play on their turf whereas Killarney just had an energy Tipp teams historically seemed to feed off.

We arrived in town on the Saturday in our blazers and suits, and stayed in the Aghadoe Heights, a 5-star hotel looking out on the lakes. With the number of supporters and people following us down, I could feel the hype and excitement.

After the drawn game we had become high profile overnight.

Cork had older and more experienced players than us on the big stage but we were determined to finish the job. There was a clarity to our thinking. If Thurles was the first-half, Killarney was the second in some ways.

I had marked John Fenton in Thurles and he was incredibly fit. He was up and down the field. I was too though, and I knew that no one would outrun me in terms of energy and enthusiasm. I tracked his runs and spent the day in Thurles trying to get a flick on the ball or take it away from him.

Before the start in Killarney they switched, and it was Tom Cashman who lined up beside me. After five minutes I was thinking… *God, what an incredible hurler he is!*

His skills, movement and first-touch made him hard to beat. Most of the game for me was about just trying to get on top in the duel with Tom. His skill level was such that he would give a little flick and swivel, and the ball would be gone in the direction he intended.

He'd rarely catch it; just double on it or keep it moving with a light touch and a strike. The likes of Cashman and Fenton were six or seven years older than a lot of us though and I think that was the difference.

We were fit, able to hurl and had a hunger about us.

Most of us were used to winning from playing on successful minor and under-21 teams, whereas older players like Bobby, Nicky and Donie were used to losing. Fear didn't come into it for a lot of us.

When Nicky got through and had a chance to take a goal, with Tipp a point down in the last minute, he hand-passed it over the bar but a lot of us thought he should have gone for a goal. We were nearly annoyed he hadn't!

Extra-time came, and we were mad for more road.

I didn't want the game to end. Tom Cashman had to go off with a cramp. Cork were fading and I just felt we had their measure. We blew them away then.

Three goals in extra-time.

I remember floating around the field in the last four or five minutes, appreciating it. It was an incredible feeling knowing history was happening as we were still playing. The game of my life, because I've never known anything like it before or since.

It was once in a lifetime stuff.

When the final whistle went the throngs swarmed onto the field. It was incredible how deep it was for people. Grown men and women and children were crying with happiness. No exaggeration.

Supporters would try to say well done but they were too hoarse.

There were no words. Pure joy all around us.

They just hadn't seen Tipp win or could barely remember it.

The emotion was overpowering.

The famous 'The famine is over' line in the speech from Richie Stakelum was very apt. That day was never surpassed after.

That day is just pure precious. It's something I hope I never forget. Needless to say, it was special to play with Conal and Cormac, my two brothers, in All-

Irelands that we later won together too, but Killarney was just awesome.

Babs Keating changed the face of Tipperary hurling. Go back a year to when I made my debut against Clare in 1986. That was a proud day for me to be togging alongside Bobby Ryan and others of that calibre.

We were leading Clare by 10 points, yet lost by one.

Same old story. I remember walking into the pub with Peter Brennan after it and the abuse that was thrown at us was something I just couldn't believe. Tipp people were so pissed off. They were on the wrong side of results since 1971 and we were the latest losers!

There was so much euphoria out of Killarney in 1987, I think that mentally a lot of the team never thought that we were going to dismantle Cork and be Munster champions from Division 2. There was a carefree attitude all of a sudden.

After being abused in the pub a year before, I noticed that a weight was gone from the county and we became folk heroes!

That tidal shift had been coming for a while, as the talent was there. Tipperary teams had started to do very well from the late 70s on, with a 'three in-a-row' at under-21 level from '79 to '81. That was Bobby Ryan's and Donie O'Connell's team. Pat Fox was corner-back and my brother, Cormac was full-back on that team so that's why I was so into it back then.

My age group, like Noel Sheedy, John Kennedy and Aiden Ryan were used to winning All-Irelands too. I think the first time I was on a losing side to Cork was in 1990 in the so called 'Donkeys don't win derbies' final.

My age group grew up having no fear of Cork or anyone else.

With quality players around, it was about getting the mix right yet things were tough for players. I think Michael Scully missed a couple frees against Clare in the semi-final and was gone then after that; that's how ruthless it became overnight at senior level.

Babs oozed confidence. My first introduction to him was when he called to the house in Cashel, opened up the boot of the car and told me to take four or five hurleys I liked. Before that, you'd be trying to mind hurleys in case you broke one but now, all of a sudden, the supply seemed limitless.

There was no money when he took over. The county board was on its knees financially. They had a huge debt after hosting the 'Centenary' All-Ireland.

Michael Lowry came in as chairperson and tried to get that debt down while Babs started up the Tipperary Supporters Club.'

The Supporters Club really ignited in Dublin and started raising huge money. Support came in from all over the world. It's common now in successful counties but Babs was ahead of his time. Tipp were the first to start it and there was no GAA rules about the Supporters Club being under the auspices of the county board.

At the time, members of the Supporters Club were as powerful as the county board in a way; not in a bad way, it was just everybody wanted Tipp to win and the revenue made a difference. The Supporters Club were in the dug-out, the same as the county board.

Babs had brought in a new style and a new way of raising finance.

Ultimately money held the power and the Supporters Club had the power in 1987. Babs was able to look after players who were living away in college or help them out financially in terms of food or in other ways, so that they would be healthy and performing well for him on the field.

Finance wasn't an issue yet they were tough times in Ireland.

We stayed in Carton House at training camps, and stayed in the most expensive and luxurious hotels. We got blazers, shirts, trousers and shoes, and arrived to championship games against Kerry and Clare and Cork in '87 in these suits.

There were people making fun of us for dressing up, but Babs wanted us to channel the glamour of previous eras when Tipp dominated. He brought playing legends from the 60s in, Theo English and Donie Nealon as selectors. Theo did most of the training in 1987 but we had a full-time trainer by '88.

After that Munster final win in 1987 we were all brought to the Canary Islands that December and a county organised holiday like that was unheard of at the time. Babs had new players on the way the following year and the new coach. Phil Conway was an athletics trainer and didn't know anything about hurling starting out, but he knew how to get us fit!

We spent 15 minutes stretching with routines before training with people looking on laughing at us. 'Ring-a-ring-a-rosy stuff' was what some called it, but it's the kind of stuff that's taken for granted today.

Noel Sheehy was into strength and conditioning, but it was new to most. We went to see psychologists, nutritionists and a whole host of other stuff too. The Supporters Club were strong in 1988 too and didn't come under the authority of the county board until maybe '89.

We were ahead of the curve for two years but didn't dominate enough.

We lost against Cork in 1990, lost in '92 and lost a winnable All-Ireland semi-final in '93 as well. That was an exceptional bunch of players so we should have got a lot more out of it. I ended up with five Munster medals but only two All-Irelands, which is disappointing.

Maybe in a way, the enjoyment was the reason we didn't push on and dominate. Killarney was so enjoyable because success was rare. There were no bans on drink or anything like that compared to today.

Teams would look after themselves coming into the championship alright but it's not like the tee-totalling regime of today, where everything is tracked.

But, the biggest changes are on the strength and conditioning side. It's about possession now. In the 1980s Galway were the only team that played a short passing possession game. The general style was get it, beat your marker and let fly.

Crowds loved it.

At our peak we had Pat Fox, Cormac and Nicky inside, so get it in to them fast was an effective plan. As an inter-county manager with Carlow in the 2020s I see that every run is checked. Every metre they cover.

How many blows, how many shots and the impact. Players have one-to-ones with nutritionists and daily meals are taken care of. There are injury prevention measures, a speed coach and so forth.

I became a full-time hurling coach in 1985, when I had completed a college course in Recreation Management in WIT. At the time, some people in Cashel told me I was off my head and I should get a regular job, but I wanted it and became the first full-time GAA officer in the country.

The role was varied and enjoyable, and I spent six months in WIT coaching all the teams in hurling, football, Ladies football and camogie, as well as going to schools and clubs across the year.

The WIT programme was pioneered by the Munster Council. Donie Nealon, one of Babs selectors in '87, was chairman of the Munster Council and from his time with Tipp he had witnessed first-hand the importance of coaching. The course was so successful it was implemented in the other colleges in Munster as well.

Croke Park got behind it then and Pat Daly took over the coaching side of it and it became more uniform. It started me on the road of managing teams from the Fitzgibbon cup onward.

I still head to a ball-alley for a few pucks every day.

I transferred to the Dunhill club in Waterford in the late 90s and in 2001 I got involved with the Waterford seniors with Gerald MacCarthy. Living there, I was helping another county to make a breakthrough similar to what Tipp had done in Killarney.

In 2002 Waterford won their first Munster final since 1963, and I ended up on the line against Tipp. I could see the same emotions in people that day.

Personally though, it didn't come near Killarney.

Nor did anything else.

CORMAC BONNAR

TIPPERARY 2-19, CORK 1-13
Munster SHC Final
Gaelic Grounds, Limerick
JULY 17, 1988

Cormac Bonnar (or simply... The Viking)

★ **TIPPERARY:** K. Hogan; C. O'Donovan, N. Sheehy, S. Gibson; B. Ryan, J. Kennedy, P. Delaney (0-3); Colm Bonnar, J. Hayes (0-2); D. Ryan (1-1), D. O'Connell (0-2), A. Ryan (0-2); P. Fox, N. English (0-9), P. O'Neill. Subs: John Leahy for O'Neill; **Cormac Bonnar (1-0)** for Hayes.

★ **CORK:** G. Cunningham; D. Mulcahy, R. Browne, D. Walsh; P. Hartnett, T. Cashman, J. Cashman; T. McCarthy (0-1), P. O'Connor (0-2); P. Horgan (1-4), K. Hennessy, M. Mullins; T. Mulcahy, G. Fitzgerald (0-1), T. O'Sullivan (0-5). Subs: C. Connery for Browne; K. Kingston for Mullins; L. Forde for Horgan.

THE ACTION

'BABS BABES' CONTINUE their march towards hurling greatness as they secured their second Munster hurling title in-a-row but, despite being 12 points down a minute into the second-half, Cork staged a spirited comeback to bring it back to a two-point game and make Tipp sweat before they found their second wind.

Cometh the hour, cometh the hero and substitute Cormac Bonnar, with the look of a Viking, became the hero that swung this game back in Tipp's favour. Scoring a match defining goal, Bonnar changed the direction of this game back in Tipperary's favour. Tipperary finally exorcised the Cork ghost that had haunted them across the 70s and most of the 80s too. Killarney in 1987 was wonderful but it took extra-time to win it; this time it was different. Tipp dictated the play from the off and called the shots. After being 1-13 to 0-5 ahead at the break, Tipp took their eyes off the ball and apart from one point just after half-time they didn't score again for the next 15 minutes.

Cork took over much to the astonishment of the 50,000 sell-out crowd. Thousands earlier in the day had searched in vain outside the ground for match tickets and were listening to the astonishing Cork comeback in pubs or on their car radios. Kitty Mackey, wife of the legendary Limerick hurling legend Mick, looked on the day the new £1.5 million stand in her husband's name was officially opened. No one could believe what was unfolding.

Led by Denis Mulcahy at the back, Cork snuffed out the Tipp attack. Scoring six points without reply, Cork drove on. Tom Cashman then floated a free which dropped by Pat Horgan and Noel Sheehy. When they checked the ball was in the net. Tipperary had flat-lined.

Nicky English and Pat Fox were in chains. Passes went astray, strikes were over-hit, and tackles were missed. Babs Keating and Theo English frantically paced the sideline and sensed the game slipping away without their intervention.

Cormac Bonnar was the name on their lips. As Colm Bonnar's older brother entered the amphitheatre, he made an instant impression. When Paul Delaney took a free it landed by Cormac Bonnar who connected and finally killed off the Cork ghost. Thanks to 'The Viking' the champions found their oars again and sailed in the direction of glory and celebrations. With the league and Munster titles under their belts Antrim now stand between Tipperary and a place in their first All-Ireland final since 1971.

★★★★★

66

IT'S FUNNY HOW it goes. By the summer of 1988, I was hitting 30 years of age and I felt that the end of my career was close. I had a lot of miles under my belt, and was living and teaching in Limerick while travelling back for club training as well as matches. It felt like there were other things to do in life.

My club, Cashel King Cormacs had been beaten in the first round of the championship each year by Clonoulty, Cappawhite or Sean Treacys. Once we lost in the club championship that was that as far as I was concerned.

Until Theo came calling.

Theo English, a selector with Babs, called into my homestead in Cashel six weeks before the Munster final and asked me if I would go into training with the Tipp panel for a trial. As strange as it sounds now, my answer was no.

I was planning on retiring and told him I had enough of it, and was packing it in after the club games finish. Theo left but asked me to think about it.

After that my father, Pierce spoke up.

'You eejit! That training will stand to you.

'If they don't go further you will have six good weeks training and will be better for the club. If they win… you'll have a Munster medal and another day!'

I knew if I said 'Yes' to Theo it would take over my life fully and I would give everything I could. But I went back to Limerick and spoke with my wife, Nesta.

We had a small baby at home and life was busy, but I decided to give it a go for six weeks and little did I know then that it would be the most memorable of games and lead to All-Irelands and All Stars, and a hurling rollercoaster!

Bonnar is a Donegal name.

We are free-spirited and move around, and my parents moved to Cashel for work in 1956. There were 13 in our family and to integrate into the town, my father got involved in coaching camogie. And the team my sister was on won a couple of county championships. Sport was always a huge thing in our family.

My mother, Maureen won a county championship playing camogie in Donegal. I had uncles and granduncles that played for years with Donegal and for Ulster in football, so there was a sporting tradition there. Declan Bonnar, the Donegal All-Ireland winning player and the manager in 2020, would be a far-out cousin, while Packie, the famous Ireland soccer goalkeeper, is still looking for a connection!

My own father had trials with Donegal as well but it didn't work out, as we moved to Cashel.

The schools helped put Cashel hurling on the map.

Monto Carrie and others were influential in the club while Brother Noonan ran lunchtime leagues in football and hurling in the primary school. Being a school teacher for many years myself, I always believed that what clubs do during the summer, schools do during the winter.

Hurling was the reason I went to school and by the time I started secondary school, I was particularly lucky that Michael O'Grady was teaching in Cashel. He was a mentor to me. When I finished secondary school to go to college, Michael had moved to Dublin and he trained the college Fitzgibbon cup team in UCD, which I was on!

So I had him for near 10 years as a coach. He was a selector with various Tipp teams at minor, under-21 and senior from the late 1970s on, and later managed the Dublin hurlers for a time, as well as contributing to Wexford, Limerick and Antrim hurling in a big way.

A lot of young people who went to school in Cashel developed as hurlers under his tutelage. West Tipp clubs Cashel, Cappawhite and Clonoulty all won county titles back then and, of course, Fox and English were from West Tipp too.

It was a long and winding road to the Munster final day in 1988. I started out as a county minor at wing back in 1977 and progressing on to under-21 level winning back-to-back All-Irelands in 1979 and '80. When the regular full-back, PJ Maxwell from Clonoulty got injured they moved me in to full-back with Pat Fox as corner-back beside me.

I was playing football with Tipp too at the time and putting more emphasis on it until a brother of mine took me aside one day and said if I wanted to win an All-Ireland I better start focusing on hurling.

My college finals took the focus in 1982 however, as I told the selectors I had to pull out of the panel. I had gone down a year in college because of my over-involvement in sport, and I didn't want it to happen again. By 1983 I made the hurling panel again.

Against Clare I came on as an impact sub but I wasn't up to it and was taken off again. It was cruel. That's the hardest thing for any player I feel, because it hits your self-esteem in a massive way.

I felt the ship was sailing and I was going in another direction.

In 1984, I spent the summer in New York and was tuned into the radio as Cork got the late goals against Tipperary in that year's Munster final. I lined out with the footballers in 1985 and then again in '86.

That summer I travelled to see the hurlers play in Ennis when Tony Wall was manager, and my younger brother Colm made his debut. Tipp lost by a point and I left there feeling sorely dejected because I felt I could have offered something to the team.

But we are all hurlers on the ditch, I suppose!

Time ticked on.

I went back to the States in the summer of 1987, to Boston this time. I was on my way to mass in America while Tipp met Cork in Killarney. I remember thinking… *Shite, I'm going to miss it.*

But I had the radio on in time to hear the famine ending! Coming home for the All-Ireland semi-final, I could feel the wave of hurling energy in the county. I was too young to remember 1971, so I had never seen Tipp play championship in Croke Park until that day. Even though Galway won the semi-final in '87, it was obvious that Tipp were on the rise. But my own career was closing, or so I thought.

Back to 1988, and the build-up to the Munster final, and in what I thought would be one of my last ever games, we played the red hot favourites Clonoulty who boasted Joe Hayes, Declan Ryan and John Kennedy from the county team.

The selectors put me in centre-forward marking Declan.

Then, as now, very few clubs have forwards so I was manufactured into one. That transition was difficult as I wasn't a natural forward with an abundance of skill. I did have speed and strength though.

The great Pat Stakelum, captain of the 1949 All-Ireland winning team, made a statement once that always stuck with me. 'You could be playing centre-forward and never hit the ball,' he said, '… and you could be the Man of the Match. The centre-back has the lock of the back-line and the centre-forward has the key to open that lock.'

In other words, keep it moving and make life easy for the other forwards!

That day I did well on Declan. I didn't score, but the fellas around me scored and we beat Clonoulty! I was thinking... *Right... one game left before I retire so!*

But life changed when I answered Theo's call and joined up with the Tipp seniors. I was overawed initially as there was a glamour about 'Bab's Babes' and I was coming in as a 'Joe Soap' who had been contemplating 'life after hurling' in my head, so it was bizarre really. Apart from myself, Pat Fox was the only one married at the time.

I committed fully.

I was one of the fittest training, as I was always fit.

From an early age my father had my brother, Brendan and myself working with him lifting blocks and shovelling on a building site every weekend so physically I was as strong as a horse. I biked everywhere in Limerick too, as I didn't have a car. Skill-wise I wasn't up to scratch, but the six weeks flew by.

There was massive hype and a buzz on the day.

There was so much colour as we travelled from the team hotel to the Gaelic Grounds. I started on the bench. Tipp went 10 up, then 11 points up with the wind.

But the game changed.

In the second-half, Cork reduced the lead bit by bit. Our lead was down to three points. Babs called me. So there I was about to run onto the field on Munster final day.

The instructions were, 'Keep the ball up there... work like hell and give our backs a break'. It was the first time since '83 that I took to the field in the championship so I fought and blocked down, and did all I could.

I wanted to unlock that defence.

I was looking at Pat Hartnett and Tom Cashman, both All-Ireland winners in '84 and '86 and household names. I was on Hartnett for a few seconds, tackling or in a tussle, and I beat him to the ball and said to myself... *You're mortal just like me.*

So I blended into it and became part of the history.

It was a fantastic thing to be hurling against Cork. Tipp and Cork games are always special, there's a timeless quality to it, as it can echo down the years.

As I was getting used to my surroundings, Tony O'Sullivan got a point for Cork, leaving just two points in it. Johnny Leahy caught the Tipp puck-out and won a free, then Paul Delaney hit it in and I pulled on it in the air.

It fell nicely and broke in front of me.

I was able to get in around my marker and just flicked it into the back of the net. With that goal we went from two to five points up. Nicky added a free and all of a sudden the Cork flow was stemmed and we went on and won the Munster final. I had got the bug and I wanted that feeling all the time.

'The Viking' was born that day against Cork. Liz Howard was the Tipp PRO at the time, and one of her nephews said I was, "Like a Viking" coming on the field that day! I wore the old style, flat top helmet, a white one.

It was distinctive and there was no No 22 on the match day programme so people didn't know who I was.

The nickname 'The Viking' has stuck with me since.

After the game, my father came into the dressing-room and told me Nesta's father had died the night before. It was a shock.

I couldn't believe it. It was a huge sacrifice on her behalf not to tell me. She wanted to wait until the game was over before saying anything about it and if she hadn't waited, it probably would have changed my whole future. I often wonder if I would have gone ahead and played the game if she had told me sooner.

It opens up the realm of speculation.

Sometimes a game is memorable because you played brilliantly, but that game stands out to me for those reasons more than anything else.

There was both ecstasy and agony.

Rather than going to a banquet, my thoughts just focused on going to the funeral. At the time our house was 500 metres from the Gaelic Grounds, and the family were all in the house during the game and could hear the crowd roaring from the stadium. We had planned to have a gathering after the game but it worked out so differently.

And on Monday morning's *Cork Examiner* newspaper there was a big article on the front page about the game, while the back page had a photo of me scoring the goal and on another page was my father-in-law's death notice.

The direction of life changed.

I didn't start the next game or the All-Ireland final against Galway in '88. I came on in the final and should have got a goal, but didn't, and then Noel Lane got one down the other end for Galway.

The team wasn't cohesive at the time, and a lot of players were tried in the full-forward position. Declan Ryan and Nicky English both played there, as did Ger O'Neill, but no one settled there.

By '89 I got to play full-forward in the league, hitting three goals against Waterford, but when it came to championship and we played Limerick in the first round, I didn't start. Instead, I came on just after half-time and set up goals for Nicky and Joe Hayes.

I was in then for the Munster final in 1989, and it was the first game I started and finished for Tipp. That was great. My first full 70 minutes of championship hurling and the adventure was just beginning.

It's funny how it goes.

I ended up getting a Munster, All-Ireland and an All Star in both '89 and '91.

DECLAN CARR

TIPPERARY 2-15, CLARE 0-8
Senior Hurling Challenge Match
MacDonagh Park, Nenagh
OCTOBER 22, 1988

When Babs Keating offered him one chance, Declan Carr grabbed it with both hands

★ **TIPPERARY:** J. Leamy; J. Heffernan, C. O'Donovan, P. Kennedy; P. McGrath (0-1), J. Maher, P. Delaney (0-3); **D. Carr (0-1)**, J. Cormack; M. Cleary (1-1), C. Bonnar (1-0), D. Fogarty (0-2); P. Fox (0-2), C. Egan, S. Nealon (0-4). Subs: N. Sheehy for O'Donovan, J. Madden (0-1) for Cormack, M. McGrath for Fox, C. Bonar for Delaney.

★ **CLARE:** P. Carmody; J. Malone, E. Giblin, J. Moroney; N. Romer, M. Glynn, T. Minogue; A. Cunningham (0-1), B. McNamara; D. Power (0-2), L. Doyle, M Meehan (0-1); M. Nugent, T. Kelly, P. Taffe (0-3). Subs: M. Clancy (0-1) for Glynn.

THE ACTION

AN EXPERIMENTAL TIPPERARY team put their hands up for the upcoming National league campaign as they put Clare to the sword in difficult conditions for hurling at MacDonagh Park, Nenagh.

Mud baths, sliding and slipping was the order of the day as both teams tried to get to grips with dreadful conditions for hurling, however Tipperary made the most of it and a number of young guns showed the grit and drive Babs Keating was hoping to see.

Of the newcomers, Declan Carr was most prominent in the middle of the field. His high fielding was superb despite the greasy conditions and, as well as getting his name on the scoresheet, his height and strength contributed in no small part to the victory. Pat McGrath, Sean Nealon and in particular Michael Cleary were others who impressed at times.

Clare were relatively inexperienced too and, despite starting well known players such as Martin Meehan and John Moroney, the Shannonsiders found the going tough in the slippery conditions.

After a slow start the teams were tied on two points apiece after 15 minutes. After David Fogarty was hit hard, Pat Fox stepped up to take a penalty but John Moroney deflected the effort away. Tipp were beginning to attack with regular frequency and Paul Delaney sent a '65' over the bar before Fox pointed from close in.

The home side lead 0-7 to 0-5 at the break and looked like they were only getting going, taking control of proceedings in the second-half and hitting 2-8 as Clare supporters looked forlornly on. Nealon and Paul Delaney registered early frees. Local hero, Cleary then gathered a Carr sideline, he turned his marker and split the posts from an acute angle.

This was Tipp's purple patch. Eleven minutes in, Carr offloaded a delightful pass to Cormac Bonnar who sprinted for goal, soloing past three of the Clare rearguard, before firing past Carmody. On 15 minutes Bonnar turned provider and laid off to Cleary who, with a powerful shot, somehow ripped the ball through the stitching of the net. From there Pat McGrath pointed a free from over 60 yards as Tipp persisted with the rout.

It was game over for Clare who looked out of their depth against a robust Tipp side.

★★★★★

66

A COUPLE OF games stand out for me. The big championship game against Cork in the Munster final replay of 1991 obviously, but a low profile game that stands out is one that was massively important to me.

It was a 'tournament' game against Clare, a competition that isn't played anymore, and it was played late in the year after Tipp had been beaten by Galway in the 1988 All-Ireland final. That game was the key to unlocking my Tipp career. Without it, I might never have got another chance with Tipp nor gone on to captain the county to an All-Ireland.

So playing and doing well that day changed the direction of my life. When you got a chance to impress Babs you had to take it, or you'd be pushed aside.

After the 1988 All-Ireland defeat, the Tipp team needed new blood and I was chomping at the bit to get a shot. My club, Holycross-Ballycahill were asked to send someone in who might be worth a look and I clearly remember realising that this could be my only shot at making the Tipperary team.

It was a dark, horrible, dirty day with lashing rain.

But I was driven and knew I had to leave a mark on the manager's mind. The lads that were beaten by Galway in the final in 1988 weren't playing that day against Clare so it was a really important trial game for those of us on the fringes.

Babs had openly said that we were losing out in the physical stakes to Galway. Nicky too, speaking to the various media of the time, said that, 'We had the hurling but we didn't have the physicality needed to beat Galway'.

There was one or two incidents in 1987 and '88 against Galway where we were bullied so I had it in my head that there's only one way to make an impression and that's to be as physical as I could. My attitude going into the game was that I'd show Babs I had what he needed. Interest was high and there was a big crowd in Nenagh.

In the dressing-room, the jersey came my direction and I knew exactly what needed to be done. In my head it was championship.

That day, I tackled and tackled again.

Every time I went in hard but fair. I made sure my presence was felt and helped myself to two points, and I knew by the reaction of the crowd that they appreciated the effort I was making.

It was physical stuff on the heavy ground and it ended up a slogging fest, full of heavy tackles with no backing down. My intention before the game was to be in the middle of it all, so it was a great feeling to be hurling out of your skin as best you could, going up for high ball and catching or knocking it away from others; and all the time shouldering fellas out of the way.

I had the engine to be comfortable there and knew I had the nerve. I was calling the shots and remember only having the ball a handful of times but made sure and used it well. The tackle count for me that day would have been exceptionally high. I was laying a marker down and made sure to get noticed. Some players let themselves go in winter, but I was fit so that helped too.

I had been training for years for an opportunity like that day.

Clare were a decent side but we won by five or six points in the end. Babs played me in every league game after that, so the foot was put to the floor and I grew in confidence, starting out with a battle against Galway in Ballinasloe.

I set out to boss the Galway lads around. That was a game I nearly got sent-off in, not from dirty play but I wasn't stepping aside and certainly wasn't taking any shit. I found that I was fitter than most others in the league and I could do what needed to be done.

Babs was happy to let me do what I was doing once it benefited the team. You knew with Babs that even if you were good today, you still had to be good the next day. There was no resting on one's laurels, the loyalty would go very quickly if you weren't playing as well as you could or weren't hitting the heights he was looking for.

I was doing a job in midfield that he needed done so I knew Babs was going to find a place on the team for me.

Making the starting team that winter's day in '88 against Clare and keeping the jersey from then on was massive to me. I had come down from Dublin at 15 years of age and I hadn't played much hurling before then. Although, while we lived in Dublin we were often down in Tipp.

With my parents being from Upperchurch, I remember playing, illegally, in the goals for Upperchurch-Drombane at Semple Stadium in a juvenile final.

I'll never forget it.

'Stick him in the goals!' is a line I can remember hearing even though I wasn't a great hurler at the time.

It was difficult moving from the city as a teenager. I grew up in Palmerstown, near Lucan, which was home until I was 15. Then the move came and I was leaving life in Dublin in a time without phones or social media. When I left, I left and that was it.

Moving down to Ballycahill I went into fourth year in the CBS in Thurles and there was fuck all to do. Playing hurling was my only option. I remember when sports time came you either went up to the hurling field or you learned the tin whistle!

The teenage years were tough, as friendships in school were already made by the time I arrived in Thurles. The hurlers hung out together.

I wasn't particularly good at that time so it was hard.

Hurling became my friend. It meant that I had something to work on when I came home from school in the evenings. I worked constantly on the skills and the fitness needed for the game. Quite simply, hurling became central to my being.

I made up my mind that this is going to be my sport. Hurling started to consume me, it was hurling day and night. I got consistently better and I was fully, and I mean fully, committed to it.

My brother, Tommy never fully moved down as he had left school when my family moved back to Tipp. He did play football with Tipperary one year; he actually played with Nicky English who was a dual player.

It's an interesting one… Tommy couldn't get on the Tipperary football team in 1983 yet he was good enough to line out for Dublin against Kerry in the All-Ireland senior football final a year later! He was in the army and was very committed to football, so he had played a bit of club football in Tipp when the family moved back.

Tipp gave him the number 25 or 26 jersey and a couple of runs but he didn't get a fair crack at it, so he togged with Ballymun Kickhams, who had been onto him all the time as he was based at Cathal Brugha Barracks in Dublin. Once he switched to a Dublin club, Kevin Heffernan called him in to the Dubs set up right away.

While he was training for an All-Ireland football final with Dublin, I was working hard to get the strength and skills needed to make my mark in hurling.

Holycross had a big tradition with John Doyle having eight All-Ireland medals, all won in an era of knockout hurling, the same as Christy Ring at the time.

But I didn't see Doyle playing, so it didn't mean that much to me. I did hurl with his son, Michael who was a very good hurler too. At 18, I went to work in England for a few months, and hurled over there, but I came back at 19 purely to play hurling.

The game had become my lifeblood.

Mick Minogue, who was in charge of the county under-21s in 1985, gave me a trial for the team and I got on the panel as an unused sub, winning an under-21 All-Ireland medal. I hadn't hurled club that time as I was in England when the club competition was on. Mick was a mentor to me when I came back and I will never forget how he kept me going by encouraging me and giving me a chance when others wouldn't.

My father too played a big part. He was an intense critic in terms of driving me on and pointing stuff out for improvement.

Having the lads my own age around when I came onto the Tipp panel that winter of 1988 certainly helped me settle in. A few of us came on the scene after that tournament game against Clare, to join the more established players like Donie O'Connell, Nicky and Bobby. That older group had played together for a long time and had seen lots of fellas come and go.

They had carried the mantle, so they trusted each other.

I can recall being captain in 1991 with things going pear-shaped after we lost the league. We had the shit beaten out of us in the league and had a massive row one night. Babs wanted to finish the meeting early, but I insisted we were going to hammer it out there and then. I was really on a knife edge that night and could easily have been kicked out of the whole thing, only for John Kennedy backing me up.

He was one of the strong players that pulled a bit of weight with the others.

I always felt I had to be assertive, as I could sense from some hurling purists in Tipperary that they didn't think I should play for the county as they saw me as a 'Dublin Jackeen'. As much as people had joked about it, there certainly was a sense that they didn't want a 'Jackeen' hurling with Tipp.

It was harder for me to make the cut than it would have been for a traditional namesake in the county. There were lots of people that made me feel welcome but I felt an undercurrent there, even from when the family moved down, as transferring clubs and uprooting just wasn't the done thing back then.

Ciaran Barr, a well-known Antrim hurler of the time, had transferred into the St Vincent's club in Dublin and it was in the news for months. Moving club or county like that seemed to unsettle people in a way that's hard to imagine now.

Looking back, I hadn't the silkiness or the skills of some of the players on the Tipp team, but I did have the hurling brain to do the right thing with the ball at the right time. I just needed the chance and when the tournament game against Clare went well and then the National League games afterwards there was no relenting.

I knew when I got in that far into the team it would be hard to get me out. Nicky would have been talking to Babs behind the scenes and pointed out what kind of ball they wanted coming in to the full-forward line, and from there I became a regular for the championship in 1989. I always felt if I got half a chance I would be determined enough to shine, so hurling against Clare in the lashing rain in Nenagh in 1988 was the chance I was looking for.

Playing well for Babs in that tournament game against Clare opened up a new world. The key was unlocked and things took off.

It wasn't a rollercoaster, it was just up and up.

Less than a year after that game against Clare we beat Antrim to win the first senior All-Ireland since 1971 and I was honoured to collect an All Star award.

The club stormed back to the top table by winning the county final in 1990 for the first time in decades. The winning club then chose the Tipp captain so I fully realised what could be achieved with Tipp.

From making the county senior team to lifting the Dan Breen Cup with Holycross, to lifting the Liam MacCarthy Cup on behalf of the people of Tipperary in 1991, it was a couple of years that I spent literally walking on air.

CONAL BONNAR

TIPPERARY 4-18, LIMERICK 2-11
Munster SHC Semi-Final
Páirc Uí Chaoimh
JUNE 11, 1989

Conal Bonnar arrived to complete one of the greatest family stories in hurling

★ **TIPPERARY:** K. Hogan; J. Heffernan, C. O'Donovan, N. Sheehy; Conal Bonnar (0-1), B. Ryan, P. Delaney (0-1); D. Carr, Colm Bonnar; D. Ryan (0-1), J. Hayes (1-2), J. Leahy (0-1); P. Fox (1-5), N. English (2-5), P. McGrath. Subs: A. Ryan for Carr; Cormac Bonnar (0-1) for McGrath; J. Cormack (0-1) for A. Ryan.

★ **LIMERICK:** T. Quaid; A. Madden, J. O'Connor, D. Nash; R. Sampson, B. Finn, D. Punch; G. Hegarty, M. Reale (0-1); D. Fitzgerald, G. Kirby (0-4), M. Nelligan (0-1); C. Carey, T. Kenny (1-0), S. Fitzgibbon (1-4). Subs: M. Galligan (0-1) for Fitzgerald; L. O'Connor for Carey.

THE ACTION

THIS TIPPERARY TEAM found a new lease of life when the game turned into the 'Bonnar show' in the second-half as the favourites left the challengers in their wake once big brother Cormac joined Conal and Colm on the field of play in front of 23,159. Limerick fought valiantly to stay in the game up until Cormac's introduction, but with Colm dictating midfield and youngster Conal playing like he belonged on the half-back line, it took 'The Viking' to storm in and sack the Limerick defence.

The two sides of Tipperary were on display in this one. Two early goals set the pace. The first for Tipp came after four minutes when a ball sent in from a Declan Carr sideline was scrappily deflected to the net off defender, Anthony Madden who was under pressure from Pat McGrath. Limerick replied instantly with a close-in Shane Fitzgibbon finish. Debutant Conal Bonnar then announced his arrival on the big stage with a fine 60 metres or so long-range effort from midfield after six minutes. That put Tipp ahead but it was the last time they would lead this game until the second-half.

Conal Bonnar is a huge find for Tipp. The Cashel hurler proved he's a skilful, lively half-back, who looked well at home on the big stage. Hurling alongside him was Bobby Ryan who cleared quick and often. Further out Joe Hayes and Declan Ryan were key to levelling at 1-7 each by half-time. Pat Fox pointed on 40 minutes to edge clear. Then the rocket went airborne.

Near the corner, Cormac Bonnar gathered, turned his marker and set the ball on a plate for English to finish in the 43rd minute. From the puckout it was Fox's turn to bury the ball in the net and then again Bonnar set up English for a point. The entire Tipp team clicked after the excellent interplay by the full-forward trio. 'The Viking' was the orchestrator for the duo of assassins.

Out the field Hayes worked his socks off. The experienced Bobby Ryan and the 'well at home' newcomer Conal Bonnar cleared more ball than they would have hit if they were pucking off the wall in the back yard. Tipp were cruising and the full-forward line chemistry was the icing on the cake for Babs Keating. 'There's a quarter of this championship year over for us,' Keating told his players afterwards.

'We have three quarters to go, now let's go and finish the job.' The former Hurler of the Year refused to be critical of his players first-half performance, saying afterwards that the team were 'under enormous pressure' being such overwhelming favourites going into the game.

★★★★★

66

A STAND OUT game for me was the first one in the championship, in 1989 against Limerick. I made my championship debut for Tipperary that day. It was the beginning of an enthralling summer of hurling that finished up in September with Tipp winning senior and under-21 All-Irelands.

Being 19 years-old at the time… it was a dream to play a part in it all!

During the start of that year, I was part of the Tipp panel while also playing hurling with the Fitzgibbon Cup team at UCD. Those of us playing college hurling were given time to fully concentrate on it. The county management, and the county selector, Donie Nealon in particular, felt that Fitzgibbon Cup was a high standard of hurling and would help develop the players.

UCD did well and Babs went along to the Fitzgibbon Cup final weekend to see how I was playing. I ended up picking up an injury though, and subsequently missed a lot of training and league games. Although I attended Tipp training and felt like I was part of the panel, my self-confidence had taken a turn and I feared my fitness level wouldn't be as good as it needed to be.

By the time I was back from injury we were through to the league semi-final against Kilkenny and in preparation played Clare in a challenge match.

I lined out at wing back, got on a lot of ball and the game went well so I felt I had a chance of seeing action for the league game. There were a number of injuries at the time and the following Tuesday night when the team was called out for the Kilkenny game I was named at wing back.

I remember going back to Dublin in the car with another newcomer, Declan Carr and we remarked to each other about how enormous an event this was; we were going to be playing in a league semi-final in Croke Park against Kilkenny.

And we ended up winning it!

For everyone else, it may have been just a league match, but for Declan and me, it mattered as it gave us a good chance of playing come championship time.

A lot of experimental players settled in during the league. My brother, Cormac was playing, Declan Carr and John McCormack lined out in the middle. I was in defence while Michael Cleary in attack was another newcomer.

We were making progress, but I suspected that the more established players would come back into the starting team for the championship.

My second year commerce exams were in UCD and were all scheduled before the first round of the championship and, in fairness to Babs, he gave me a lot of support and told me to focus on the exams. I stopped travelling down for training but he wished me well, and didn't close any doors regarding the summer.

Then, towards the end of my exams, my brother, Brendan who was the Cashel manager, called me. Cashel King Cormacs were playing Eire Og Annacarthy in a big club game at Bansha, and he was really keen that I'd come down from Dublin to play.

Annacarthy had a strong team with Pat Fox as their main player. I decided to go down to play for Cashel and the game went well for me, scoring a couple of points in the first-half, and overall just contributing to the team.

After the game, I got a lift back to Dublin with Nicky English and I remember him asking me in the car, 'How come you're not back training with Tipp?'.

I explained about my exams, and said that Babs hadn't called me since.

'If he calls you… will you come back?' Nicky asked.

I had just four exams left, so I said I would.

That night Babs phoned me.

It was awkward living in Dublin and not having a car, but that Thursday I cycled to Heuston Station straight after an exam, got the train to Thurles and trained with the Tipp team. I got a late train back to Dublin, studied on the train, cycled back to the house in Ranelagh and then headed off to another exam the morning after!

We trained again on Sunday and I was absolutely wrecked when Danny Morrissey came over to me. 'I think you will be on the team against Limerick next Sunday,' he told me. 'John Kennedy's finger is broken… and you're going well.'

For the first time that year I thought… *Maybe… just maybe I'll make the starting team.*

Later that evening Babs told me I didn't have to travel to training the following Tuesday because it would be a light session and he'd be naming the team.

I didn't know what to think.

But then he told me, 'You're going to be starting'.

I nearly got a heart attack!

On the night of the team announcement, my teammates were training in Thurles, and I was drinking a pint at the UCD hurling team pub quiz.

The radio was on as Seán Óg Ó Ceallacháin was reading the sports news and calling out the starting Tipp team for the game. I hadn't told anyone, because I was still doubting myself and was questioning… *Why would Babs tell me not to go training the week of the game if he's going to start me?*

But sure enough, my name was called out on the radio and the lads in the pub couldn't believe it! In a way I couldn't believe it either, but I was delighted.

It was surreal to be in a pub in Dublin and hearing my name being called out on the radio, and knowing I was going to be playing for Tipp the next Sunday.

The night before the match, the Tipp team were staying in a hotel in Blarney. I had the final exam that day in Dublin, so I rang Babs and told him my last exam wasn't finished until half past five that day.

'I will pick you up Conal!' he told me, adding, 'But look, I'm in an awful hurry… any chance you can finish it by five?'

Being young and naive I said, 'No problem, Babs'.

I left the UCD sports hall at five, joined Babs and Christy Roche in the car and felt fine, not giving the exam a second thought.

But looking back now, Babs would have had no problem waiting I'd say!

On the way down Babs asked how I was feeling about making my championship debut and I got my excuses in early. 'I could be a lot fitter,' I told him. 'And I haven't trained fully since April.'

I will never forget Babs' answer.

'Look, I completely understand that you're not at your best at the moment… but you'll get fitter and better.

'I've no concern whatsoever about that.

'The only thing is… Conal… there will be 40,000 or 50,000 people at the match and they won't know that. They will judge you on how you play when you cross the white line.'

I realised from then on that it doesn't matter what challenges you have in life, as nothing else matters when you cross the white line to play; you just have to perform.

In the hotel in Blarney later that night, we had a team meeting and I was looking around the room at all the established and quality players. I expected us to win, but I still felt that I had to keep mistakes out of my play and not be the weak link.

I remember saying to Paul Delaney that I was nervous.

'Have no fear. Every hurler plays well in a championship match.' He told me. 'Every fella starting at this level is a really good hurler.'

One of our coaches, Liam Hennessy knew that the fitness issue was on my mind and said to me, 'Are you fit enough for the first 15 minutes?'

I told him I was, and he said, 'Go for the next 15 then, and if it's too much we have loads of subs who are mad to play'. When it was broken into 15 minute slots like that my fears evaporated slowly.

I was marking Limerick's Maurice Nelligan who was a debutant as well. We saw a lot of the ball early on. One of my first touches was a point and I got a great boost from that.

The next ball I hit went to John Leahy and he scored a point.

But as a whole, Tipp were going terrible. Shane Fitzgibbon scored a goal for Limerick and Nicky got a flustery goal and the teams went in more or less level at the break.

Changes were made and my brother, Cormac was introduced.

He had played in the league and was on the fringes until that point, when he took over the main stage. Coming on that day at full-forward, he pushed Nicky out into the corner. Cormac created a massive buzz and made the full-forward position his own.

The performance levels went up in the second-half and things were going well for me. A ball came into the square and I half controlled it as it bobbled in the air, so I flicked on the ball and connected mid-air sending it out the side then raced over to it and drove it down the field. It was a moment that stands out, the crowd reacted and I grew more confident.

I remember afterwards, Padraig Hogan, who was playing under-21 with me at the time, said, 'You were on fire… even when things went wrong for you, things went right'.

Also, in the second-half I missed a pick-up and kicked it on, tipping the ball off my hurley and into my hand while getting fouled at the same time.

As the free was given, Nicky came over.

'Bonnar... you're some piece of stuff!'

During the game, Liam Hennessy kept coming in from the sideline.

'Well done... now have you 15 minutes more to give?'

There was so much support and reassurance from people I admired and respected. Little things like that stand out when you're 19 years of age and hurling in your first big game for the county.

Halfway through the second-half we were on top and stayed the course from there. My brother, Colm was playing midfield just in front of me which was a huge sense of security. Colm was like a horse, he would just tackle and tackle again.

I knew what ball to go for, and what he'd pick up.

Equally, Colm was as likely to tackle my man as I was. With 10 minutes to go I shouted, 'Colm... would you come back here and help me, I'm really tired'.

I can just remember him looking at me and saying, 'Fine', and he played a bit deeper. After the game he said more or less what Babs had said to me:

'Once you cross the line it's your responsibility.'

That match was the first time the three Bonnars lined out together for Tipp. The buzz was about Cormac afterwards, but Pat Fox had a storming second-half too.

We stopped in a pub in Oola on the way back and watched *The Sunday Game* inside in the snug. Pat got Man of the Match but myself and Bobby Ryan got a mention. It was an enormous feeling going from wondering if I would even last 15 minutes, to being half disappointed that I wasn't picked for Man of the Match by the time I got home!

Afterwards Babs asked, 'How did those exams go by the way?'

I told him that I probably struggled in one of them and he replied, 'Don't worry... I'll sort it out!'

With the aura that he had, I half believed that he knew somebody, or something that I didn't! That's just the way he was, he had such a confident way about him.

There was a big lesson in the game too, about performing in both halves.

I remember Theo English giving a team talk to the whole panel on the Tuesday after the match at training where he said, 'No one hurled well in the first-half bar young Bonnar and Bobby'.

Little things like that would make you believe you're good enough for that level. The under-21s didn't train that evening, as John Madden, Declan Ryan, John Leahy and I were playing in the Munster under-21 championship semi-final against Cork at Páirc Uí Chaoimh the following night.

It was a year of highs with Tipp.

Every championship senior match we played was followed up a few days later with an under-21 championship game all the way to the All-Ireland finals in September.

We won the senior final against Antrim, bringing an All-Ireland to the county for the first time since 1971. And then, with the county on a high, we followed up a week later and won the under-21 final against Offaly. It was unbelievable to be a teenager and experience so much success in a short few months.

Of all the matches though, it was the game against Limerick that sparked the journey.

DECLAN RYAN

TIPPERARY 2-18, LIMERICK 0-10
Munster SHC Semi-Final
Semple Stadium
JUNE 9, 1991

The style and calmness on the ball of Declan Ryan steadied Tipperary on so many big days

★ **TIPPERARY:** K. Hogan; P. Delaney, C. O'Donovan, N. Sheehy; J. Madden, B. Ryan, J. Kennedy; D. Carr, J. Hayes; M.Cleary (0-5), **D. Ryan (0-3)**, J. Leahy (0-3); P. Fox (0-4), Cormac Bonnar (1-1), N. English (1-2). Subs: M. Ryan for Kennedy

★ **LIMERICK:** T. Quaid; B. Finn, P. Carey, J. O'Connor; D. Nash, M. Reale, M. Houlihan; A. Carmody (0-1), G. Hegarty; F. Carroll (0-1), G. Kirby (0-5), M. Galligan (0-1); P. Heffernan, T. Kenny, G. Ryan (0-1). Subs: P. Howard (0-1) for Carroll; P. Farrell for Nash.

THE ACTION

THE FULL MIGHT of Tipperary hurling was on display as Babs Keating's charges steamrolled the Limerick challenge and set up a fifth successive Munster final since 1987. This lethal display of skill, steel and style will match up favourably with any performance. In front of an attendance of over 35,000 the winners looked like a driven side who are in the form of their lives.

Limerick started with a roar but tiptoed home after. The first-half had an edginess about it as the Shannonsiders tried to mix it with Tipperary physically but they came off second best. Losing Anthony Carmody to a red card for a wayward strike in the first-half was a blow for Limerick but Tipp suffered too as John Kennedy hobbled off to injury after a separate wild swing. The Clonoulty defender was replaced by former minor and under-21 dual star, Michael Ryan, who was making his debut.

The turning point in this game came two minutes before the break when Cormac Bonnar collected a low drive from Joe Hayes and turned for goal. Jinking one way 'The Viking' turned Pa Carey and soloed on goal before a clever kick from the former county footballer sent the ball out of Tommy Quaid's reach.

Tipp hit the dressing-room 1-5 to 0-7 up having played against the considerable wind. In the second-half the difference in class told on the scoreboard. It was one-way traffic as the mean Tipp defence held Limerick, who were missing Ciaran Carey through injury, to just two points in 31 minutes of action. Declan Carr and Hayes dominated the middle and sent angled ball to the lethal six forwards.

The versatile and skilful Declan Ryan opened up the defence from centre-forward. Having previously lined out at centre-back and midfield, it looks like Babs Keating is offering Ryan the No. 11 jersey to make his own in the summer of 1991. Working back to help out midfield or offer assistance to the full-forward line, Ryan was wherever he was needed.

The balance of the Tipp attack looks good with all six scoring from play, and all six potential match winners on any given day. Michael Cleary and John Leahy flanked Ryan and were industrious while the inside trio caused constant menace with Fox and English complimented by 'Viking' Bonnar.

The thoughts of the All-Ireland champions of 1989 against the All-Ireland champions of 1990 in knockout hurling by the Lee is one to whet the appetite. Cork haven't lost a championship game in Páirc Uí Chaoimh since it opened, but after this performance Tipp will travel full of confidence. If their form in this game is anything to go by, this is a classy Tipperary team approaching their peak.

★★★★★

66

MY MOST MEMORABLE game. That day we produced what was probably the best team performance I remember in my time playing with Tipp.

I started playing for Tipp in the league of 1987, but made my championship debut the year after and hurled straight through until my last game which was the All-Ireland final of 2001. I hurled under quality managers, including Fr. Tom Fogarty, Len Gaynor and Nicky English who all brought their own abilities as managers. But Babs Keating was the right manager at the right time for Tipperary.

He revolutionised the role of the manager within the county. Thankfully, he came to the helm when he did and got us back to the top. And I was lucky enough to come on to the county scene at the same time.

The supporters were starved of success as we had won less than a handful of championship matches between 1973 and '87. Supporters were hungry and a team can feed off that, so when we won the All-Ireland in '89 everything was great until Cork beat us in '90. That stung hard.

We let Babs down.

We didn't play to our capability and came in for a lot of criticism around the county after that Munster final. So when 1991 came around the players made a decision that we'd put in a huge effort to right that wrong.

In the lead-up to the game, we had bowed out of the league too easily and people around the county were wondering if we'd fade away again; so no matter what team we might have played against in that first game in 1991, I think we would have beaten them.

The mix was right.

We were driven and energised.

After the league exit, Declan Carr held a meeting inside in the dressing-room where everyone spoke honestly about their disappointments with the league campaign. I think it was the first time I'd been involved in a group that spoke so sincerely about what went wrong and how we could change direction for the championship.

We were an ambitious bunch but our league campaign just wasn't up to scratch and we were soundly beaten by Offaly in the semi-final. There was great openness during and after the discussion at that training session.

It was there and then we made up our minds.

Preparation matches for the championship were intense and fierce and for once, we carried that into the Limerick game. We were driven.

Everything we did had purpose.

I felt it was important that we as a group didn't let Babs down again the way we did against Cork the year before. It was all about getting the performance on the day. Crucially, we felt we were able to find a new gear for the championship.

Liam Hennessy was our physical trainer at the time and he was top class in his preparation methods. He had a lot of success with teams and individuals in other sports afterwards. Having such a high calibre coach with us meant we were in prime condition. We were well prepared for the summer which would define that team's legacy.

The Limerick game provided the foundation and the attitude was to give it one hundred percent from all involved. Everything was geared towards getting back to a Munster final. My own preparation had gone well and we were all primed for summer hurling.

The Tipp public came out in force to support us.

They craved success nearly as much as the players did at the time. Limerick had beaten Clare in the quarter-final and weren't far off a breakthrough, so some thought we were vulnerable. There were switches made, as Colm and Conal Bonnar were both out injured.

Bobby went back in at centre-back. The first 15 minutes was particularly intense. Sharpness was needed early on to lay down a marker. We went in a point clear at the break but really took control in the second-half.

We clicked into a new gear and the season took off.

We had dug deep and found a whole other level of performance. It was a game in which I felt everyone made a contribution. It was one of the best performances from that group with every player standing up and being counted on the day, so it was a supreme team effort. We found that badly needed form and felt we were back.

There was a great spirit in that team and it came to the fore that day and carried on for the season. As a group we repaid the faith Babs Keating had shown in us.

After that performance we felt we were genuine contenders going down to Páirc Uí Chaoimh against that Cork side that turned us over and won the All-

Ireland the year before. It's notoriously hard to beat Cork in Cork but we had a new belief after the Limerick game.

We did enough to get the draw and then we won the replay in Thurles, in what was a pretty decent game of hurling by any standards. The skill levels and pace of the replay in particular were very high and would shine in any era.

After beating Galway we played Kilkenny in the final.

It was a great occasion and believe it or not, but that final in 1991 was the only time I played against Kilkenny in 15 years hurling with the county. Tipperary hadn't played Kilkenny in the championship since the time Babs was playing back in 1971.

After 20 years without clashing in the championship everyone expected a classic. The pace of it never got going and it was as poor a final as was ever played but we didn't care, we got the result we wanted.

It's hard to believe we didn't win an All-Ireland for 10 years after that.

The game changed as the 1990s went on. Offaly, Clare and Wexford had their successes after that. Clare in particular, set a new standard and a new level for fitness and physicality in the game. It took us a couple of years to get up to a level to match Clare in that respect.

There were some other great games in those times, particularly in the Munster championship. Some of the games we played against Clare in the late 1990s up to 2001 really stood out. The atmosphere around those games in Páirc Uí Chaoimh against that Clare side was pretty spectacular.

We had a very good team in 1996 too, and at one stage we were 10 points up against Limerick. They beat us in a replay with a lot of the same players that lined out against us in 1991.

From playing in the 1980s up to 2001 I noticed that physical training and preparation went up year-on-year across the 1990s and had changed completely by the late 1990s from where it was when I started out.

I think with all the time given to the game now in the 2020s that the skill levels of players has risen again. Hurley styles have changed too, and I know from the young lads' hurleys at home that the shape of the stick is adapted for controlling the ball and striking it rather than perfecting it for ground hurling.

The ball has changed obviously, I've seen minor hurlers at club level now putting the ball over from their own half-back line in the championship. That's incredible to see.

A lot of the skills on display are probably because there's a lot more time given to coaching young players now than there ever was before. By the time they reach 15 or 16 years of age, players have so many hours of organised coaching put in compared to the equivalent age group a generation or two before.

All those things influence the ball striking and skill levels of today. The game has changed, probably as it has always, but pitches are better now, there's more coaching and the focus is on strength and conditioning much more than it was before.

Growing up in Clonoulty Rossmore the game was, and still is, a part of everything. Tony Brennan had been the old hero from the parish, winning three or four medals back in the 1940s and 50s.

PJ Maxwell then captained Tipp under-21s to a Munster title a decade before my time. Joe Hayes played midfield on the winning minor team of 1980 and after that John Kennedy captained the Tipp minors to an All-Ireland in 1982 before winning an under-21 final. It was great that both of them were part of the county's hurling journey under Babs, who was a huge influence on us all back then.

Tipperary owe a huge debt to Babs Keating.

He was always larger than life. I know he's outspoken in the media, but when he took over the county senior team he changed the hurling landscape. I was in Ennis in 1986 to see the Tipperary hurlers playing Clare and it was a fiasco.

There's a story of one guy playing with another fella's boots, as one of his own boots broke in the warm-up and he had to borrow a pair! Any of the lads that were playing would tell you that they had to look after their own boots and gear which would be unheard of today. Babs took over in the league of late 1986 and early '87 and he changed all that around; he changed the attitude and brought in a greater awareness of looking after the players properly.

When you're playing for the blue and gold, you're playing for the guy beside you and for all that the county jersey means. But I was also playing for Babs Keating.

And just like those on the field that day, Babs had a big part to play in that clinical, top class display against Limerick in 1991. It was probably the best overall Tipp display I can remember.

MICHAEL CLEARY
(PAT FOX, MICHAEL RYAN & JOE HAYES)

TIPPERARY 4-19, CORK 4-15
Munster SHC Final Replay
Semple Stadium
JULY 21, 1991

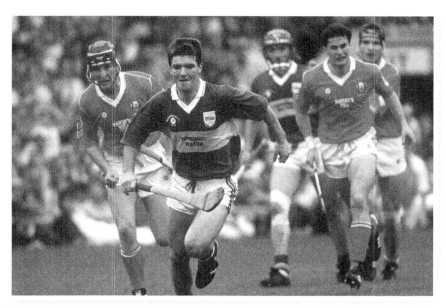

Michael Cleary races through the Cork defence in typical fashion in 1991

★ **TIPPERARY:** K. Hogan; P. Delaney, N. Sheehy, **M. Ryan**; J. Madden, B. Ryan, Conal Bonnar; D. Carr (1-1), Colm Bonnar; D. Ryan(0-2), D. O'Connell, J. Leahy (0-2); **P. Fox (1-5)**, Cormac Bonnar (0-1), **M. Cleary (1-7)**. Subs: A. Ryan (1-1) for O'Connell; **J. Hayes** for Madden.

★ **CORK:** G. Cunningham; S. O'Gorman, R. Browne, D. Walsh; C. Casey (0-1), J. Cashman (0-3), P. Hartnett; B. O'Sullivan, T. McCarthy; T. Mulcahy (0-1), M. Foley, T. O'Sullivan (0-6); G. Fitzgerald (1-2), K. Hennessy (1-0), J. Fitzgibbon (2-1). Subs: P. Buckley (0-1) for B. O'Sullivan.

THE ACTION

RARELY DOES A game capture hurling's utter magic in the way this game did for all who witnessed it. This was one of the greatest Munster finals in living memory. Probably once in a lifetime stuff. After a drawn thriller two weeks ago, both teams produced even greater stuff in this replay which had all the ingredients of a classic. Honours go to Tipperary, in irrepressible form, as they hit 3-9 to Cork's 1-2 in the last 20 minutes.

On a humid, warm and windless afternoon in Thurles, Cork led 2-8 to 1-7 at the break. Tasty exchanges saw John Madden and Declan Ryan's name go into the book but the game was sporting.

Newcomer at corner-back, Michael Ryan looks made for the big stage. He had to settle fast alongside Noel Sheehy as the defence was busy but so too was Cork's defence. Michael Cleary, who was simply outstanding throughout, kept the scoreboard ticking over along with the team's star forward, Pat Fox. For all their efforts though, Cork looked likely winners until three key moments changed the course of this game.

Warriors, Joe Hayes and Aiden Ryan, were called by Babs Keating as he looked to stir in a magic ingredient before it was too late. Added to that, Babs moved John Leahy to half-back and then the 'fire starter' arrived, a Pat Fox goal, in the 52nd minute.

This was one storming comeback considering that when a Kevin Hennessy goal put Cork 3-13 to 1-10 ahead with 23 minutes to go Tipp looked down and out. There is a spirit and determination about Tipp this year though that suggests they realise the potential they possess. The capacity 55,000 crowd got entertainment and magic in equal measure. Point by point Tipp kept going until an injury-time goal from Aiden Ryan sealed it.

It's one that will be played on long winter nights in pubs across Tipperary for years to come. Like a whirlwind he dispossessed one Cork defender then went past a second red shirt before slotting past Cunningham.

It completed a 14-point turnaround. The supporters, bursting with excitement, stormed the field. They had done so already for Pat Fox's goal and now the moment of destiny was closer still.

★★★★★

66

THE 1991 MUNSTER final replay was the standout game of my career for many reasons. Cork were the reigning All-Ireland champions at the time and after getting a draw against them down in Cork we found ourselves nine points down in the second-half in Thurles but managed to get back level, and win it.

There was a massive rivalry between the counties at the time, with us winning the All-Ireland in 1989 and then Cork beating us in '90 and winning the All-Ireland. We had beaten Antrim in the '89 final and there was a notion thrown about at the time that we hadn't beaten an established hurling county in the final.

So after losing to Cork in 1990 it felt like the reputation of the Tipp team was on the line in '91.

I had a hurley I played with in every Tipp match back then and I minded it like you'd mind a child!

It was one I absolutely loved, made by Phil Bourke of Upperchurch.

I had discovered Phil's hurleys when I was a minor with Tipp. In 1983, our manager Brother Perkins organised it so that we all got a hurley from Phil as a 'treat' for winning the Munster final. I can still feel it and see it!

From that day until the day I stopped, I never used anything only a Phil Bourke hurley. I always had three hurleys and would be very particular about them. In 1990 Phil gave me my favourite hurley of all time.

I used it straight through until I broke it marking Gerry McInerney of Galway in 1993, but I had it for the entire '91 championship and it was in my hands during those two epic contests against Cork.

We trained on the Sunday between the draw and the replay in Thurles Sarsfield's 'outside field' and there was a great feeling. It was as though the senses were heightened. It was a privilege to be there on what was a balmy summer's evening; the ball was hopping nicely, and I remember thinking … *God, this is magic to be part of… there's such great energy.*

Going home in the car after training with Conor O'Donovan I felt really good and knew we were ready for something special.

There was an excitement in the county about it at the time.

There was no 'backdoor' so the stakes were high, but I felt that all the ingredients were mixing in the pot for what I sensed was going to be a titanic battle.

The Sunday morning of the game, Fr Tom Fogarty said mass for us in Templemore. It was private and had been organised just for the team, and afterwards we went for a few pucks. We then headed by bus to Thurles for the game and having our own superstitions, I always sat beside Conal Bonnar on the bus!

I can remember saying…

'Conal, I've a great feeling about today!'

It wasn't something I'd normally say and we knew we would have to be at our best for the full game to win. We weren't ultra-confident or anything like that but there wasn't any fear of Cork there either.

As we got to Thurles there was a phrase going round in my head that Fr. Tom Fogarty had used in mass that morning. Crystal Palace were after being beaten 9-0 by Liverpool and Fr. Tom made reference to it in his sermon.

'Form comes and goes… but class is always there.'

It may be a well-known phrase now, but that was the first time I heard it and it stuck in my head and gave me the reassurance I needed. He was making reference to the fact we had a poor league but were still a great team, and it was time to go out and show it.

One thing I always hated was meeting someone I knew when I got off the bus at a big stadium on match day, be it family or friends.

I didn't like making eye contact with anyone, just wanting to get into the dressing-room, tog off and prepare for the game in my own way; then get out on the field and play. That was the usual routine but that day my uncle and godfather, whom I was very fond of, Tommy Gavin, from county Clare was there.

I got off the bus and this fella shook my hand without me seeing him, and who was it only Tommy, who gave me a big hug and I was pure delighted.

As it was a replay there was no minor match beforehand, yet as we were going out the tunnel there was a big crowd even an hour before throw-in.

It wasn't sunny, but a warm day and a sense of occasion with a hum from the crowd. After a couple of minutes, I had a feel for it and headed back into the dressing-room.

I don't remember any speeches beforehand, but I was playing Fr. Fogarty's words over in my head.

Nicky English didn't play that day as he was injured. After the draw he made the famous remark, 'If I had ducks… they'd drown' about his accuracy but he was still winning ball and was generally involved in everything.

In Nicky's absence I was moved into corner-forward and started on Sean O'Gorman. It was the only time I marked him and he never shut up! He was talking all the time, almost a commentary on the game.

'Oh… I thought that was a great score down the other end.

'Michael… what did you think of it?'

Things like that!

I don't think it was any kind of gamesmanship, it was just his way and I remember thinking… *Will he ever shut up!*

Until I ignored him, and focused on my own game.

Getting an early point really settled me into it and then further on in the half I remember that Cormac Bonnar came through with a ball and it was a two-on-one situation. It was obvious that he was going to give me the pass but I was 10 or 15 yards away.

With the greatest respect, and I know he will enjoy me saying it, I remember thinking at that moment that if 'Big Bonnar' was giving me a pass it wasn't going to come into my hand and I'd have to move left or right or some way for it!

It came at my ankles, and thankfully I put it away and the roar went up. I had got a goal in 1990 but that was my first one in a big championship match that we won.

The goal sticks out as a clear memory in my mind.

I keep going back to it; how privileged I felt to be playing for Tipp and for my father to see me play that day. I grew up at a time that my father, and his peers at the time, spoke nothing but hurling.

It centred on the 'three in-a-row' Tipp team of the 1949 to '51 era more than the 60s team. I carried that, and felt privileged to wear that Tipp jersey, be it in a league game, challenge match or that day against Cork.

That was the ultimate honour in life to me at the time.

To be holding my own and scoring a goal that day was powerful. I was fully cognisant of everything it meant to be wearing the jersey and to be the embodiment of that tradition. That game just flowed for me. I wanted the ball all the time and I felt and understood the magnitude of it being a Tipp and Cork final in Thurles.

By half-time, both sides felt it was their day but in the second-half they pulled away and went nine points up after Kevin Hennessy scored a goal.

I wasn't worried at the time, as they had gone seven up in the drawn game and we pulled it back and on the day of the replay they weren't nine points better than us at any time during the game.

When they were nine up they couldn't consolidate it.

We kept hurling. Our comeback started.

Declan Ryan pulled and hit Jim Cashman under a dropping ball. Cork lads, to this day, will say Declan should have been sent off but Declan never took his eyes off the ball.

People say it took Jim Cashman out of the game but he wasn't dominating at the time. Within two or three minutes we had a couple of points and a goal scored. I'd say they only had a nine point lead for five minutes, and then it was back to four points very quickly.

That day, the crowd came in on the field from the Killinan End terrace and I was down that end. Those days, a corner-forward didn't drift out too far from the goal and I was only about 10 yards from the crowd.

Declan Carr got his famous goal with an overhead flick, and then Pat Fox found room and got a flick on the ball turning it into the net ahead of an on-rushing Ger Cunningham, so the tables had turned.

The game was held up for two minutes as the ref pleaded with supporters to go off the field as they were starting to get onto the Cork goalkeeper Ger Cunningham over pucking out the ball.

The guards came in and got the supporters back.

The next thing, my hurley was gone!

Some young fella had run in from the crowd and took my hurley!

The ball was about to be pucked out and just before I went to roar for a new stick the same supporter came back to me and said, 'Oh sorry… here's your hurley back!'

The place was throbbing, there was a fantastic atmosphere. Everything was magnified. They were the moments you knew would define the future.

Towards the end, Cork were still in it, still lurking and they were used to winning in Thurles too. When Declan Carr drove in a ball to the forwards, the Cork defender Sean O'Gorman gathered it for a long clearance but the speed of Aiden Ryan meant he got up to the '45' and blocked him down.

Then the ball broke to the Cork full-back, Richard Brown who went to clear. But Aiden kept racing away; won it, rose the ball, and headed for the goals.

He fired it low to the left of Cunningham and into the net.

The place erupted again!

Thousands streamed onto the field in a sea of blue and gold.

That goal put us five points up. It was an extraordinary day. There was such an outpouring of emotion at the full-time whistle you'd think it was an All-Ireland we had won.

In fact, we did go on to beat Kilkenny in the All-Ireland final that year. But in 1992 we lost to Cork in the first round of the Munster championship. My father died suddenly of a heart attack in January, 1993 and looking back, that Munster final replay against Cork in '91 was probably one of the last matches that my father was alive to see me play really well in.

He was a big part of my life and hurling had a language of its own in our house. That day in Thurles playing Cork brought treasured memories.

PAT FOX

Nobody lifted the spirits of the Tipperary fans like the scorching Pat Fox

"

THERE'S NOTHING LIKE an epic Munster final.

The game in Killarney in 1987 was great too, but the emotion was nearly overpowering that day and it was better in '91 when we realised how to savour it, and we could appreciate it more.

We were playing for our hurling careers that day.

After losing at the same venue to the same opposition in 1990 a lot of us were written off. Time can easily move on and leave you behind. And it wouldn't take much for Babs to get rid of you if you weren't performing!

Babs was still a bit upset over losing in '90 and there was an edge to us in '91 to get everything right and perform consistently. I was putting in the effort both for me to stay on the team, as well as do good for the team.

It was a relief getting the draw in Cork but we had a few niggly injuries going into the replay and we knew we had to perform and step up. The game started at a hundred miles an hour. It was tight marking but then Cork got a run on us and we found ourselves seven or eight points down, when I remember getting a ball outside in the corner.

I didn't know whether to head straight towards goal or have a go for a score, because we were so far behind. A Cork clearance at that point might mean another Cork score, so I had a go and it went over the bar.

Michael Cleary added one soon after and we brought it back bit by bit. We were catching them on the scoreboard when a long ball came into the corner.

It was exactly what I wanted. I was marking Denis Walsh and he was sticky but the ball went in over my head. Denis was a little hesitant, but went for it.

Ger Cunningham came off his line but was hesitant too, and in that split second of delay from them, didn't I get a little flick on it; to hit it into the net.

Well the place erupted!

There was great excitement, the crowd burst onto the field and I remember the fella in the wheelchair on the pitch and all the supporters from the terrace and the sideline! It added to the excitement seeing Ger Cunningham getting so upset with the Tipp supporters all around him!

Just after I got that goal some fella jumped up on top of me, onto my back but I ran on and knocked him over by accident. When play resumed we had caught our breath and the big lead they had was gone.

Aiden Ryan's goal was magnificent.

Coming in like that from the wing, blocking down a couple of Cork defenders, one after another and heading straight for the goals… it was a goal worthy of winning any final. The excitement of the comeback was powerful but Cork had dangerous forwards like John Fitzgibbon and they were getting goals too in the last quarter of an hour.

That Munster final feeling is hard to top on a hot summer's day.

We had such a history built up with Cork over the previous years, and that added to the day. The games with Cork were always epic. Players had a mutual respect for each other, it never spilled over against them.

The colour that Cork and Tipp supporters bring to a big occasion like that is powerful, I genuinely think both counties bring out the best in each other.

The Cork players and supporters call in to the pub regularly in Cashel since I got it in 1993. They drop in on their way to or from a big match. It isn't as easy to call to pubs as it was before, but Kevin Hennessy calls frequently, and so does Denis Walsh who I was marking that day.

I made so many contacts out of hurling and through the pub. I remember one time there was a cameraman in the pub and they asked me to bring down any jerseys I had from upstairs for the interview. I gave out three or four jerseys for youngsters to put them on and add colour to the day, but at the end of the interview the youngsters were gone and so were the jerseys!

In fact, I gave all my jerseys away and I regret it now as I don't even have one jersey left… of any description!

I gave away a lot of my hurleys too, to different charities for raffles over the years. I was very particular about my hurleys and went to JJ O'Brien in Cahir and in the latter stages of my career I went to Phil Bourke.

The lighter the better, but I always wanted a hurley with a good strike off the base. Certain hurleys just can't be replaced and if it would break, you'd do all you could to see if it could be fixed.

I used to go in to get a hurley repaired by Noel Ryan in Thurles and he would notice me looking at the other hurleys and say, 'Go on… take it. It's there ages and no one will miss it!'

I still have a lot of hurleys in a shed but a lot of the special ones are gone.

I was coming to the end of my career when I got the pub and it didn't help my hurling career I can tell you! But everything went well in 1991 and that season was the pinnacle of my career. It was a glorious time to be involved in Tipp hurling.

It was magnificent to get the Hurler of the Year award but it was a testament to those around me.

I started out at corner-back on under-21 level with Cormac Bonnar at full-back one year and Peter Brennan another year, with what was a very successful team that won three in-a-row of All-Irelands. Little did we think that 10 years later, Cormac would be full-forward and I'd be in the corner!

He was a savage player for the team.

We discussed in training what we'd do and we had our signals. Nicky and I only had to wait for the breaks and Cormac would always deliver it when the time was right. Big Cormac was the playmaker and we would never have won so much without him.

Babs would love you and hate you.

He was very direct. He'd ring and say, 'Is everything ok with you Pat?'

With Babs it either was or it wasn't. If it was fine then it was fine; if it wasn't then Babs wanted a solution.

There was always good humour and a great spirit in the camp. The craic used be mighty, mainly because we had the great Joe Hayes playing at the time! At one stage Joe was being dropped for a while. Babs was going around the panel and was dropping players and had decided Joe was one of them.

Both of them were great friends at the time and Babs was after speaking with a couple more players around the fringes of the panel when he saw Joe pucking around at the far side of the pitch before training started.

Babs strolled over.

Joe had guessed what was coming and he wasn't making it easy for Babs to drop him, so he ran off away from him! Babs said, 'We're going to give you an aul break Joe'.

'Look Babs,' Joe replied. 'I don't want any break at all. I will be here doing extra training… now just wait and see!'

Babs relented and Joe had a stormer after!

Jody Grace was another great character in our panel. Babs was mad about him as he was training a few racehorses and Babs loved the horses. After we won the All-Ireland in 1991 we were back in training and selling both calendars and framed pictures to raise a few bob for spending money on the team holiday.

Babs asked me how many had I sold and I told him I had about 20 sold, but in reality I had no more than about five sold! Babs went around the dressing-room one by one and asked us all. Jody, who was late, came into the dressing-room and Babs asked him as well.

'I can't even give them away Babs!' Jody said.

The room burst out laughing and that was the end of the calendars. I'd say he never bothered collecting the calendar money off us either!

We had some great trips and did two cruises, but they were just too much for me. I came back more than a stone heavier than I was going! The weight went up across the team!

Babs was great at organising holidays in fairness. He enjoyed them too and only the best was good enough, with all expenses paid.

We enjoyed it and we sure did hurl for him too.

99

MICHAEL RYAN

As a player and manager, Michael Ryan made the essential difference on winning days

❝

WE WERE IN real trouble in Páirc Uí Chaoimh and managed to salvage it with a draw. But in the replay in Thurles, we found ourselves well down on the scoreboard in the second-half, and then all of a sudden there was a vast wave that swept up the game, before it culminated in Aiden Ryan's famous goal.

And Tipp were back again!

It was my first year with the team and I was barely inside the camp, being almost a fan as much as a player, and I remember being awe struck by those around me and somehow enjoying the journey that it was.

There wasn't time to even take a moment to take it in, as it was a phenomenal hour or so of hurling and is something one seldom gets in a lifetime. It was the pinnacle for me as regards the spectacle of hurling; that game had everything.

To come back from being so far behind and run out such convincing winners was phenomenal.

It was a blistering hot day as I remember, and it was knockout hurling with the All-Ireland champions of 1989 against the champions of 1990.

It was winner takes all, the loser had to wait a year for another go so there was depth and a strong rivalry between the teams. I remember no pre-match speech, no words uttered that day, just the feel of it all.

It was quite the introduction to senior hurling to be marking Ger Fitzgerald, who was pacey, tall and experienced. I had come on as a sub against Limerick and again in the draw two weeks previous, but it was my first championship start.

Babs picked me at corner-back and I had an absolutely brutal start!

The first ball that came in was across the field from a line ball that was taken on the old stand side. It was a long ball that came in diagonally and was heading my way so I went for it.

I got out in front and Ger beautifully caught my hurley, got in on the turn, caught the ball and stuck it in the net! I can now imagine Babs looking in and thinking… *What am I after doing playing this lad!*

What can you do at that moment only draw breath, keep going and get ready for the next ball. When an early goal like that happens you need to break even, get beside him all the time and definitely don't let him in again.

I settled into the game after that and just got on with it.

In the second-half, when the game was in the melting pot, it was fairly robust and physical. At one stage I wrestled for possession with Ger and the ball hadn't even come in! I lost my hurley in the tangle and without it I had to hold and wrestle him away from the ball. Thankfully the ref didn't spot it and the ball broke behind us, where some of the boys tidied it up and moved it on. But I got this flake of the hurley from him and what else could he do after I had stopped him by whatever means necessary!

The emotion of the day was very strong. Aiden Ryan's spectacular late goal to seal it stands out and after it there was the sensation of the crowd swarming the field at the end, and I was thinking… *Get off the field… the ref could call off the match.*

But of course he was never going to call off the match, but those types of thoughts rush through your mind.

And then came the final whistle!

That hurling era seemed like a wave and I was being carried along.

I was 21 years-old at the time and everything was wonderful… being part of such a hurling journey. The underage success we had before '91 had made it easier to settle in to the seniors. We got to a minor All-Ireland final in 1987 but we didn't win it.

The manager of that minor side was Jimmy Doyle's brother, Paddy. He was an incredibly successful manager having led Borris Ileigh to the club All-Ireland. Wherever he went, success followed.

Our minor team threw up a lot of senior hurlers, including Johnny Leahy, who was unheard of at the time and by the following year he was playing senior hurling under Babs. In 1989 we beat Offaly in an under-21 All-Ireland final with a team that included Declan Ryan, Conor Stakelum and Conal Bonnar, so the confidence was flowing.

Mick Minogue and Danny Morrissey were in charge of the under-21s for that win and they were outstanding over a team. Coming through successful minor and under-21 teams definitely gave us confidence.

1991 had been up and down for me until the championship started.

Back then the league started before Christmas and continued into the spring. I hadn't featured in the early league but kept the full effort going over the Christmas period and got a league start against Dublin in Croke Park. I didn't settle at all, got caught for an early goal and didn't make it out for the second-half.

That was the kind of season it was!

That's how it can be in sport, one day you're ordinary and then you catch a break at training, get a chance. Then it may slip and you feel like you're at the bottom of the hill again. In fairness to Babs, Donie Nealon and John O'Donoghue they were very supportive.

I remember talking to one of the selectors after that Dublin game and I said I was disgusted with how the game went for me. Afterwards I realised I had made too much of it in my own head.

It was that kind of season, it ebbed and flowed, and I even got a couple of runs at full-forward! Babs sent me up there in training and then I came on as a sub playing full-forward in a knockout league game against Offaly! I somehow managed to get a score from play but in a very low scoring game.

We were desperate that day and were beaten.

Babs was disgusted afterwards and we had a real 'clear the air' session before the championship began. By then, we were firing on all cylinders and the season came alive as we beat Limerick and drew with Cork, before getting our wind to win that replay. We beat Galway next before playing Kilkenny in a final that never lived up to it's billing, but we didn't mind at all as it was a massive win.

It was amazing to play those games and win that All-Ireland in my first year.

Having won an All-Ireland as a player and manager the parallels are there between then and now. The management back then was extraordinary.

Even going back to what Mick Minogue and Paddy Doyle were doing with us as minors was incredible, they were passing on what they knew. They were conversational about the game and made us *think* about hurling.

I remember sitting down one evening at under-21 training with the lads on our team sharing ideas. Conal Bonnar, John Madden, Declan Ryan, Johnny Leahy and Conor Stakelum led us to a certain extent because they were already playing senior. Sometimes as a group we'd chat on the grass about the game, about how we wanted to play.

Everyone had a view and everyone was listened to. But it was more educational and mind-opening as opposed to laps-of-the-field type training. We didn't need to be doing laps as we were fit as fiddles at that age anyway.

The Tipp connection to and interest in hurling – tradition I suppose we call it – is an incredibly powerful stimulant. This is going on for generations, and it's hugely important to our identity in Tipperary. It reflects the skills, the commitment and passions of the game and it means so much to the people.

If there was one glass ceiling that I would give Babs massive credit for breaking, it's that he didn't mind where someone came from. If you look at the teams Babs put together, but particularly the 1991 team, I would say half of us playing came from junior or intermediate clubs. It didn't matter where the talent came from, it was always about what you brought to it for Babs. And it wasn't just the hurling, it was what you could give to the team.

Babs found out what type of character you were.

If you were positive by disposition or by nature, those were the things he looked for. The same things certainly made a difference to me when I first got involved with Liam Sheedy and Eamon O'Shea on the management side of things with Tipp. You're really testing the character because that's the whole thing… it's the player.

I'm convinced that we, from Tipp, can always hurl with anybody.

When I went in with Liam and Eamon at the end of 2007 we hadn't won an All-Ireland since 2001 but I wouldn't have thought for one second that we were inferior to Kilkenny or anyone else. Not for a second.

And that's not to be mistaken for disrespect. I absolutely believed we could get there. Take where we were in early 2008 and go to the quality of the game we played in 2009. Between that time people would have said to me, 'Ye were lucky ye didn't meet them in 2008!'

And that sickened me.

We were beaten fair and square by Waterford in the All-Ireland semi-final in 2008 and people were suggesting we would have got a beating in the final that year against Kilkenny. But to me, it was a lost opportunity.

We lost the chance to play them. I would always give a Tipp team a chance in a final once the work has been done, so 2008 felt like a year of lost possibilities to me. The following year, 2009, tells its own story and we won in 2010 and then finished that decade with three titles. The Tipp and Kilkenny teams from 2009 until 2019 brought the best out of each other. Those games rarely disappointed.

Hurling is just such a fantastic game and playing at that Munster final against Cork at 21 years of age left a big impact on me. I enjoy playing other sports now but hurling is a special game.

People say it's about winning in Tipperary but I always say, while winning plays a big part, the key thing always is to perform. The Tipperary public want to have a team that they can be proud of and who are trying to play the game the right way, to the best of their ability.

One of the key things I learned at a young age was that if players are honest and give their best in every way, then that's all you can ask for.

JOE HAYES

Triumph and some heartbreak awaited Joe Hayes in a glorious era

❝

THE REPLAY AGAINST Cork in 1991 was as good as any match ever played.

I watched it recently, during the Coronavirus lockdown, and I was getting excited just watching the video of it! We had a great rivalry with Cork.

We were caught on the hop in 1990 and really, a team should never be. Mistakes were made that year, but we were rectifying them in '91, starting with the win over Limerick, then the draw against Cork which was fierce exciting too.

The referee, Terence Murray gave us a late free down in Páirc Uí Chaoimh to balance the books, so we got out of there alive. The replay was a truly brilliant day and it worked out perfectly for us, on a smashing day in Thurles.

I was gutted ahead of the replay as I was dropped.

It was very disappointing. I felt I had played well in the first game but found myself sitting on the bench watching it all happen in front of me.

So I was really down until I got the call.

Just before half-time, I was brought on for Donie O'Connell. The atmosphere with all the colour was electric, the place was bursting; well beyond capacity. There must have been near 60,000 at it and you couldn't help but feel the magnitude of the day.

Things went well for me.

It was a frantic pace. I'd always be doing something or saying something, like telling the fella I was on that, 'I have you now'… when I hit a great ball.

I'd talk plenty when it was going well, but I wouldn't be saying much when it wasn't! But that day, there wasn't a lot of talking because I didn't have the breath to talk!

Calling out to the sideline for water, that's about all the calling I was doing!

We had a great camaraderie with the Cork lads but it was all about the game when we were on the field. Teddy McCarthy was the Cork man in midfield alongside me that day. I don't remember a lot about the ball coming near me but the main thing for me was the sheer excitement of the day, in particular Aiden Ryan's goal and that pitch invasion after!

There was actually a steward that day letting Tipp supporters onto the field! Rumour has it he brought a wire cutter in with him so people could get onto the pitch as fast as they could! I don't think he did steward after it!

When Aiden Ryan got that goal to put the nail in Cork's coffin, a man was pushed in to the middle of the pitch in his wheelchair, but with the excitement of it all, whoever was looking after him lost track of the wheelchair!

You wouldn't see the likes of it now!

The atmosphere in Thurles in those minutes stays with me and I think it did for the crowd too. I have heard so many stories from family and friends since.

My mother, who celebrated her 94th birthday in 2020, often went to the matches back then. On one occasion I went for a point but missed it and the fella sitting behind her said, 'If 'twas a pint of Guinness… you could be sure he wouldn't miss it!'

She wasn't best pleased.

A day like that is for your family and your county, and you only get one chance at it. I had a great friend called Jimmy Morrissey, he tragically died later in life, but he was also at the match and he brought a big teddy bear with the words, "Bring on Joe!" written on it.

A Cork fella beside him said, 'Take down that teddy bear!'

He wouldn't take it down and the next thing the Cork fella says, 'Who's this Joe fella anyway?'

'That's my friend,' Jimmy told him, '… Joe Hayes and he should be playing.' At the end of the match the Cork fella admitted, 'By God now, Joe wasn't so bad at all!'

Afterwards we had a great time in Thurles and I remember ending up in Declan Carr's pub in Holycross that night. It was brilliant craic and I will never forget that Monday. The place was packed all day in Holycross.

The atmosphere and the supporters were fantastic.

Our team had a very close relationship with supporters. They both celebrated with us and commiserated with us. It didn't matter.

We knew them and expected to see them after a match.

Times were different. There was no such thing as swimming pools or gyms after playing. After the game that day I thought Babs would say, 'Well done, Joe!' but he surprised me when he said, 'You're fair lucky I dropped you because it meant you got to finish on the pitch… you were out on your legs when that match was over!'

The previous week I had gone off down to Clonmel and the South Tipp bars, on a bit of a 'tour' as I was so mad he had dropped me from the starting team.

I suppose it caught up on me in the last few minutes!

Looking back, the 35 or so minutes on the pitch were enough for me; the gas was running low by the time it was over!

We trained hard coming up to the matches and then had great craic after the matches. Some of us were two days missing after that one! We'd make it back in time for training on the Tuesday night.

Declan Carr had the pub at the time so we gave him as much support as possible! It wouldn't have been half as good without the craic. Those days are special so you have to appreciate them. There's no point celebrating 10 years after them.

Celebrate the here and the now.

These are the days of our lives, and you must live them as best you can. The very sad thing about it now is that so many that were part of our lives then are dead now. Like my great friend, Jimmy Morrissey and our bus driver, Matt Kavanagh, who died in 2020. We probably didn't fully appreciate the times when we had them, so my advice is live and appreciate the 'here and now'.

I was a guard at the time and it was hard at times to get out of night duty and get cover for the big matches. Inter-county was a big commitment but nothing like today when they can't go out without it ending up on social media and people writing nasty comments.

I wouldn't care for it now to be honest.

The game has changed and not always for the better.

Letting fly on a moving ball was great, and it has just gone from the game. My hurleys were 37 inches and I see six foot lads now using 30 or 32 inch hurleys which is unbelievable. I have one in the wardrobe at home I used in the minor All-Ireland final in 1980 and it's the nearest thing to a billhook one could imagine!

Back then, it was the real deal and was made by a master craftsman, Phil Bourke. The hurley changed, much like the times, and the game is still an amazing game. Back then we trained hard, played hard and celebrated hard.

We had the craic too. I remember one time Babs got a psychologist in for us, but we were doing enough talking so in the end the psychologist was concentrating more on Babs and the selectors than the players!

He was gone after less than three weeks I'd say!

We had great fun under Babs even though I was hurt and disappointed with calls he made the rest of that year. After beating Cork in the replay I only got in for five minutes more that year. A cameo role against Galway.

I didn't get on the field against Kilkenny in the final and I was gutted with that. Ger Canning said it on the telly that day... 'Joe Hayes will be in now soon' ... but I didn't get in.

Look, that's the way it goes but I was so heartbroken that the All-Ireland didn't mean anything to me after.

The win meant nothing.

After the final, I was gone away out of there as soon as the whistle sounded.

I was so gutted I went straight to a tavern at the final whistle and met the great writer, Con Houlihan.

That was my All-Ireland.

It was played out in The Shakespeare.

When they were getting the cup in Croke Park, I was supping in that tavern on the northside. Con was a genius that I greatly admired. He was never critical of players but could put words together about a game like no other.

Brandy and milk was what he drank.

'Why don't you drink a pint?' I asked him.

'I only drink a pint when I'm thirsty,' he replied.

I didn't go to the reception in The Burlington Hotel. Instead, I enjoyed the evening with Con. It was a beautiful evening. He gave me a great write-up the following evening in the *Herald* newspaper. If I had gotten the Man of the Match award I wouldn't have received the write-up he gave me!

Even though I was hugely disappointed it is a great memory to have and I became good friends with Con after. Mick Malone of Cork, the only player to win four under-21 hurling All-Irelands, was with us for a while too.

That evening in The Shakespeare stands out, as the rest of them were celebrating at the other side of the city. The following day I met Con again in The Palace Bar before heading back to Tipp.

When we came back to Thurles I got a wonderful reception from the people. There was 35,000 or more in Thurles all chanting my name when I got the cup and lifted it up in the air. I got great solace from that to be honest about it.

The supporters meant a lot to me and they were on my side. At the end of the day, they are the judges really. They gave me a great reception because they knew I was bitterly disappointed.

My last match was against Galway in the league final in 1994.

We were underdogs and probably peaked too soon and were out of the championship a fortnight later. Clare beat us.

They were an up-and-coming team and won the All-Ireland the following year. As a county we faded from the big days for a while. Personally, it was hard leaving the jersey. I didn't accept it for two or three years.

It was devastating.

It's leaving your life. Remember I played minor, under-21 and senior, so for all my adult life I was a Tipperary hurler. Then you're gone and someone else lives the dream. I found it hard to move on.

It's about accepting those things.

I don't remember a lot about the matches I played in; more about the people that were there. Only for the lockdown during the Coronavirus I wouldn't have seen any of the matches I played in! You enjoy the friends you make from hurling more than the matches.

I enjoyed the 'afters' from it too! In one way, I didn't enjoy playing at the time because I'd be so tensed up. One mistake and it could be the losing of the match and it would be remembered. I needed to play well, as it would eat me up if I didn't.

I'd be embarrassed and would take it very personally.

I had a lot of anxiety around those matches, getting sick after and maybe before too. I'd be on a high or low during and after the game. The right way is to be in the middle, then you can play your best.

Some handle it well like the main man, Pat Fox.

He used to be as cool as a breeze!

That time for the team was like that song *Glory Days*. Hurling was in a state in Tipp until Babs came along. We were winning under-21s and minors but it wasn't translating until Babs brought a touch of magic to those times. For me, that replay against Cork was the match of all the matches.

I was talking about the game lately, with Pat Fox, when we were out fishing, and by the way, he's a better fisherman than he was a hurler!

One thing I'm glad of is that I never threw in the towel. I kept fighting and kept going. And to be young and hurling with Tipperary was truly a beautiful thing.

No regrets.

99

LIAM CAHILL

TIPPERARY 1-16, LIMERICK 0-19
Munster SHC Final
Gaelic Grounds, Limerick
JULY 7, 1996

The brilliant Liam Cahill was always his own fiercest critic

★ **TIPPERARY:** B. Cummins; G. Frend, P. Shelly, M. Ryan; R. Ryan, Colm Bonnar, B Carroll; B O'Meara, Conal Bonnar; M. Cleary (0-4), L. McGrath (0-1), J. Leahy (0-2); **L. Cahill (1-3)**, D. Ryan (0-2), T. Dunne (0-2). Subs: A. Ryan for Carroll; N. English (0-1) for McGrath; K Tucker (0-1) for Leahy.

★ **LIMERICK:** J. Quaid; S. McDonagh, M. Nash, D. Nash; D. Clarke, C. Carey (0-1), M. Foley; M. Houlihan, Sean O'Neill; Shane O'Neill (0-1), G. Kirby (0-10), TJ Ryan (0-3); O. O'Neill (0-1), P. Tobin, D. Quigley. Subs: M. Galligan (0-1) for Shane O'Neill; F. Carroll (0-2) for Quigley; B Tobin for Owen O'Neill.

THE ACTION

THIS WAS MUNSTER hurling magic. Rollercoaster hurling, and afterwards everyone just wanted to go again. Tipperary were at their brilliant best in the first-half, but roles were reversed in the second. A game of two halves then played out in front of an official attendance of 43,525.

In the previous round Limerick beat last year's All-Ireland champions, Clare and eventually the character shown that day came to the fore but Tipp refused to quit.

In a remarkable Munster final, teenage sensation Liam Cahill announced his arrival on the big stage. The talented forward struck a stylish goal on the run, after a set up by the excellent Declan Ryan, to put Tipp 1-2 to 0-1 up and in the driving seat after just six minutes of action. They made hay while the sun shined and piled on the scores until half-time. Tipp were magnificent, with Cahill in particular causing all sorts of problems for the Limerick defence. The former minor star slotted over just before the break to put Tipp 1-11 to 0-4 up as they headed for the dressing-room.

The game looked over and some Limerick supporters were contemplating slipping away home to beat the rush. They'll be glad they stayed.

'We were so quiet. We knew we hadn't hurled,' Limerick forward, Gary Kirby said afterwards, when talking about half-time in their dressing-room. 'Tom [Ryan, the Manager] came in and told us a few home truths straight away'. A different Limerick emerged for round two. After failing to score from play in the first-half, the Shannonsiders hit their first score just 16 seconds into the half. Between the 41st and 66th minute they outscored Tipp 0-10 to 0-0 before part three of this game arrived.

The Man of the Match, Liam Cahill pointed with five minutes remaining to give Fr. Tom Fogarty's team a lifeline. Kevin Tucker added one in the 69th minute as Tipp went two points up and looked to have come back into the game just in time. Limerick fought back though with a Kirby point from a dead ball. before Frankie Carroll landed the equaliser from play to uproarious cheers on 73 minutes.

A ceasefire was finally called and supporters carried the Limerick players shoulder high after their magnificent second-half comeback.

★★★★★

66

TO ONLY DRAW against Limerick was a killer.

It was my first year on the team. We played a really brilliant brand of hurling in the first-half. Limerick had no answer to us in any area of the field.

We were really playing well as a team. Ball was being pinged to hand and we were well clear on the scoreboard. The second-half started reasonably well. I remember getting a chance early on when we were 10 points up.

Declan Ryan won the ball down in front of the covered stand right down at the Thomond Park side. He hit a super ball across to me.

I had made a run just on to the edge of the square.

It was a brilliant pass.

Just about three or so foot off the ground, travelling like a rocket across. I controlled it on the hurley, but out of the corner of my eye I saw Quaid coming off his goal line towards me.

I was going to bang it off my left but when I saw him, I spun around on my right. And blazed it wide. I blazed it between the umpire and the side net just over the umpire's head.

After that, Limerick started to come back into the game.

If I had buried that it would have put us 13 points up.

We wouldn't have been caught. Limerick got on a run after that and we got done. I just remember that being a sickener afterwards. I was so young at the time as well that it definitely had an effect on me.

Real good forwards shouldn't let that happen to them.

With the quality of forwards that came after, like Eoin Kelly and Lar Corbett and Seamie Callanan, they never really dwelled on the ones they missed, but I did.

It should have gone in.

I missed a chance to put us 13 points up.

That's what stands out.

That was the game to win. I had controlled it so well from Declan; I was thinking in a split second… *This is it… I'm gonna burst the net.*

When Quaid came towards me, I turned and got the angle slightly wrong.

Millimetres wide.

Even if it hit the post it wouldn't have been as bad because Michael Cleary and Liam McGrath would have got onto the break, but that's always the case.

Those millimetres are down to the individual. Some players beat themselves up more than others, and I was one of those players. People might not have thought that about me but that ate me up.

Those little things can eat you up for years.

Nowadays teams have fellas watching for these things to figure out what needs to be done to prepare a player to kick on. For me, I let those things get to me.

Not just that individual miss but poor performances or a mistake really got to me. I'd get down over it. Take the Munster semi-final against Clare, down in Páirc Uí Chaoimh in 1999, for example. It was a dinger of a match.

It was a draw after Davy Fitzgerald scored a penalty.

That day anyway, myself and Paul Shelly were on the two Lohan brothers and we were on top. With five minutes to go, a high ball came in over Paul Shelly and Brian Lohan. I was out in the corner and I made a run in front of Shelly for the breaking ball.

It broke lovely and I ran on to it.

I had the ball in my hand. I went on to kick away from Frank Lohan and had lost him, when I got this massive bulge of a cramp right down my calf muscle. A shooting feeling.

I lost my balance and the ball fell into Davy's hand.

He drove it up the field and it came back down alright but it was Davy who stuck the penalty for Clare at the end. If I had to nail that chance?

I think I had three points scored but that one near the end was the easiest chance of the day.

It wasn't lack of preparation but maybe I wasn't tuned in right to nail it.

I hadn't covered all the angles, I was dehydrated.

Drained and not tuned in. I shouldn't have been cramping because I was fit enough but that was a real hot day and I didn't think of everything. We lost the replay a week later.

I can still remember having the ball in my hand.

The outcome of a full season's hurling depended on what I did with that ball. Or so I thought, anyway. We had a lot of near misses.

Careers could have been a lot different and it's not hard luck stories, it's just reality. Fine margins.

From 1996 to '99 we missed one or two chances to kick on and make a success of those years. In 1996 Fr Tom Fogarty was manager and brought in a couple of players and looked for more. He worked hard to make progress but didn't get the luck needed that can turn a game in your favour, as we drew in that Munster final with Limerick.

Like every year, it was competitive.

In 1997 Len Gaynor came in and got the most he could out of players but maybe we just hadn't the quality required against a really good Clare team that time. We lost a close Munster final to Clare. Then in 1999 we drew with Clare under Nicky English before losing the replay.

I think I wasn't as ruthless as I needed to be for inter-county hurling. I often went home thinking... *Where am I in the manager's plans?*

Instead of just asking them.

All the managers I trained under were fair and none of them had an agenda. Times were different though because you just came in and trained away without the manager communicating to players in the way they might now.

I never took a central position with Tipp, even though I had the ability. I just hadn't the belief in myself. That can manifest with the ball going the wrong few millimetres one side of the post.

I remember one time being brought on and taken off again by English.

I looked out to the line and knew I was in trouble. I had a fear of missing the ball and then I did. It was an awful feeling, but my body language wasn't right for the game and maybe we could have lost the game if I stayed on.

After a couple of good seasons and being in my early twenties at the time, it was a setback. I was never one of the great forwards nor claimed to be, but I was a decent forward with the potential to be better, and was up-and-coming, but when I think back on it I have no issue with being taken off as being a manager myself now, I know calls have to be made.

In the 2001 Munster final I came in as a sub with 10 minutes or so to go.

It was a real tight game and I gave a pass to Brian O'Meara for a score to put us on the way home. I remember that alright and that was something I felt good after. I did miss a chance of a point late on the same day and can remember Declan Ryan saying to me, 'That's as good as a score' ... because time was just up, but it still bugged me going home on the bus that it should have been nailed and it wasn't.

No one really appreciates the value of Declan Ryan for what he did for players behind the scenes. He was a huge motivator and leader. Everyone saw his exploits on the field, they knew how great he was and the skill and touch he had for a left handed hurler. His vision to spot players and lay off a good pass surpassed all others. His calmness stood out; you'd never see him losing the head. He had the perfect temperament for inter-county hurling. If he was a greyhound or a racehorse, he would be perfect for the big day because he just would perform. He wouldn't have his race left in the kennel or the horsebox!

Some players don't need guidance while others do.

Tommy Dunne was so tuned in all the time, he was just so focused every night he came to training. Others needed to be in the right frame of mind to train and play at one hundred percent and I was in that group.

It happens at all levels, even in professional sport.

Now, there was days I was cocky as hell and going really well, but if my form slipped and confidence fell, with new players coming into the panel... that's when the 'mentality' matters.

The biggest regret I have as a player is that I used to dwell too much on a mistake or a wide. With Ballingarry I could hit a goal and nine or 10 points in a club match but I'd still be mentally beating myself up over what scores I missed.

I had the desire to be the Man of the Match every day I went out but no one wins every ball they go for. When I got older, I figured it out but by then inter-county was getting further away from me.

For most of the time I played with Tipp I'd be thinking about a miss or a mistake for ages after a game. Dwelling way too much. We lost to Limerick and Clare those times in Cork when the talk afterwards was about Tipp's inability to win a championship game in Cork and this type of craic, and that could sink in.

They were all close games we could have won if a single ball or moment went differently. But the worst thing is the fear of losing, or fear of making a mistake.

That's something that now as a manager I wouldn't want any of my players to experience. With the Tipp teams I managed the last few years and Waterford too, it's straightforward. If they make honest mistakes I will stick with them within reason.

I thought a lot about my own time playing and it has benefitted me as a manager, as I go to a field now and ask myself… *Where's that fella's head now?*

If I was him what way would I be thinking?

The game has moved on so much now in terms of preparing mentally. That's why there's so many cliff-hangers of matches where a fella might be getting buried for a few balls and then get one and bury it in the net.

Teams might be getting beaten off the field for 10 minutes and come back and score eight or nine points in-a-row. That has become the norm.

I'm learning all the time as a manager.

Communication is so important. It's about your player knowing where he or she stands and helping them progress. I always say it to teams I'm involved with, 'If you're going out the gate as a player thinking you're flying, and I'm sitting in the car going home thinking this fella needs to do this and this, then we have a problem.'

If there's five or six fellas not informed and coming for the manager then communication must have broken down somewhere. Communication and guidance are key elements for me as a manager.

I was hard on myself as a player, definitely.

I still remember that miss against Limerick to put us 13 points up and my career with Tipp is full of regret. But that is what drives me now.

99

EAMONN CORCORAN

TIPPERARY 0-18, CLARE 2-12
Munster SHC Semi-Final
Páirc Uí Chaoimh
JUNE 6, 1999

Eamonn Corcoran beats Clare's Jamesie O'Connor to the ball in 1999

★ **TIPPERARY:** B. Cummins; D. Fahey, F. Heaney, L. Sheedy; Conal Bonnar, D. Kennedy, **E. Corcoran**; E. Enright (0-1), C. Gleeson; T. Dunne (0-7), D. Ryan (0-1), J. Leahy (0-1); L. Cahill (0-3), P. Shelly (0-2), B. O'Meara (0-1). Subs: E. Tucker (0-1) for Leahy; P. Kelly (0-1) for Tucker.

★ **CLARE:** D. Fitzgerald (1-0); B. Quinn, B. Lohan, F. Lohan; L. Doyle, S. McMahon (0-1), A. Daly: E. Flannery, C. Lynch (0-1); J. O'Connor (1-2), N. Gilligan (0-2), A. Markham (0-1); D. Forde (0-3), S. McNamara, B. Murphy (0-1). Subs: O. Baker for McNamara; C. Clancy (0-1) for Markham.

THE ACTION

DAVY FITSGERALD WAS the villain for Tipperary supporters as a late penalty was dispatched home as the net-minder snatched a draw for Clare just 11 seconds before the final whistle. As if that wasn't enough, Fitzgerald had produced a stunning save at the other end with three minutes to go to deny Tipperary a match winning moment.

A new look Tipp team came valiantly close to knocking out a Clare team seeking three in-a-row of Munster titles. In the dust bowl heat 42,382 attendees were left mesmerised by the drama.

The conclusion evoked memories of the All-Ireland final of 1997. On that occasion Fitzgerald stopped a John Leahy shot to win the All-Ireland for Clare. This time round Davy Fitz denied Paul Shelly. The drama wasn't just confined to the end, it rolled right through. The terraces were heaving with colour, foghorns, flags and the Clare bodhrán.

The hurling was furious and fierce before eventually a pattern developed. Eamonn Corcoran matched Jamesie O'Connor ball for ball and as a result Clare's main scoring threat was shackled. It allowed Tipp freedom to thrive. Liam Cahill, who roved out the field, levelled it up with a sweet strike on 12 minutes for Tipp as the half flowed by.

At half-way Tipp led 0-8 to 0-7. On resumption Brian O'Meara and Shelly stretched their lead while the defence was composed with Eamonn Corcoran looking like a natural on the half-back line alongside Conal Bonnar and David Kennedy, who hurled the world of ball at centre-back.

The old war general, Ger Loughnane summoned Ollie Baker from the bench. Nine minutes into the half Baker broke the ball to Gilligan, who sped away from his marker forcing Corcoran to go to him. O'Connor calmly collected and in a flash fired past Brendan Cummins for his first championship goal. Clare were back level but a focused Tipp edged 0-15 to 1-9 clear with 10 minutes to go. Corcoran, who was one of the key reasons Tipp were in the game, marshalled the half back line. Tommy Dunne, Liam Cahill and Paul Shelly dictated before Seanie McMahon and Daly drove it on. All that before Davy Fitzgerald rewrote the script and saved the day for Clare.

★★★★★

66

I NEVER WITNESSED an atmosphere like the first game against Clare in the Munster championship in 1999. I will never forget it. In all the games I played before or after, there was nothing else like it.

The hatred, the rivalry, the Ger Loughnane factor… it all stands out as a vivid memory.

The teams hadn't met in the championship since the All-Ireland final in 1997. I probably wasn't ready for what was in store.

You couldn't be for such an intense rivalry!

Now, we had played them in the league with big crowds but this was different. It was the heat of knockout hurling. On the way to Páirc Uí Chaoimh, the song *Slievenamon* was being played on our bus, while outside the Clare supporters were banging on the sides and windows of the bus with their flags!

They were making hand signs at us and the cans of cider were flowing! It was a raw festive atmosphere outside in the sunshine, but on the bus we were trying to ignore it and focus on what we had to do.

You wouldn't fit 15 or 16 players in the dressing-room in Páirc Uí Chaoimh, never mind a full panel! It was so cramped and had only one toilet.

Our manager, Nicky English got the room beside the dressing-room for space. It was a gym but to get from our room to the gym we had to go through the supporters who were passing by us and bouncing off us even! Up close, before we went out on the field, the Clare supporters were in our faces, roaring at us!

There were a few of us making our debuts and Nicky had told us what it would be like but I don't know if anything can prepare you for it really because it was a totally different atmosphere than anything before.

I'll never forget running out onto the pitch that day. I wouldn't even say I soaked it in, I ran around in the warm-up with my senses overloaded.

At every angle there was colour, flags and sounds like bodhráns and chants!

I was probably in shock until the ball was thrown in!

That summer I was starting to establish myself at wing back and knew I was going to be marking Jamesie O'Connor. I had picked him up in the league game that year and before the championship game started, Nicky put me at ease.

'Just expect he's going to score three points off you… as a given!' he told me.

Nicky had relaxed me so I wouldn't drop the head or panic if an early score went sailing over the bar. Mentally I was ready.

I knew I wouldn't doubt myself if Jamesie scored. Jamesie was the type of player that just wanted to hurl and I just wanted to play ball too.

Liam Sheedy was at corner-back behind me marking the Clare forward, Niall Gilligan and just before throw in I looked back and Liam was after belting him with the hurley and you could see the red mark on the leg and the white mark in the middle!

Liam had drawn, and Niall Gilligan had drawn back too!

Back then umpires and linesmen didn't care! Liam stood up, chest out as he does! The crowd were roaring, with digs being given and timber being used all over the place; yet the game hadn't even started!

The pace of the game and the dry heat of the day meant you were gasping to stay ready for the next ball. It was manic and fierce.

Colin Lynch hit a long ball in and Niall Gilligan gathered it, and took off soloing towards the goals. He was free so I had to go to him. As I met him the ball was laid off to Jamesie, who had drifted away and from there he buried it in the net.

I often get slagged since then as Jamesie O'Connor had never scored a goal in the championship until that day, but that's all he got from play! It worked out for me that day and having marked Jamesie in the league it helped take away any hesitancy.

There was a huge roar from the stands and terraces whenever a goal chance was on. I hit one ball up the field and it seemed to be back down near us before you'd have a breath taken, and you're trying to win it again a couple of seconds later. It was that frantic in the heat. Relentless.

Everyone will probably remember Davy Fitzgerald coming up the field to take the penalty just at the end and stitching it. That earned them a draw.

That was the day for us to win but we didn't.

We were so disappointed we had let it slip while Clare were on a high by comparison. Their supporters were roaring and they knew they had escaped. A lot of their players were experienced while a lot of us were new to the championship.

Mentally, we weren't ready for a replay.

Going back on the bus it felt like a loss and our heads were down. Everything was geared towards Clare in the first round of the championship. Everything we had worked for.

All the training camps away, every training session, every plan was based on winning that first day. Nowadays it's not just one day out with the format that's there. But in 1999 it was a lose-and-you're-gone type of situation.

We weren't thinking of the replay, only asking ourselves how we didn't get over the line and the replay was just a week later.

It finished 1-21 to 1-11 in the replay.

Clare found that level of intensity needed, but it was too much for us so soon after the draw. That was it, gone out of the championship after that.

Hard to believe that after all the training and effort, even leading most of the second-half of the drawn game, it was Clare who pulled through. There was positives though, a number of us were breaking through with the likes of Paul Ormond and Donnacha Fahy getting established. We learned so much from the experience of that atmosphere and those events.

Playing against that Clare team of Davy Fitz, Brian Lohan, Anthony Daly, Jamesie O'Connor and the rest of them wasn't enjoyment: it was going to war!

It was a duel to the death, your whole year of hurling hinged on the result.

That year was so intense but things changed in the following years. The rivalry with Clare settled a bit, as back then it was boiling over! You'd hear stories of what Ger Loughnane was doing with Tipp jerseys and how he was motivating Clare, but our manager was different. That game in 1999 against Clare was the start of Nicky's journey with us. A lot of Clare's big players were coming near the end. We were building, and Clare were fading.

I was fortunate enough to hurl with players of the calibre of Declan Ryan in those early days with Tipp. Like any other young player I was in awe and starstruck by some of the older lads and then they are like anyone else when you get to hurl with them. You enjoy their company and socialise with them and if you were 19 or 32 years-old on the panel, it didn't matter because we mixed well.

Nicky brought us off on a number of training camps and did things not many managers would do to build a bond. I remember going over to Sunderland on a training camp and being a student at that time, I didn't have a lot of money.

Nicky would put a few pounds in your pocket and say, 'Go off now and enjoy the craic with the lads'. He did things like that and he included the young players with the older lads, who were all brilliant to help us fit in.

They helped me along the way.

No one gets to that level of hurling without a lot of support starting out at county level, and even in the years beforehand.

Believe it or not, swimming was the first love for me when I started off at sports as a child. My mother and father were both teaching swimming in Templemore and it wasn't until near the end of primary school, when Brian Kenny from Borris Ileigh introduced me to hurling, that I started to play with the club at about nine or 10 years of age.

The game took over from there, but I was probably a late enough developer when you see young children nowadays at five or six with hurleys in their hands.

When I went to Our Lady's Secondary School in Templemore hurling became a huge part of my life, with John Costigan running the show. From Rice Cup at under-14 up along we were fortunate that some very good players from different clubs around the area were going to school there, like Paul Ormond from Loughmore, Denis Kelly from Toomevara and PJ Sweeney from Moyne Templetuohy among others; and so growing up I got to play on different teams along with them.

I went to college in Waterford and was hurling down there when I first joined the Tipp panel. Len Gaynor was the Tipp manager in 1997 and I remember getting a call about joining the panel.

When Len first got the panel together that year he asked, 'How does it feel to play with Tipperary?'

And my comment was, 'I'm just glad to be here'.

I think that was the worst thing I could say, as I could see from Len's reaction that it was the wrong answer! It just shows how naive I was at the time.

It was an honour to get the call to go in with the team and I was in awe, looking up to the players around me, instead of going in and establishing myself as a player. They culled the panel at the All-Ireland semi-final stage that year, and I was dropped.

Tipp went on to play Clare in the 1997 final that September. I didn't get back in for '98 but then in '99 Nicky took over.

Nicky met the players individually. I remember being in a meeting with the selectors, Jack Bergin and Ken Hogan alongside Nicky, who put a blank piece of paper on the table and said, 'That's my panel for the year and it's up to you to go for it and make sure your name is put on it'.

My game had come on a lot by then.

In Waterford we were going well in the college, and we went on and won the Fitzgibbon cup in 1999. It was a higher level than club and was probably a step up from under-21 and a step down from inter-county senior level.

Looking back, that's when my hurling career took off. I was living for hurling down there. It wasn't why I went down to what's now called WIT, but looking back it really was four years of hurling!

There were hurlers from all over playing in college in Waterford back then. Henry Shefflin was the big name. Michael Kavanagh, Andy Moloney, Ollie Moran and Colm Cassidy were there too. Tipp were well represented with Mikey Bevans, Mark O'Leary and William Maher, who had captained the Tipp minor hurlers to the All-Ireland.

Declan Browne, who was already a top footballer with Tipperary, was one of the best hurlers in college in Waterford too. The following year Paul Curran came down, Neil Ronan of Cork, Declan Ruth of Wexford and a few more arrived. My first year there I was wing forward at 10 with Peter Barry of Kilkenny on the other wing wearing 12 and, ironically, both of us ended up in the half-back line after! The Fitzgibbon team was full of county players so it was great to make it in whatever position!

That time spent in Waterford was a great hurling education.

Playing Clare in 1999 was a hurling education too! At that time I was 21 years-old and was kept on the team for a few years after, playing wing back mostly with some games now and again at corner or centre-back. I have to say that I do believe that if we had taken Clare that roasting hot summer's day in 1999 we could have gone on a right good journey, because we had so much training done.

Mentally we would have been in a great space had we won the first day but we didn't win and, while the replay was beyond us, progress was made. We learned enough to beat them in 2000 and again in 2001 on the way to the All-Ireland final.

99

TOMMY DUNNE

TIPPERARY 2-18, GALWAY 2-15
All-Ireland SHC Final
Croke Park
SEPTEMBER 9, 2001

Tommy Dunne raises the Liam MacCarthy Cup high after victory over Galway in 2001

★ **TIPPERARY:** B. Cummins; T. Costello, P. Maher, P. Ormonde; E. Corcoran, D. Kennedy, P. Kelly; **T. Dunne (0-5)**, E. Enright; M. O'Leary (2-1), J. Carroll (0-1), L. Corbett (0-2); E. Kelly (0-7), D. Ryan (0-1), E. O'Neill. Subs: D. Fahey for Costello; P. O'Brien (0-1) for O'Neill; M. Ryan for Paul Kelly; C. Gleeson for Kennedy.

★ **GALWAY:** M. Crimmons; G. Kennedy, M. Healy, O. Canning; D. Hardiman, L. Hodgins, C. Moore; D. Tierney, R. Murray; A. Kerins, M. Kerins (0-2), K. Broderick (0-5); J. Rabbitte (0-1), E. Cloonan (1-5), F. Healy (1-2). Subs: B. Higgins for Hardiman; O. Fahy for Rabbitte.

THE ACTION

A LITTLE TOUCH of class brought euphoria to Tipp fans as Tommy Dunne's charges secured Tipperary's 25th All-Ireland senior hurling triumph. Unbeaten in competitive and in challenge games this season, this latest win caps a remarkable season as Tipp finish the year off nicely with 15 wins and two draws. Apart from a short spell before half-time and a 10-minute period in the second-half, the blue and gold played with a fluency that has become their trademark this season.

Right from the first whistle Tipp were up for this and performing. A tense opening saw both sides scuffling for possession and when Tommy Dunne burst through a cluster of players and struck on the run from the sideline for the first score, the Tipp supporters knew the team had the right mindset. The captain was driving it.

The other leaders shone too. Brendan Cummins controlled from the back while Declan Ryan, Tipp's most influential forward, was the playmaker for the forwards. Everything went through him. As the focal point of the attack, ball was launched on top of Big Dec where younger players Mark O'Leary, Eoin Kelly and Lar Corbett flourished from the lay-offs.

Tipp led from Tommy Dunne's superb opening point and kept ahead. With Tipp 0-5 to 0-2 up on 22 minutes Declan Ryan laid off a delicate pass to Mark O'Leary, who gratefully fired to the net. Eugene Cloonan and Eoin Kelly traded scores, but Cloonan kept Galway in the game when he finished home a rebound from a Cummins save.

Tipp led 1-9 to 1-7 at half-time and, playing against the wind, got a break at the start of the second-half when a missed Cloonan free was followed by a scrappy kicked goal from O'Leary at the other end. Galway refused to die though and fought their way back as Fergal Healy soloed through and beat Cummins with 10 left. Tipp, with their noses in front, led 2-13 to 2-12 as the crowd got behind their teams.

Tipp held their nerve and the subs gave them a second wind. Galway, at the same time, will ponder the 'what if' scenarios when they consider Fergal Healy hit the post twice in the second-half. Late on, a controversial refereeing decision saw Tipp awarded a free out as Broderick raced away to put the ball in the net.

★★★★★

66

WHEN I WAS a child I used to say a prayer every night before going to bed that I'd be as good as Nicky English. That's what it meant to me when I was a kid.

Hurling was everything, and Nicky was the player I wanted to 'be'.

I didn't want to do anything else with my life only hurl. One of my earliest memories is of the 1984 Munster final between Tipp and Cork in Semple Stadium. I was hugely affected by that and can still feel the colour and the excitement of the day, the sense of atmosphere and above all, the passion of the players and the crowd.

I will never forget it. I was very young that day in Thurles but even before that I'd have given anything to hurl with Tipperary.

Fast forward to All-Ireland final day in 2001 against Galway and that's the game for me. We hadn't won an All-Ireland since 1991. In those days there was one chance only in May or June, so it was a harsh environment.

Quality teams were often knocked out after the first game.

Nicky English was in his third year in charge and the team had been knocking on the door for a few years without ever reaching the final, but that year we went on a run and were unbeaten in every game, league and championship, right up to September.

It was the day that shines brightest from my 14 or 15 years hurling with Tipp. Being the captain of the team made it extra special but it was a long, long road to get to that day.

Babs Keating brought me onto the Tipp team for the National League at the end of 1992. I came on as a sub against Offaly, marking the great Brian Whelehan, so that was my first introduction to county hurling!

I really came onto a Tipp team that was full of superstars, so I had to wait to get established. I was a sub for the Munster final win over Clare in 1993 and started in '94 when we were beaten by Clare. Then Limerick, led by Ciaran Carey and Gary Kirby, beat us in Munster in '95 and again after a replay in '96. That powerful Clare team beat us in the provincial and All-Ireland final in 1997, so there was a lot of hard luck stories.

In 1998 we were beaten in the first round, so I spent some time that summer hurling in Chicago.

At times I thought it would all pass me by and that the team of our time wouldn't win an All-Ireland at all. We tried as hard as we could but it was tough because so many other counties were strong then. We just had to get on with it.

Some of those years I found it challenging to mix work and hurling. I can recall working nights with Intel in Kildare, where I went to work at 7pm on a Saturday and finished at 7am on Sunday morning, then travelled home to train with Tipp.

That was just the way life was at the time.

When Nicky English came in as manager for the 1999 season he asked me to be captain. You never forget those kind of things.

Being asked to captain Tipp by the person I had looked up to when I was a child was a dream come true. To develop such a close friendship with mutual respect… well, that was incredible. It was a massive honour to be chosen and I held the position until 2002.

I look back very fondly to think that people thought enough of me to make me captain of a team with powerful personalities such as Brendan Cummins, Philip Maher, Eamon Corcoran, David Kennedy and Declan Ryan. We had some extraordinary players so to lead that team on the pitch was really special.

I really enjoyed those years from 1999 on.

By then I was working day-time hours locally which aided my routine and allowed me focus on hurling. Progress was gradual year-on-year. There was a professional approach, new players were uncovered and the ante was upped as to what was required from players.

Jim Kilty was our strength and conditioning coach, with Ken Hogan and Jack Bergin in as selectors. We had cracking games at that time, particularly with Clare, and when we finally broke the Clare stranglehold on us, our world grew broader.

We pushed them hard in an outstanding drawn game in 1999, eventually beating them in 2000, then again by a point in the 2001 Munster semi-final. After that we beat Limerick to win Munster and then after a replay we overcame Wexford to qualify for the All-Ireland final.

It was an amazing time.

I really felt the buzz the week of the game. To have a Toomevara player as captain meant a lot locally and there were visitors to my home with relations, friends and neighbours coming over. I liked it but I was always superstitious coming up to big games. I'd chat away about everything bar the match. I only liked talking about the match with the people I was training with and those in the backroom team.

That was just my way of preparing mentally for it.

I was very particular about my hurleys.

Phil Bourke of Upperchurch was an absolute genius who made special hurleys that just fitted me perfectly. He has a wisdom and an approach to life that made me feel grateful to know him. I felt in a good frame of mind that week and felt we had every possibility covered for the test ahead.

We travelled up to Dublin by train the night before the final and I remember waking up early on the Sunday morning.

On the day in Croke Park I remember wanting to be sure to introduce the players appropriately to President Mary McAleese. It all felt a little surreal once the moment arrived. When I look back now at highlights of it I remember knowing there was a lot at stake.

You carry the hopes and the expectations of the people when you're hurling with Tipperary, and more so in an All-Ireland final. It's bigger than you. It's a stand-alone day but at the same time you have to trust what you're doing and focus on getting the basics right, just as you do in every other game.

You have to grasp the opportunity.

Once the game started it was frantic.

There was an electric atmosphere and we fed off the crowd. The Tipp supporters were vocal early on and we got some confidence from it. Both sides were trying to break the stalemate. A couple of minutes passed without either team scoring so there was a lot of nerves around the pitch.

Alan Kerins was wearing No 13 for Galway but playing out around the middle of the field early on. I remember making an early tackle in the middle of the field; he got on the ball but we turned it over and the ball broke high up in the air and I got a good touch onto it and into my hand.

Next I broke another tackle, ran down the touchline and suddenly found a bit of room to get a good strike on it and watched as it sailed over the bar. We settled and started to play then.

It felt like we made a statement early on which was important to us.

While Galway had a good win over Kilkenny in the semi-final, they hadn't won it since 1988 so they were as nervous as we were!

Being tight all through, there were lots of scores and saves. We were probably dictating the game but we weren't dominating.

Mark O'Leary got a great goal in the first-half off a pass from Declan Ryan, so we were out in front. Declan was influential for us and was on top at 14, laying off some great ball. Eoin Kelly got a great score off his left hand side that lifted the crowd again.

Coming towards half-time though, Galway closed the gap.

It was very seldom players spoke at half-time, even the captain. I don't ever remember speaking at half-time during the year but for some reason I spoke that day. I remember reinforcing the message that I was sick of getting beaten with Tipp all my life and it wasn't going to happen today.

I let that out.

We knew we had the ability to win but we needed to make sure we did. That was the point I wanted to make to the team. Getting a good start again and not letting Galway catch their breath kept us focused.

We were playing into a stiff breeze which was blowing into the Railway End. We got a boost when Mark O'Leary got an early goal, a scrappy enough goal and I pointed a '65'. Our play was measured but Galway were in the game all the way through.

Kevin Broderick, who was a really important player for them, got through one-on-one against Brendan Cummins who made a really important save. We got a bit of luck at times in fairness, but I thought we used the ball very well.

As the game wore on in the second-half we could feel that we were getting closer to the finishing line. There was a fair bit of pressure in the closing stages.

Micheal Ryan came off the subs bench and made a big difference, as did Paddy O'Brien and Conor Gleeson. The pitch wasn't in the best condition as the Hogan Stand was under construction but it was the same for both sides.

As the clock ticked by I was taking it moment by moment and second by second, as I'd been through too many dark days with Tipp to get ahead of myself.

The frame of mind I was in was that if it went on for three or four more minutes over time, no problem… let's play away! There was no shortcut.

I was conscious that we needed to be smart and not do anything stupid. It was one thing drilled into us over and over again.

'Play smart.

'Be smart on the ball.'

And we did that.

Two very special people came straight over to me at the final whistle which I clearly remember. My brother, Terry who was also on the panel that year, raced over. We had played on so many teams and soldiered together for a long time with Toome.

The other was Brian O'Meara from Mullinahone, who had missed out on the final through suspension. Brian and I had played with Tipp since 1994, sharing many disappointments and an odd good day!

He missed out on playing that day through a very harsh suspension which he picked up against Wexford in the All-Ireland semi-final replay. It was incredibly hard on Brian to miss out on it and he was a huge loss to the team.

There was a motivational drive within the team to perform *for* Brian as he was missing out on the final. So in some ways he contributed, albeit in a different way than he had during the year.

The three of us just locked into each other at the final whistle.

With the Hogan Stand under construction the cup presentation was on the pitch but we didn't care where it was once we had the cup in our hands! I often drift in my mind back to those moments of lifting the cup and sharing it with the people around me.

Some family and friends got in through the security and onto the pitch.

The joy that win brought was immense. We took the cup to the supporters and then sat on the pitch for a long time after. To finally win something that was so elusive for so long stands out and when I reflect now, certain people were there encouraging all along the way, people like my parents, Recie and Tony as well as my uncle Jimmy.

Also Neil Williams, who was over juvenile teams in Toome was a huge source of learning about the game for years as were John Costigan, Jody Spooner and

Willie Butler in school at Our Lady's, Templemore.

I met my wife, Deirdre in Templemore too and had a brilliant time hurling in Our Lady's, winning a Kinane Cup and a Rice Cup medal. While I did well at soccer and badminton in school, hurling was the be-all and end-all, so captaining Tipp that day meant everything.

When you play for Tipp you *feel* the history.

Maybe I didn't understand it fully, but I know it's there. It's a really exciting, powerful brand from way back in time right through to the present day.

Periods of dominance are exceptional; we've no right to expect to win all the time but just like the success, the years of failure and famine are part of Tipp hurling too. The 1987 breakthrough was special because of it.

There will be lulls again and, hopefully, Tipperary hurling will come through it stronger. The challenge is to keep the lulls short and stay competitive.

Our win in 2001 is proof that you can reap what you sow.

SHANE MCGRATH

TIPPERARY 1-19, CORK 1-13
Munster SHC Semi-Final
Páirc Uí Chaoimh
JUNE 8, 2008

Shane McGrath produced his very best in the home of Cork hurling in 2008

★ **TIPPERARY:** B. Cummins; E. Buckley, P. Curran, C. O'Brien; E. Corcoran (0-1), C. O'Mahony, S. Maher; J. Woodlock, **S. McGrath (0-1)**; S. Butler, S. Callinan (0-3), R. O'Dwyer; E. Kelly (1-7), L. Corbett (0-4), W. Ryan (0-1). Subs: P. Kerwick (0-1) for O'Dwyer; B. Dunne for Woodlock; M. Webster (0-1) for Butler; J. O'Brien for Ryan; D. Egan for Callanan.

★ **CORK:** D. Óg Cusack; S. O'Neill, D. O'Sullivan, B. Murphy; J. Gardiner, R. Curran, S. Óg Ó hAilpín (0-1); J. O'Connor (0-2), T. Kenny (0-1); B. O'Connor (1-3), K. Canty, T. McCarthy; P. O'Sullivan (0-1), P. Cronin, C. Naughton (0-4). Subs: N. McCarthy for Canty; K. Murphy for McCarthy; B. Corry (0-1) for Cronin; P. Horgan for Niall McCarthy

THE ACTION

THE WEIGHT OF history was lighter by the end and Tipp could look to the future. Having last won a championship game by the banks of the Lee way back in 1922 this side made light work of it. Granted the teams haven't met regularly in Cork, but it's a fact worth taking notice of as it was a convincing win in the end. This Tipp team outscored Cork 1-15 to 0-5 from the 23rd minute onwards. An experienced Cork side were going in search of their fifth Munster title this decade but they met a hungry Tipp team whose last provincial title success came in 2001.

A capacity 42,823 turned up to see the game which was a number far exceeding the expected attendance beforehand. It caused unforeseen issues though as thousands arrived when the game was due to start. Pitchside gates had to be opened to ease pressure on the Blackrock End. GAA officials ordered an investigation after 400 fans, including children, had to be led onto the pitch to avert a crush.

Cork built up a 1-8 to 0-4 lead after 20 minutes with Ben O'Connor and Tom Kenny along with Sean Óg Ó hAilpín clearing ball while Cathal Naughton helped himself to three points. Then rapidly things turned around. The Tipp half-back line got a grip on Cork while Shane McGrath and James Woodlock took over in midfield. Eoin Kelly finally started getting the supply lines he craved. On 24 minutes, in a whirlwind, he turned Brian Murphy and sent the ball flying past Donal Óg Cusack to the adulation of the Tipperary supporters.

With the backs, midfield and now forwards on form, Tipp realised they had Cork's measure. The engine room of Conor O'Mahony at six as well as midfield pair McGrath and Woodlock were more in control as the game wore on ensuring constant ball rained in on top of the Cork full back line. Half time left Cork with more questions than answers while Tipp began attacking more frequently. A missed penalty by Paudie O'Sullivan on 42 minutes had forced the pendulum shift.

Cork held on as long as they could but in the last 10 minutes Tipp, with more energy in their legs, pulled clear. Subs Micheal Webster and Pat Kerwick added power to the attack as the Premier county hit five straight points. Eamonn Corcoran pointed a sideline in the 63rd minute that had supporters in the stands on their feet. It felt like a changing of the guard in Munster hurling as the Tipp supporters swarmed the field at the end.

★★★★★

66

THE ODDS WERE stacked against us in 2008 when we travelled down to Páirc Uí Chaoimh to face an experienced Cork team. For me personally, I was looking across at Jerry O'Connor, who was Hurler of the Year in 2005 and also Tom Kenny who was in midfield for them.

Tom was one of the top athletes in the sport and took midfield play to a new level in regard to the distances he could cover on the field in a match. To be able to say that you could match up to those guys, well that was brilliant.

It's a day that I loved.

Supporters just weren't sure if we could win, as Tipp hadn't won in Cork since 1922 at that stage!

I will never forget the atmosphere that particular day. I think they oversold the terraces and the crowd came onto the field. People were everywhere and every word was amplified. It was the last of the big championship games where they would have had that issue in relation to health and safety.

People had to literally sit on the sideline a foot or so from the players.

It was that old Páirc Uí Chaoimh atmosphere, cauldron-like and fierce intense. The crowd was on top of us. The dressing-rooms were tiny and to get there at half-time you could end up walking past your next door neighbour on their way to the shop or the toilet!

At the very start of the game, Larry Corbett won a ball and he threw it out to me. I touched it down, controlled it and put it over the bar.

The Tipp crowd loved it.

There was a minute or two gone and that settled me for the whole game. I just really, really enjoyed that game. Wherever the ball was I happened to be. I loved being in that zone. I loved the adrenalin of it, the atmosphere, winning rucks.

And I remember jumping high up to catch one ball in the second-half with three or four other players going for it and it felt like nothing was going to stop me! I jumped and came down with the ball, then hand passed it off.

That's some feeling. Nothing major came of it but I got confidence from performing that day against the two best midfielders of the time. You knew if you could perform against them, you were doing something fairly right.

The experience of the day stood to me in other games.

Some of those Cork players had a pace of thought that could leave you stunned. There was a piece of skill that I never saw happen before or since.

Jerry O'Connor won a free and he put the ball down and actually hit the free from the ground. Quick as lightening he hit the ball along the ground 20 yards to his brother, Ben!

That's the understanding they had with each other.

It tells you of the confidence he had in himself, as well as his brother. I was looking on, thinking… *Imagine having that level of confidence in yourself… we're here in front of 40,000 plus people and you just don't care like!*

I remember that moment clearly.

I was delighted with how the game went but when we finally got back to the dressing-room the tiredness hit me. It was such an intense day. I was drained but satisfied. The physical, as well as the mental preparation that goes into a championship game is hard to believe.

That 70 or so minutes would have been the focus for months, so when it's over it's like a new reality. Add in the atmosphere in the sapping heat and it just becomes a relief that we won. As I've said, the old dressing-rooms in Páirc Uí Chaoimh were tight, and John Casey was trying to do physio in the showers while everything was going on!

That 15 or 20 minutes in the dressing-room after winning was special.

I knew I was part of something big.

That day announced to the rest of the teams that we were a serious side and weren't the soft touch that we were seen as a few short years before. It was my third year on the team and we didn't have a win as big as that up to that point.

To go down to Cork and beat them - being the first Tipp team to do so since 1922, and then power on and win the Munster final that year was tremendous.

Winning the Munster final was very special as I was the first from our parish of Ballinahinch to be starting on the Tipp senior team. We collected the league earlier in the year, beating Galway in the final, but it's always nice to get that first championship medal in your pocket. I'm proud to have won five Munster medals with Tipp. Each one tells a story and is treasured.

While that summer of 2008 was my third year on the senior team it was my first big year and the Cork game was the first big match where people would have taken notice and said, 'This guy Shane McGrath… he's not too bad now'.

As a teenager I hadn't made the Tipp minor hurling panel which was really devastating at that age, but I kept at it. A couple of years later at college in LIT, hurling under the Clare legend Davy Fitzgerald, I was part of two Fitzgibbon Cup winning teams.

Davy brought me on a lot skills-wise, and then Babs Keating brought me into the Tipp panel in 2006. I was doing fine in there and got nominated for an All Star, but 2007 didn't go as well. 2008 was the year it took off for me.

It had a lot to do with the new management team. Cian O'Neill came in as a coach and had a big impact on me. I learned how to train properly and how to perform, and thanks to that, I got the best out of myself on big days like that one in Cork.

Times were different then in that you didn't have the Munster championship week-on-week-off as you do now. We had a good few weeks between that Cork game and the Munster final and a lot of us stayed down in Cork afterwards and had a brilliant night together. They are great memories to have and I remember being back in the hotel getting a singsong going.

It was really great craic. We actually ended up meeting a lot of the Cork players out the same night!

The next few years were magic.

Whatever it is about that group, on and off the field, we're very close, even with Liam Sheedy, Eamon O'Shea and those guys that were part of the management.

It's a testament to the group we had. We still meet up regularly. I'm still in touch with a lot of the boys and that's gone out of a lot of inter-county groups now because lads are so busy and don't have time. Whatever it is about that group… the wives, partners, girlfriends; the whole group was very close and that day down in Páirc Uí Chaoimh was one of the big days for us all.

From there on, I was midfield all the time.

Woody was there beside me in midfield and I just know we both loved every minute that year. We eventually lost to Waterford in the All-Ireland semi-final, but that year was huge progress. In 2009 I thought we were just phenomenal.

We came so close but it didn't happen that year. I think a lot of our belief to win the 2010 All-Ireland came from what we did in the years leading up to it.

That day in Páirc Uí Chaoimh in 2008 was the end of that particular Cork team with their older stock coming to the end of what were fantastic careers. They were spent and we took over in Munster after that, claiming four of the next five Munster championships.

Winning that glorious day was hugely important as it heralded the emergence of a new and ambitious Tipp team. It was a serious day for me too as it established Woody and I as a genuine midfield pairing that had arrived on the big stage.

We knew we could mix it with anyone after that.

JAMES WOODLOCK

KILKENNY 2-22, TIPPERARY 0-23
All-Ireland SHC Final
Croke Park
SEPTEMBER 6, 2009

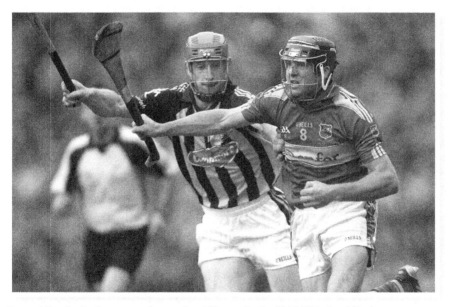

James Woodlock wins possession against Kilkenny in the 2009 All-Ireland final

★ **KILKENNY:** PJ Ryan; M. Kavanagh, JJ Delaney, J. Tyrell (0-1); T. Walsh (0-1), B. Hogan, J. Tennyson; D. Lyng (0-1), M. Rice; E. Brennan (0-3), E. Larkin (0-3), R. Power (0-1); R. Hogan (0-2), H. Shefflin (1-8), A. Fogarty. Subs: TJ Reid (0-1) for Fogarty; M. Fennelly (0-1) for Lyng; M. Comerford (1-0) for Hogan.

★ **TIPPERARY:** B. Cummins; P. Stapleton, P. Maher, P. Curran; D. Fanning, C. O'Mahony, B. Maher; **J. Woodlock**, S. McGrath (0-1); N. McGrath (0-2), J. O'Brien, S. Callanan (0-3); P. Kerwick, E. Kelly (0-13), L. Corbett (0-4). Subs: B. Dunne for O'Brien; W. Ryan for Kerwick; M.Webster for Woodlock.

THE ACTION

AS EPIC FINALS go, this was one of the best. As a game it had it all from flicks, hooks and blocks to breath-taking scores, controversy and history being made in front of 82,104 spectators. It was up there with the greatest of finals ever played. Tipperary gave their all but the experience of playing on the big stage for the last number of years allied with a slice of fortune from a controversial penalty call meant the coin flipped the Noresiders way in the end. They had the will-power and energy to claim four in a row and create their own history.

Days like this go beyond sporting occasions. The memory will funnel back and forth through time. Tipp hurled well in the first-half and even though Kilkenny hit two stoppage time points to lead 0-13 to 0-11 at half-time, Eoin Kelly's team looked like they would last the distance. Tipp had their chances to win it. PJ Ryan, the Kilkenny goalkeeper, produced two fantastic reflex saves to deny Seamus Callanan on 37 minutes and Eoin Kelly on 45 minutes. Despite a red card for Benny Dunne for a high pull on Tommy Walsh in the 54th minute Tipp regrouped and, even though they only had 14 players, looked the better team.

Noel McGrath's 62nd minute point gave Tipp a two-point lead but then Richie Power surged towards goal and was judged by Diarmuid Kirwin to have been impeded illegally much to the consternation of the Tipp players. The penalty, duly dispatched by Henry Shefflin, was the spark that ignited the Kilkenny blaze that saw them outscore the challengers 2-3 to 0-2 over the closing seven minutes.

Afterwards Tipp manager Liam Sheedy said, 'The penalty was probably the changing of the game because the other 14 definitely went up a notch after Benny Dunne was dismissed. It was a big call and matches are won on big calls. I've watched it again and it looked a tight call. He started outside the square and finished inside it. Did anyone count the steps? These are big calls and the day you get those calls is the day you win the match'. When pressed on the penalty call by RTE reporter Marty Morrissey after the match, Kilkenny manager Brian Cody said, 'Diarmuid Kirwin certainly gave a penalty. If you want to start wondering about all the frees in the course of a game you will have a fairly busy time. Did you think yourself it was a penalty Marty?'

★★★★★

66

THE HEARTBREAK OF it was something else, but the 2009 All-Ireland final is a match I don't even have to look back on or watch again, it's simply ingrained in my memory.

I think it's the greatest match I've ever played in.

It will live in my memory forever. That game had everything. It had skill, work rate, power, hits, and that ever-present deep history between the counties.

They were a seasoned team while we were an up-and-coming youthful side. It was an amazing game, but my overriding emotion was that I had given it everything, that we had given it everything.

We never fell.

We never faltered. We never broke. Our character was tested in every way and held firm. Our destiny was taken out of our grasp by a controversial refereeing decision, which was the penalty call. We were the better team up until then.

Goals win games.

We missed our chances and while we will never know, I think we would have edged it without that penalty. I look back on it as an unbelievable game but it cost us an All-Ireland final win and all the joy that goes with it. But that is hurling for you!

I got the taste for hurling in primary school underneath the guidance of Paudie Butler and, I swear, I used to pray to God that I would play for Tipperary!

Getting to play on All-Ireland final day meant everything to me since the first time I wore a Tipp jersey to represent a primary schools team in 1998. Clare were playing Offaly in the All-Ireland semi-final in Croke Park that summer and I was one of the lucky children to get to play at half-time that day.

From there, I just wanted to hurl with Tipp!

I knew if I worked hard enough I could get there. I had the passion but I needed to work on my hurling skills more than other players. It was my determination that got me there. If people told me I couldn't do something, I was always able to say to myself... *I can do it.*

I treasured wearing the Tipperary jersey, be it in a training session, a challenge match in the wind and rain or in the All-Ireland finals at under-21 and senior level. My parents and later my wife, Michelle and family always supported me in every way.

It took a few years to build our hurling up to the standard needed to reach an All-Ireland final. Tipp went from 2001 until '09 without playing on the biggest day in hurling. We were building all the time though, and a young bunch of players were gaining experience.

At under-21 level in 2006 we won a Munster title but got beaten by Kilkenny after a replay in the All-Ireland final. I got Man of the Match that day and progressed further when I got the start with the senior team in 2007 under Babs Keating.

The trilogy of games with Limerick was a good stepping stone, and we learned from it. The breakthrough at senior level wasn't far away. Tipp won back-to-back minor All-Irelands in 2006 and '07. Liam Sheedy came in as senior manager for 2008. I started at wing forward in the league of 2008 before being moved out to the middle of the field alongside Shane McGrath.

That's where I was most comfortable, linking the play from the backs to the forwards. We won the Munster championship in 2008 and '09. All stepping stones. It followed on that we played in the All-Ireland final against Kilkenny.

I knew all about the historic rivalry with Kilkenny but we hadn't played them in the final since 1991. We had a young team coming up against one of the all-time great teams who were going for four in-a-row. We had youth but they had experience.

It was my first senior final.

The occasion and the colour was everywhere, all the time. Driving along the road I was thinking about it and if I turned on the radio, there it was as well. It consumed me and I loved every minute of it. There were flags out on the road, the prayers were being said, the phone was hopping, and there were callers to the house.

It really would take you over!

At the time I was a guard in Kilkenny.

I was working one day and decided to create a bit of an atmosphere for myself and put my Tipp flags up on the patrol car going around Kilkenny city!

Anyway, I was stopped by a former player, Charlie Carter who told me take down those colours quick! We had a bit of banter!

I had a good semi-final and was full of confidence after it. Kilkenny had an experienced midfield pairing in Michael Rice and Derek Lyng, who were having serious campaigns and were overwhelming favourites, but we had no fear of them at all.

I was young enough to be carefree and I always liked playing Kilkenny at all levels up along. I was looking forward to the crowd, to the feel of it, to the roar. I had played in under-21 All-Irelands, county finals and Munster finals, but this was my first senior final and the one thing I had in my head was that good players always play well on the big days.

The day before my routine was always the same. I'd farm away at home, out in the fresh air all day and make sure I wasn't overdoing it but I was making sure I filled my lungs with fresh air all day.

I was working to keep my mind off it to some degree, but I was still thinking about what I would do when I got the ball and what I needed to do to be sure I got into the game early. On the day itself, we met in the 'Midway' stop in Laois and travelled on.

It was a lovely calm day, but it was a bit greasy undersod.

The atmosphere was huge but I knew we were ready for an onslaught. We were two traditional teams, no sweepers, no surprises, just pure hurling. We had won back-to-back Munster championships and felt we were ready to go another step now and win in September.

We had experienced players like the leader himself, Eoin Kelly and also Brendan Cummins and Lar Corbett, who had won in 2001.

John O'Brien too was experienced but it was new to the rest of us. I loved it. Walking around in the parade I looked up at the crowd and thought… *This is what the nation wants… it's us and them.*

We're ready.

I looked up to heaven and said a quick prayer to those above to make sure it went well. It felt like seconds 'til the ball was thrown in.

It was relentless.

There is nothing else like it. I remember thinking it must be near half-time but then looked up to see that there was only 12 minutes gone in the game!

My tongue was out!

The ferociousness of the tackles and the hits were so intense. There was no air. It was hard to catch your breath. We were working non-stop hurling against the breeze but we were going toe-to-toe with them. There was no space and the physicality was huge.

The first score came when I blocked down Eoin Larkin and we turned it over and delivered it in to Eoin Kelly, who won himself a free and it was pointed. That really got me into the game.

Brendan Cummins made a fantastic save and I knew we would match them. Seamie Callanan went to 14 while Lar moved to 11 to bring Brian Hogan out from the centre-back position. It worked.

We got some great scores.

We had no fear, sampling everything for the first time.

Kilkenny pumped ball to their full-forward line and tried to bully us but it wasn't working for them. They looked to bury early goals to kill us off early like they did to Limerick in the 2007 final and Waterford in the 2008 final.

Paidi Maher was new to the scene so they fed ball to the more experienced Henry Shefflin, but Paidi was well able for it. We were matching them all over, so the hits got harder.

Seamie took a full frontal charge from Jackie Tyrell.

Amazingly no free was given for it.

That set the tempo for me. I loved the battle! We were dominant in the hits but couldn't translate it to the scoreboard. For all our work and hurling we weren't putting the ball over the bar.

Kilkenny and Tipp is always on the day; whoever edges the breaks and takes their chances will win.

Kilkenny were living off scraps but were still in touching distance.

We were going well at that stage. It was 0-11 apiece coming up to half-time when Richie Power was lying on the ball and Paidi got blown up for picking the ball but, to me, it wasn't a free. Those types of calls by the referee weren't going our way.

Kilkenny added another point.

The scoreboard didn't reflect how well we were playing but we had missed one or two chances as well as the calls going against us. We were mixing short and long puckouts and that was working. Declan Fanning was having a huge game; he would catch balls or break them down to me and I loved seeing him going for it as he was such a dependable player. Eoin Kelly was on fire, winning every ball that came into him. He was a huge leader for us.

JJ Delaney pushed over to pick him up but Eoin was winning ball coming in high or low. Lar was roaming and creating space for himself. Both half-back lines were doing well too. Tommy Walsh for them was winning a lot of ball while on our side, Brendan Maher was having a stormer on Eddie Brennan.

Our centre-back, Conor O'Mahony was dealing with Larkin and later Shefflin, who had gone into that position. The crowd were loving it. The players were too!

At half-time both teams caught their breath. The mood in our dressing-room was good. As usual, players washed their face or changed socks or had Jaffa cakes or wine gums. Liam spoke and it gave us great confidence.

My role was to support the half-backs and half-forwards, and to man the middle. It was overcast again for the second-half but it was atmospheric. I remember coming out for the second-half and feeling it.

History would be created one way or another.

By us or by them.

Time would tell. So off we went again.

Scores were hard to come by. We were even more determined. The more the game went on the more I felt myself and Shane in the middle of the field were starting to get on top. Any time a Kilkenny player got the ball, we absolutely swarmed them in the middle.

We did that to prevent quality ball going in to their full-forward line. Our half-backs were sending in ball but we hit some wides. We wanted to rattle the net.

Seamie Callanan had a goal chance denied when Pat Kerwick, who was by the Canal End side, crossed one ball over into Seamie but the Kilkenny goalie, PJ Ryan made a fantastic save. They were hanging on by a thread.

Shortly after the '65' was missed and when a team is hurling well you just have to put the scores on the board, but we weren't doing it.

We didn't finish them off.

Seamie got two massive scores for us and we were well on top, however Richie Power was catching ball and winning frees for them with Henry Shefflin keeping the scoreboard ticking over so we weren't going clear. It was intense and still up for grabs.

We had another chance when Eoin got through but slipped and didn't unleash his usual unstoppable shot so PJ Ryan got to it. Pat Kerwick was hit high and Paidi Maher was hit too but the cards weren't shown for all challenges.

Larry then hit a massive point and the crowd was roaring.

We were flowing and attacking non-stop but couldn't create that gap on the scoreboard. It was tense and the stakes got higher as the game went on.

Then in the blink of an eye, Benny Dunne was sent off and we were down to 14 players. Benny left the field and I felt so sorry for him as he wasn't a dirty player.

It didn't change the game though; we were still hunting in packs. Michael Kavanagh in their full-back line was their free man.

I was happy the free man wasn't further out.

We were well in the game and the sending off never fazed us. With 10 to go, Eoin Kelly got an unbelievable score and we were two up!

Then three!

We were dominating the game but on limited possession they were getting scores and we were still hitting wides. I couldn't get that out of my head.

That's experience.

However, when the chips were down we were able to stay with them and were leading them. They got one back. The crowd was sizzling at this stage, it was high stakes stuff! Martin Comerford came on for them. I remember a high ball dropping on our half-back line and Conor O'Mahony slipped.

Comerford got it and gave it to Richie Power.

I could see Paul Curran and I thought it was a free out. All I can remember is the referee's arms going out for a penalty. I couldn't see it clearly but can remember Brendan Cummins rushing out to the ref and all the Tipp players gathering around him.

A couple of decisions had gone against us but I thought the ref had done a fair enough job up until then. But he completely got that call wrong.

My heart sank.

There was seven minutes to go and we had them until then, but they got a lifeline. Henry Shefflin stood over it and scored.

The next play was a goal by Martin Comerford.

BANG!!!!

Another shot fired for them. It was still winnable but we just couldn't change it. That three-minute spell cost us the game. We still had time, but we didn't have the experience needed to close it.

The tide didn't turn but they did get on top. Their half-back line won the ball we had been winning.

We stayed going but spilled ball. Eoin Larkin got his two points then. For us, Noel McGrath had a shot blocked, second by second it was slipping away. Our inexperience told. We ran out of time.

Looking back, Seamie, Noel and Eoin had goal chances and there were chances for points too but the penalty changed the course of that game.

Diarmuid Kirwin got the call wrong.

I think Kilkenny couldn't believe their luck!

They got two goal chances and took them. It was absolute heartbreak. But it was an amazing game.

We returned to Thurles on Monday night to a massive reception, the supporters really loved that team. There was only one thing to do and that was to go back to Croke Park the following year and bring the cup home with us.

The tone was set for the decade ahead.

BRENDAN CUMMINS

(EOIN KELLY, MICHAEL CAHILL, BRENDAN MAHER & LAR CORBETT)

TIPPERARY 4-17, KILKENNY 1-18
All-Ireland SHC Final
Croke Park
SEPTEMBER 5, 2010

Brendan Cummins celebrates Tipperary epic victory over Kilkenny in 2010

★ **TIPPERARY:** B. Cummins (0-1); P. Stapleton, P. Curran, **M. Cahill**; D. Fanning, C. O'Mahony, Padraic Maher; **B. Maher (0-2)**, S. McGrath; G. Ryan (0-1), Patrick Maher, J. O'Brien (0-2); N. McGrath (1-0), **E. Kelly (0-7)**, **L. Corbett (3-0)**. Subs: C. O'Brien for O'Mahony; S. Callanan (0-2) for O'Brien; B. Dunne (0-1) for McGrath; D. Young for Fanning; S. Hennessy (0-1) for Brendan Maher.

★ **KILKENNY:** A. PJ Ryan; J. Dalton, N. Hickey, J. Tyrrell; T. Walsh, J. Tennyson, JJ Delaney; J. 'Cha' Fitzpatrick, M. Fennelly; TJ Reid (0-4), H. Shefflin (0-1), E. Larkin; E. Brennan, R. Power (1-9), A. Fogarty (0-1). Subs: M. Rice (0-1) for Shefflin; D. Lyng (0-1) for Fitzpatrick; M. Comerford for Brennan; R. Hogan for Fogarty; J. Mulhall (0-1) for Reid.

THE ACTION

THE SWEETEST FEELING overcame Tipp supporters at the final whistle as the old familiar 'Slievenamon' rang out heralding in the new champions of Ireland. With last year's final still raw, Tipperary made no mistake this time as hat-trick hero Lar Corbett led the way to the Promised Land. The 'five in a row' Kilkenny t-shirts were already printed, but weren't worth tuppence after the match, as Tipperary claimed their 26th title overall and first since 2001.

Once more, courage and selflessness were key traits in the champions. An awesome display of power meant Kilkenny were denied their 'drive for five' in front of 81,765 that marvelled at the spectacle. Splendid scores put them clear, the pick of them an early Lar Corbett goal as he fetched Shane McGrath's touchdown pass above Noel Hickey's head and swivelled around to finish. Brendan Cummins, with the aid of the strong breeze, fired over a memorable long-range effort from a free and Tipp went on to lead 1-10 to 0-7 after 32 minutes. A minute later Richie Power fired in a goal and added two points to leave just a point in it at the break.

Tipp had done most of the hurling, yet Kilkenny were right beside them despite losing Henry Shefflin on 13 minutes to a cruciate injury which he had picked up in the semi-final. Kilkenny had survived without him when he got the same injury in the 2007 final against Limerick, but Tipp were to prove a different story altogether. Kilkenny's shortcomings in the forwards cost them in the second half. Eddie Brennan, Aiden Fogarty and TJ Reid were all replaced. The Tipp defence was excellent, working as a unit. Michael Cahill had a storming game in particular, as did Padraic Maher at half-back while Brendan Cummins was solid as ever in goals.

Although the four Kilkenny forward replacements did well, the Tipp subs did even better with all five making telling contributions. Tipp were on top in more sectors as the game went on. Brendan Maher shined in midfield and linked up play well between the backs and forwards. Eoin Kelly showed immense leadership and when the game was close, Kelly popped up with a point before Noel McGrath and Lar Corbett fired in goals on 42 and 44 minutes. Tipp attacked down the middle and the approach worked with Corbett and Kelly in lethal form. After the two quick goals, Tipp looked uncatchable at 3-11 to 1-10 up but Kilkenny stayed in the game and a lesser team could easily have been caught.

Lar Corbett completed his hat trick late on with a lovely touch on the stick before angling the ball past PJ Ryan to become the first to bury three final goals since Cork's Eddie O'Brien did so in 1970.

★★★★★

66

I WAS BORN and reared with hurling as a central part of my life and being on the team on an All-Ireland final day was always a dream. My father used to take me down to the field to play football when I was small and then, one day, I decided I'd go down to Ballybacon and have a few pucks.

I met a coach by the name of Jody Spooner, who was helping out in the club and he brought us on so much by organising training which gave us structure, and so we progressed. We won an under-16 B county final and it put me on the platform to play with Tipperary.

I've had a lengthy career and one constant jersey throughout: from the time I was a minor hurler I wore a Manchester United jersey under the team jersey for every match. Since I finished up with Tipp, I haven't worn it once, not even now when I play with the club as the last thing I want is for it to be robbed out of a dressing-room.

It's hung up at home, but I still mind it.

My intention is to frame it. It's been a good luck charm since I was a minor in 1993 and has the sponsor 'Sharp' written on it, and has some strings by the collar on the front of it. I wore it underneath the team jersey in every single match for Tipp, every club game and challenge game.

If it was a training game or a trial game I always put on that jersey; it was like my brain telling my body… *This matters, this is serious…* and so I wore it.

In the early days with Tipp I was a dual player, and both football and hurling were an integral part of my life. I used to train with the county footballers on Mondays and Wednesdays, and the hurlers on Tuesdays and Thursdays.

And then I played whatever game was fixed for the weekend!

There were a few times I played two games in the one day.

I remember playing the commemoration game for the 75th anniversary of 'Bloody Sunday' in 1995 with the Tipp footballers and togging after then with the hurlers that same day. I was in goals for hurling and a half-forward in football, and generally the football managers didn't mind me playing both sports but the hurling managers did.

Hurling-wise, I played for the Tipperary senior team under so many different managers, from 1995 to 2013, and if the team was no good we'd often just blame the manager! One night in training I remember we were running in a group and a player said, 'Ah sure look… if it doesn't work out this year we'll all be here next year… it's the manager who will be gone!'

I was there across decades and generations of players, joining the panel under Fr. Tom Fogarty in the mid-90s after we won an All-Ireland under-21 final against Kilkenny in Thurles in 1995. That year in the senior Munster championship Paul Delaney and Mick Ryan got sent off and suspended after a row against Waterford below in Cork, and we ended up having to play a midfielder like Colm Bonnar at corner-back.

The following year I had the privilege of getting to play with Nicky and Pat Fox in the Munster final. We were 10 points up against Limerick who had Gary Kirby and Ciaran Carey playing that day in the summer of 1996 and I think if we had won that day we'd have won the All-Ireland.

Look, the swings and roundabouts of it all are that when we were right we actually won the All-Ireland. I knew we were right in 2001 and 2010.

Of all the games I played in, the All-Ireland final in 2010 is the one that sticks out the most with me. Maybe because of the journey to get there as much as for the final itself. That year we had carried the disappointment of 2009 and felt we had unfinished business, but then we got beaten by Cork in the first round in Páirc Uí Chaoimh and it was back to square one.

We had worked too hard to let it all fall away, so first off we had a meeting in the Jockey to clear the air and then our comeback began. We got motoring after beating Wexford, then got over Galway in a close quarter-final, and Waterford then to make it back to the All-Ireland final.

Against Kilkenny, again.

Stopping the 'five in-a-row' didn't mean an awful lot to me, it was more about redemption for the year before when we had been in the driving seat but didn't win.

At a training camp in Carton House the week before the final Eamon O'Shea walked by me and he said, 'Can you hear that?'

I hadn't heard anything and told him so.

'Exactly,' he said. 'There's 15,000 people below in Nowlan Park tonight watching them train.' It really struck me then that Kilkenny were under serious pressure going into the final. I had a great feeling before it that we were ready to win and I felt very relaxed and prepared on the day.

Before the parade we were on the field and, cool as you like, I went in towards the toilet and passed two fellas just sitting by the dressing-room and I said, 'Well lads, how's it going?'

They responded, 'Well Brendan… best of luck'.

And we chatted for a bit.

It was surreal because I was going back out to play in the All-Ireland final in a few minutes! I opened the door and sauntered out with Paddy Stapleton saying to me, 'You nearly missed the parade'.

On an emotional level I felt we were going to win.

I felt it in 2001 and again that day. So while I didn't enjoy the match in one way because there was so much at stake; in another way *I felt* the belief that was instilled in us. It was an emotionally charged day but when the whistle went to play it was just great, as it was time to express ourselves.

I scored a point that day and it's a special memory for me.

Believe it or not, there are times that I'm driving around in the car feeling a bit depressed with work or whatever is going on in life and I just think about standing on my own '45' saying to myself… *I can do this.*

The ball went up and flew and it carried as the volume of the crowd went up and up, nearer and nearer Hill 16… and then it dropped over the bar!

The run back to the goals was adrenaline-filled but I had to take my heart rate down as my job was to stop the ball, not to be too excited at getting a score.

It was no good scoring unless you could save the ball.

Goals were on our mind. We felt going into the game that we needed goals, and that if we raised green flags it would knock their confidence because thinking about Kilkenny in that era, when they got you under the cosh they scored a goal, and every time we played Kilkenny a goal for either team seemed to be worth five points.

Think of their goalkeeper, PJ Ryan the year before; he stopped everything because we struck the ball from maybe three or four yards too far out.

I listened to our forwards talking in 2010 and they were saying they were going to be able to see the colour of his eyes before they pulled the trigger. In the first-half, Lar Corbett caught a dropping ball, turned fast and buried an early goal at the Hill 16 end. Just knowing what they had discussed beforehand gave me huge belief up the other end in goals.

Just before half-time Richie Power bagged one for them.

The way he turned his body to receive the pass, you just can't coach to people. TJ Reid or Larkin gave him the pass but the way he stepped back to get room to swing was something else.

I came out but I knew the next hurley I was going to have in my hand was the pucking out one. I hadn't a massive amount of balls to save; TJ Reid had a shot in the first-half that I broke out to the side and really when defending starts from the front it makes life easier in the goals.

We got the hooks and blocks in all over the field. Bonnar Maher did his usual thing, Noel McGrath linked up the play and Larry scored the goals.

The final whistle came with so many emotions. Being the goalkeeper when we won in 2001, it felt like it was the first of many, and then I was gone from the starting team in 2007 so an All-Ireland seemed light years away before I got back into the team.

And at that moment, when the whistle went in 2010, I had some clarity of thought in relation to the journey over the previous months and years. I also felt the end of the road for me playing at that level wasn't too far away so I appreciated the moment a bit more.

I'll never forget 12 months before, after the final whistle in the 2009 final, I went out to Paidi Maher and he was lying face down with the tears rolling down his cheeks and onto the field. Paddy Stapleton also and Conor O'Mahony, who's never an emotional fella. I will never forget that dressing-room after the 2009 final as long as I live.

The relief in beating Kilkenny in 2010 was that the younger players wouldn't have to go through that again, more so than an... *I have won an All-Ireland...* feeling.

At home I have the picture up of Mick Ryan, Eamon O'Shea and Liam Sheedy lifting the cup that day. We owed the management team a huge amount for trusting us to do the job. The talk from some people beforehand was that some of us players were washed up so it was the management team that gave us another opportunity and for that I'm grateful.

I'm delighted we didn't let them down.

Whenever I left Ballybacon to go and play a big game I used to get a good luck card from the primary school. I'd be invited down to the school the week of the game and it was always a very special place for me so I always told them in the school that… 'When I play the game on Sunday I will have all of you in the goals with me'.

That is what it's about and it carries you.

Everywhere you go around the village you can see the pride of the people in what you're doing. That final win was sweet and it was for everybody back home at the butt of the mountain.

EOIN KELLY

Eoin Kelly enjoys the greatest moment for any hurler in the game, lifting the MacCarthy Cup

❝

THE 2010 ALL-IRELAND was my day of days.

It was the way we played. It was everything we prepared for.

I remember thinking on the bus in to Croke Park that the day felt exactly like 2009 and I was thinking… *This is half time!*

It was like the 2009 final had only been played two hours beforehand and we were going back in to play the 2010 final as the second-half.

It just felt so real.

There was a drizzle of rain in 2010, the same drizzle was there in 2009, and I kept thinking… *2009 was half time… here's the second-half!*

The script was written and it was just meant to be.

Playing and winning with an intensity instilled in us by Liam Sheedy was amazing. To cap it all off afterwards, our half-forward, Pat 'Festy' Kerwick sang the *Galtee Mountain Boy* in a way that felt like it captured a moment in time.

I heard after of people that left the stadium and came back to hear the song.

That day ticked the box for the fighting spirit that was in the team right up to the singing of that song, and I've heard that from supporters too.

For me, it pulled everything together.

In Tipperary we have the hurlers but when we don't bring the physicality and intensity, we don't do so well. Then when we do bring it, we are very hard to beat.

Emotions were let out on the field that day and the only disappointment is that we didn't have that feeling more. I'd love to have experienced that more but, then, some never experience it, so I'm grateful I had that day.

That time left an everlasting connection with that squad which is an unbelievable feeling.

I've strong memories about the day itself and also the preparation for it. I put my speech together before the final. I got one of those little plastic containers that a school bus ticket would come in, a little plastic slip, and I had the speech put in that because I had said if it's raining on the day I don't want my speech getting wet!

That's how convinced I was we were going to win.

I gave the speech in the slip to our kit man, John 'Hotpoint' Hayes a few days before and said to him, 'Mind this… I'm going to need it on Sunday'.

The preparation was unbelievable but that's the way Liam Sheedy had us.

On the Tuesday before the game, John O'Brien had caught me on the face in a drill and I remember being cut and thinking… *Ah jeez, that cut is going to be there now on Sunday when I'm collecting the cup!*

It's just how convinced you'd be.

I had on-going back trouble though and it flared up the week of the game.

On the Wednesday morning before the match, I couldn't get out of bed. I was absolutely crippled so I actually crawled out of the bed to get to my phone.

I rang our physio, John Casey, panicking, and saying, 'John this is over!'

'Relax,' he told me. 'It's Wednesday. Get into the car and come up to me.'

I pulled myself up using the wardrobe, got into the car and drove up to John in Nenagh. My back had gone into spasm but somehow John managed to fix it. Players often have to deal with these sort of things and I feel so lucky that it didn't stop me from playing that Sunday.

Going back to the start of the journey when Liam became manager in 2008, we were breaking through walls slowly but surely, and the belief was coming in to the dressing-room. Step by step, and game by game.

There's a massive difference between believing you're going to win an All-Ireland and *hoping* you're going to win one.

They are oceans apart and Liam had us believing.

Improvement mattered. From the start of my career to the finish, the time on the ball decreased. It started out as one on one marking but changed to two or three swarming the player with the ball for a finish. Players just got fitter and science played a bigger part, so I had to adapt.

During the season I didn't want anyone to interrupt my thought process which centred on winning the All-Ireland. My constant focus was on preparing for training, performing in training, setting targets with the strength and conditioning coach and reaching them.

I was living through hurling.

I was due to get married in February, 2011 but it was hurling that was on my mind and preparing to reach the goal which was the All-Ireland.

Hurling was in every part of the day. I mean, everyday things were done with more intensity, you were just pumped up. We changed and adapted our style of play and Eamon O'Shea introduced a lot of movement into the team.

It was enjoyable as we were constantly learning and that's the thing with hurling, you never stop learning.

By match day, 2010, I was still convinced that we weren't going to lose. We were prepared for everything. The attention to detail was immaculate and all scenarios were covered. For example, if Henry Shefflin would go down injured, Eamon O'Shea would go in to the backs to tell them to stay focused, because with Shefflin gone, heads could switch off for a second.

In those two All-Irelands, in 2009 and 2010, we performed, but we didn't take the goal chances in 2009 and with that Kilkenny team you needed to be six or seven points ahead of them because one or two points just wasn't enough.

Every goal we got in 2010 was a nail in their coffin.

What I remember most from the game itself is Noel McGrath coming back out the field after scoring a goal. I just remember saying to him, 'Keep the head', and that was after putting us a few points up but I suppose it was the experience of 2009, when we went three points ahead, 0-20 to 0-17.

That time we were down to 14 players and it got away from us.

Definitely, when Kilkenny got the goal they were still only a point ahead and we probably lost our composure and they got another goal just after, and then it was 'game over' really. In 2010, at that moment when Noel was passing by, I pointed and said, 'Keep the head', relating to the fact we have them on the rack now… let's drive on.

Noel's goal was the third goal to put us clear.

But it was Kilkenny we were playing, so focus was key.

The intensity of lads going into tackles was something else, they just didn't care if they came out alive or not. The work rate was phenomenal and it had to be because Kilkenny came back at us, there was only a point in it at half-time, so it was a ding-dong battle until we got two goals after half-time.

We didn't care who scored the goals as it was often said in the dressing-room, 'If you have a 99% chance you get the ball… if it's a 70% chance then that's not good enough'.

We were really united, we were a real team.

TJ Reid was the Kilkenny captain, and I remember shaking hands with him after the game. The blue helmet I was wearing in 2010 was a helmet I got from TJ Reid years before.

I went to school in St Kieran's College in Kilkenny, and when I was in 5th or 6th year, and TJ was in 1st or 2nd year, we swapped helmets. I definitely got the better deal as I got a perfect blue helmet for a green helmet that wasn't in great condition. When I shook hands with TJ Reid after the All-Ireland final I said, 'I got a better deal on you before and I'm getting it again today TJ!'.

At the end, for me, it was just a relief that we had won it because 2009 was so devastating. As a captain, you have a job to do in making the acceptance speech and that's a big moment too so you're not in celebratory mode until you go back into the dressing-room and that's when you go bananas with the group.

That's the couple of minutes that definitely sticks out because that's *your* group and it's a rare time. I can still remember Brian Cody coming into the dressing-room and the respect he got, and I will always remember his words.

I don't know if he was having a hint at 2009 when he said, 'Look lads, the best team always wins the All-Ireland final'.

He was very gracious in defeat.

He came in the year before, and the year after too when they won.

I was in the dressing-room when he came into the winning Tipp room in 2019 as well. It just shows the sportsmanship of him. When he talks, everyone listens.

That's also a moment that stands out.

A month after the final, Liam Sheedy stepped down as manager which was heart-breaking at the time. He had started out as manager in 2008 and told us we were going on a 'journey' which was a word he often mentioned.

If we ever look back on it as a group we can say it finished for us where he wanted it to finish. It brought us to different environments like training camps in Portugal, Spain, Wales and the Curragh, and we bought into everything. There was a family atmosphere for those couple of years and we had something special.

To be lucky enough to be chosen captain added something for me. Coming from a place where Kilkenny were after beating us so many times, also meant that the 2010 final stands out.

Tipperary is definitely based on skills, the skilfulness of the players.

And that's what I've grown up seeing and admiring. As I was growing up, the teams of 1989 and '91 ignited it for us. The charisma attached to those players as well, they were icons. I remember the cup coming to the school in 1989 and '91.

In Mullinahone we had John Leahy in the dressing-room with the minor and junior county final in 1989 and the intermediate in '90. My dad was involved in those teams as manager and selector, so I'd be in the dressing-rooms listening to all this which was all I wanted to do. A couple of years later I was playing for Mullinahone as we went on a journey of our own at senior level. I won my first All-Ireland in 2001 at 19 years of age and then the county final with Mullinahone at 20, and was thinking this will happen every year!

But I later learned that it doesn't, and you really have to cherish the wins. There's ups and downs but that All-Ireland final in 2010 is one of the fondest memories I have.

99

MICHAEL CAHILL

Kilkenny's 'Drive for Five' in 2010 met a major stumbling block in Michael Cahill

"

THE 2010 FINAL against Kilkenny was the big one for me, and it probably was for anyone playing or watching that day. There was a group of us involved that had come up along from minor with some success, including Brendan Maher, Noel McGrath, Paidi Maher, Gearoid Ryan and a couple more who all broke onto the senior team at the same time.

We were in it together growing up, but the stakes were higher at senior level.

That final was a big occasion for a group of young lads like us.

To have a chance to claim an All-Ireland and to stop the 'Drive for Five!'

In the lead up to the final, there were whispers that Kilkenny had the 'five in-a-row' t-shirts and banners already printed and were writing us off, so we saw that as a chance to make our own history.

As a young player I felt fearless, plus a lot of us had played in minor and under-21 finals previously in Croke Park but, it's still a massive occasion.

Unbeknownst to myself I was doing a lot of mental preparation before matches. I see it now, in hindsight, that I did a lot of mental preparation for that game. I went over the game in my head the night before, figuring out when to go forward or wait; how I'd approach whoever I was marking, and all that would be in my mind, so visualisation was something I did before it became the norm.

There'd be no surprises on the day then.

I knew I was prepared for Henry Shefflin, Richie Hogan or whoever else, but I knew I'd be corner-back on Eddie Brennan for most of it. It's a different type of game in the current era but back then it was positional and I was probably known as a bit of a man-marker, so I would have backed myself to stop him at all costs.

I had a ritual the night before finals, and other games too, that I would drink a 'half one' before going to bed! Whiskey was the routine for county finals with Sarsfields or All-Irelands; it just helped me relax and chill out.

I began doing it from a minor final on and it worked so I kept it on.

I'm not massively superstitious but it fed into my mental preparation routine. For the senior final that year I remember the night before the game watching *Up for the Match* on telly at home with my mother and father, and having a hot whiskey!

On match days I was big into pumping myself up!

Some lads would have headphones on with music playing and when we headed to Croke Park I had 1980s rock tunes going!

I loved the *Rocky* films so the theme music was a big favourite at the time! Being relaxed or feeling at home is the key because when you run out on the field in front of over 80,000 people it's easy to get overwhelmed. You're already full of adrenalin but when the roar arrives, you're ready to burst! But with that, it was important to be grounded and find clarity to be able to play your best.

That game was like a tidal wave. A lot of the time you're swept in one direction or another but you keep trying to do the simple things well.

At one point in the first-half, the ball broke in front of us.

Eddie Brennan positioned himself well but I stretched and let fly on the ball one-handed and drove it to a roar which set the tempo from my point of view.

During the game I was thinking… *Can I get it out of here quick enough?*
Or… *Next ball is mine.*

There's times you don't want to see the ball coming in at all but you have to set the tempo. Those games from 2009 to 2016 were played at a ferocious tempo and it was all about winning your own corner, then relying on your teammates to win their patch.

That day I was thinking… *Where the hell is he?*
And… *I will beat him to that ball.*

I didn't want to give him a sniff of the ball, that was in my head, because if he got it I knew what he could do with it.

We had debates over the years whether or not to man-mark or stay in position. I thought confusion was created at times if we stayed in the same position and the fella you were marking drifted off with no one marking him at all.

Hip to hip and man to man marking usually worked better for the backs, so I stuck with Eddie Brennan wherever he went.

A massive part of our game at the time was Eamon O'Shea's influence and helping the forwards find room and angles for passes and shots, so Larry's goal at the start of the second-half was huge.

I can still picture the play.

Gearoid Ryan got the ball in midfield and sent a sharp angled pass in to Noel McGrath, who spun around and without looking he palmed the ball off to Larry who took it on the run, then buried it.

Larry could end up anywhere, but he was a great man for ghosting into space.

I got such energy from that, it was like electricity; I was buzzing. Noel and Eoin Kelly were pointing to the helmets just after to remind themselves to keep switched on.

Kilkenny would often catch teams on the bounce after a goal because you could switch off for a split second when the ball was near and the goal you just got would be cancelled out with one the other end. Staying in the game was vital, so pointing to the helmets was a trigger to us to stay in the moment.

The roof was lifted by the roar for our goals and the rush was like electricity going through you. Near the end, one ball came dropping from the sky and I wasn't strong in the air so I didn't catch it but knocked it down to Paidi, who cleared it.

It was a serious team effort and had to be.

At times it would creep into your head… *Will we ever beat Kilkenny?*

But that day we reached the heights and again under Mick Ryan in 2016. It was a pleasure to hurl against top players like Tommy Walsh, Henry Shefflin, JJ Delaney and Eddie Brennan. Across the decade, both teams were just going to war and scrapping for inches whenever we met.

Thurles, on the night of a homecoming, is special too.

I remember when Tipp won in 2001 and The Square was alive for the homecoming with thousands there. I was about 12 years of age but could feel the depth of emotion with that many people in the one place.

Growing up, Tommy Dunne was a hurler that I looked up to as well as Eddie Enright who was from my own club. By the time 2010 came around I had hit 21 years of age and experienced it from a player's point of view.

The supporters loved that night in town and it was a special time for the players and those close to them as well.

It was some week after beating Kilkenny. We had an under-21 All-Ireland final the following weekend. The party continued. Thurles was decked in blue and gold when we beat Galway, winning the first under-21 and senior double since 1989.

A few of us played in both finals within the week. Paidi lined out full-back, I was in the corner, Noel was in midfield with Seamus Hennessy, Bonnar and Brendan Maher were playing too.

I'd like to think I will always be involved in some capacity in hurling but the injury I got in 2018 put things in perspective. I did the cruciate in the county semi-final in October, 2018. I worked hard to overcome it and my goal was to make the club and county team again.

Six months after the first injury, I made it onto the field but just three training sessions back into it I broke my kneecap in two. It was a hammer blow, a bad injury.

I was never one to hold back at training and always drove myself to the limit so maybe I had pushed my body too far and too soon trying to come back quick from the first injury. Mentally, at that time, it was difficult to adjust.

My home life changed and my hurling life changed as I was then on the outside looking in at the Tipp team. I was a bit unlucky in ways but it brought home to me the importance of hurling in my life. The pleasure of going out meeting your friends and pucking a ball around is something I really missed when it was gone.

For your mental health, being active and meeting people is so important.

My years are filled with hurling.

Living in Thurles and playing with Sarsfields, there was a history there growing up that you couldn't ignore. I remember Paidi Maher and I watching the seniors train when we were young. The likes of Johnny and Eddie Enright were on the field. We'd watch the training games from the sideline.

I knew Jimmy Doyle from going into the Sarsfields Social Centre with my father where he'd be playing cards on a Wednesday or Thursday night. He was a nice, quiet, unassuming man. You never would have thought this guy was an absolute folk hero!

Years later, going to his funeral, I realised what he meant to people with crowds as far as you could see. The history in Sarsfields is unreal, the wall outside the Social Centre has a mural of the club's All-Ireland winning captains and it hits home every day I'm going training.

That kind of thing drives young players on to want to make their own history.

BRENDAN MAHER

Brendan Maher is typically relentless against Kilkenny in 2010

❝

WE SAW THE happiness that winning in 2010 brought to everyone.

It was an unbelievable feeling to be able to stand on the stage in Semple Stadium at the homecoming on the Monday night, seeing people cheer for you and knowing you were after achieving something special.

Something unique.

I had a picture of the moment saved on my phone for a good few years, just a picture from the stand in Thurles looking across the field and it felt like there were 100,000 people there! It was one of those occasions, one of those times where you nearly have to pinch yourself to prove it's real.

You're thinking… *Is this really happening?*

I was 21 years of age and it was only my second year on the Tipp panel, but it was the first year I was a regular starter all through the year.

The All-Ireland final against Kilkenny stands out as a special game.

Going into it, the main motivating factor would have been to right the wrongs of 2009. We felt we performed but ultimately lost the game in '09. There was a lot of things we felt we could change or do differently.

So for every game in 2010, we were trying to right the wrongs of the previous year and previous games within the season. We focused on ourselves and whatever was going on in Kilkenny was irrelevant to us. All that mattered was our own performance.

The talk outside the camp was all about stopping the five in-a-row.

There was so much talk about the large crowds watching Kilkenny while they were training. There were all sorts of rumours that there was 10,000 or 20,000 or a 100,000 people even at the Kilkenny training sessions!

But I can remember the support that came for us at the open training sessions we had ahead of the game. We were cheered off the pitch in Thurles at one of the sessions and the buzz, the energy of the crowd really got us going. That's one thing that sticks in my mind in the lead up to the game.

The supporters needed the win as much as the team did.

The importance of us being able to come off the pitch with our heads held high regardless of the result was stated over and over again. So that was the motivation we had then, and it's always the motivation really, but it's great to have that focus as a collective.

You go out onto that pitch and your focus and goal is to give everything you have. Then, afterwards, you can come off the pitch with your head held high, regardless of the result.

The day of the game was smooth right from the start to the finish. We always warmed up in Clanna Gael Fontenoy, the GAA club that's not too far from Croke Park.

Cian O'Neill was training us and doing the physical work with us at that time. Our warm-ups were quite intense now. We did about 45 minutes of intense stuff before we got onto the bus and into Croke Park.

Those 45 minutes were always interesting, to say the least!

My memory of that one is actually of Larry Corbett and Paul Curran rolling around the ground tussling with each other in the middle of a possession game! We were kinda thinking… *Lads will ye go handy!*

But that just shows the way we were feeling. The team was willing to do anything to get a win that day.

The first-half of that game was the most satisfying 35 minutes I've played in a Tipp jersey. Early on in the game I broke onto a ball and managed to get it through the middle and won a free. It just settled me into the game.

And then, it felt as if no matter where I moved, the ball was going there; or no matter what move I made it had a positive outcome whether it was a tackle, a hook or a block, getting possession, making a pass or winning a free.

I also got a couple of scores!

It was one of those games where you feel as if every move you make is the right one.

Then in the second-half, myself and Shane McGrath were in midfield and the stand out memory in the half is breaking out with a ball.

I was flicking the ball over JJ Delaney's head and running onto it, then laying it off to Larry. That's something you wouldn't even think about trying!

For me, that was a sign of the mindset I was in.

Just playing off pure instinct and treating it as if it was a game in Borris Ileigh or a training session in Semple Stadium or Dr. Morris Park. I was in a 'flow status' I suppose and I can remember thinking a couple of minutes after that flick… *I might regret that one, JJ Delaney will probably line me up now for an aul hit!*

With a couple of minutes to go, I was cramping up and I was brought off.

Shane and I both came off and we were sitting beside each other on the sideline. Larry got a third goal; then our fourth goal went in and I was thinking… *Yea, we have it!*

When the final whistle blew I took off running.

I didn't know where I was going but I just ran! I remember catching the number seven jersey; it was Paidi, over the other side of the pitch and he was running towards the Cusack Stand. I stayed running towards him, meeting him at the sideline.

I was running towards the Hill too, climbing the barrier and just seeing the

Tipp supporters on Hill 16. Just absolute scenes, as they say!

It's pure elation.

You don't know where you are or where you're going. It's just a state of pure joy.

Sunday night in The Burlington was unbelievable too, over a thousand people and absolute carnage with people just in a state of joy and happiness. I was sitting with my family at one stage, and it can be hard to get those moments with your family at the banquet or after the match.

Spending time with my three brothers, their partners and my parents and just having a drink with them was a rare treat. The following day, we got an open top bus from the train station around Thurles and into Semple Stadium.

Being on the bus and looking out at the crowds was unbelievable. It's days like that which give you that appetite for success and then you want it again and again.

The legacy of Tipperary hurling also feeds into that mind set.

There's a picture inside the door of Stapleton's pub in Borrisoleigh of a Tipp team, from a by-gone era, being led by Sean Kenny.

He was captain of the Tipp team that won the All-Ireland in 1950.

In the picture they're in the parade before the game, behind the band with someone holding an umbrella over Sean at the front. I think they were protecting him from the sun rather than the rain.

It's something I just remember, that photo captures the whole thing of marching behind a pipe band and the honour of it all. That image is hanging on the wall 70 years later and that, in turn, becomes something young people want to achieve.

They want to be remembered in that way.

To have your name put down beside such hurling greats as Liam Devaney, Sean Kenny, Jimmy Finn and these guys is something I'm really proud of.

We have a strong tradition of hurling in Borris Ileigh and to be part of that history and culture really means a lot to me. To be one of the captains to bring back the Liam MacCarthy cup to the parish is something I will carry with me for the rest of my life. Our winning group in 2016 had an amazing few days after the final, the craic was unbelievable and the people of Tipperary gave us an amazing reception.

Of all the other games over the years with Tipp another one that has a special place in my heart is the Munster championship game in 2019, against Cork. It was my first championship match back after being out for a long time because of injury.

I had a different perspective after not playing for so long. Training on my own had been a major struggle at times and there were some tough days but I trusted the recovery process and stuck to it.

When I got back to the field my hurling became more about enjoying being able to play rather than overthinking things, and being worried about making mistakes. Getting a win in Páirc Uí Chaoimh is rare enough for Tipp teams, so going down there and winning from a personal and a collective point of view meant a lot.

Being able to perform well in a big championship game after a long rehab from a serious knee injury was memorable.

It was a joy to go on and win another All-Ireland with Tipp in 2019 and then it meant the world to me that Borris Ileigh won the county hurling final soon afterwards. Adding the Munster club title was a glorious end to the decade.

LAR CORBETT

Lar Corbett broke Kilkenny's heart in 2010, again and again and again.

❝

I ALWAYS HAD goals on my mind.

2010.

All-Ireland final.

No better day for goals. Back then, once I got inside the '21', I would have been disappointed with a point. I would never have been thinking any different going into challenge matches, training matches or All-Ireland finals.

I knew if I got a chance in front of goal, I wanted to see that net shake.

My percentage chance in front of goal in 2008 and '09 was fairly high, and the same in the earlier games of 2010. Kilkenny were going for the 'Drive for Five' and the whole country thought they were unstoppable.

No one was giving Tipperary a chance.

We thought differently. I was fairly confident.

Those of us that were a little older were after gelling well with the younger players, like Paidi Maher, Seamie Callanan, and Noel McGrath.

We were blending nicely together. We just needed to make it work on the day and we did. Teamwork is the key word.

Take the first goal. I know it's so easy to blow things up and change the narrative but in game situations like that you only work on your memory of what you have done before, and what you're capable of doing.

Shane McGrath sent in the ball for that goal the same as he would do in training or challenge matches. You do what is instinctive to you. So in those situations I was used to Shane McGrath dropping a ball to the edge of the square.

Shane was on the back foot so I knew it was going to come in high.

What I look for in those situations is to see if I can get the defender on my left hand. I know then that my right hand is free to catch the ball. If you ask any left-handed hurler they always like to get the defender on their left side because the other hand is free to catch the ball.

Also, they are catching the defender off balance.

That's how it was for me, as I caught Noel Hickey in that situation. It was a little trick I learned over years of playing. There was nothing special about it because we had done that in training and in challenge matches; the difference was we did it on the day of an All-Ireland final.

We had belief in what we were doing and things fell right for us as they had for them in 2009. Kilkenny were going for the five in-a-row but little things like that first goal fell right for us. But the mentality has to be right all year.

A team can't just switch it on when they get to Croke Park.

It's how a team trains and how they go about their business. You have to be getting goals in training and goals in challenge matches and creating chances. I never minded missing but I needed to be creating chances.

If the goalie saved all three goals then that's fine once I did what I could. If you create goal chances you will get the percentages that you're due. I was lucky I got the percentages all on the one day, and finished with three goals.

The highlight was the referee blowing the final whistle.

That might seem strange but going back to 2009 we thought we were on the right track and most thought we had it won with 10 minutes to go. We took our foot off the gas and they got two goals in one minute.

We said after that final that it was about hurling till the end and not easing off with 10 minutes to go. In the 2010 final, before the third goal went in, they had our lead down to four points. They were still in the game and it wasn't until the final whistle that I felt we had it.

Back then, a team wouldn't beat Kilkenny on points alone.

Goals were essential and we knew that. I don't think it happened in those years that a team beat Kilkenny without scoring a goal. An exceptional team, like that Kilkenny team was, needed a team like us to put it up to them.

One great team on their own are never going to get recognition. We played in three All-Irelands in-a-row and we weren't too far away at all but we probably played second fiddle to them. We lost the 2009, '11 and '14 finals but in the last few years the balance of power changed with Tipperary winning the 2016 and '19 finals against them.

I always had a great respect for the Kilkenny players. We are linked in some way after those years. Off the field they were real nice fellas, to be fair. We went on All Star trips with them so I've nothing only the utmost respect for them but on the days of matches, like us, they fought tooth and nail for what they wanted.

They fought for what they believed and we did the same. The one thing they have over us is that they beat us on a lot of the big days, but the relationships we have now are good.

I was probably lucky to be there in 2010.

I had been hugely inconsistent in my performances in previous years as I struggled with injuries in 2002, '03, '05 and '06. I had a long career with Tipp but the managers came and went. Nicky English, Michael Doyle, Ken Hogan and Babs Keating came in and were straight into matches and often the season was over before you know it.

When Liam Sheedy and Eamon O'Shea came into the set up for 2008 I felt they had a different kind of belief in me. I think I responded well to that and found consistency in my game.

After the 2010 season, Liam Sheedy left as manager. Declan Ryan came in for two years and then Eamon O'Shea from 2013 until '15. That's seven managers I played under.

There was a new manager coming in every two years on average. I always think of the comparisons between business and sport. For example, if a county team go back in around October and continue with the same managerial set up and structure as the previous year, they are starting ahead of their opponents who are starting from square one with a new manager, a new backroom team and maybe new players.

I think that's a huge thing and should never be underestimated.

The constant change hampered Tipp at times. When a manager comes in first time round the players and managerial set up have to get to know each other very quickly, if they are to be competitive. If a manager is in place for a few years then it's easier for everyone involved as a lot of bridges are crossed already.

Often a player doesn't know where he stands at the beginning of the year but they usually find out fairly soon if they're in the plans or not!

I'm very grateful for the years I got out of it and don't have any regrets. We lost games but that's not a regret because we tried to do all we could in 2009 and '11 and as well in '14. I was very lucky to play for 15 years with Tipperary.

I was delighted with everything I got out of it and the games I played in. When you go into that system you know it's not long lived. You know you're going to leave someday or be asked to stay home someday without any reason.

We went into the set-up knowing the people that came before us were either dropped or told to stay at home, often full of disappointments. We all know that lads were hard done by or never got called in for a trial, and that's the nature of sport.

I enjoy being a supporter now and going to the matches. When I started out with Tipp, I was a single man and serving my time to be an electrician but it's different now; I'm married with a family and have four lovely girls so different priorities take over in life at different times.

I think that if you stand still on the Tipperary hurling team and it is everything you are, then there could be huge disappointments when it's over. It was always one part of my life along with other parts, like family and career among other things.

I think it's important that when it finishes, players can fall back into society in a right kind of way, and without a crash landing.

The big thing for me is that I'm still going up to my club, Thurles Sarsfields for training. I absolutely love going up there training with the intermediate or senior team. I know it was difficult on players and supporters not having sport during the coronavirus lockdown because sport is good for your heart and your mind.

I'm hitting 40 years of age now but I absolutely love running around the field with lads half my age and I test myself against them for an hour at training in the outside field in Thurles. That is great for my mentality, and I hope to be going up training at 50 years of age!

Do what you love in life if you can.

I'm going to play the game as long as I can. A lot of lads give up playing because they slow down a bit or are wondering what others think and then they regret not being able to play longer.

The only thing is not to expect the same out of yourself that you expected when you were 20 years-old. The performance and the fitness won't be the same as when you were 20 but at least you're still in the game.

If a manager doesn't start me in a match, I don't think about it too much, just come back the next day and train away. It's a great way to be. Often with working careers or jobs you start off at 20 years of age and work your way to the top, but the GAA is totally different.

You start off at the very top at 20 years of age and then are lucky if you make it to 30, but then it's a downward curve. You have to accept there are other players coming that will take your spot.

That has to be accepted because if it isn't, you retire and put on a few pounds and need to find a new hobby. I chose to stay pucking the ball in the outside field, to stop thinking about making the team for the weekend and I accept it for what it is.

Stay in the game for as long as you can because the game never ends.

99

JAMES BARRY

TIPPERARY 1-28, KILKENNY 3-22
All-Ireland SHC Final
Croke Park
SEPTEMBER 7, 2014

James Barry was always a man on a mission with Tipperary

★ **TIPPERARY:** D. Gleeson; C. Barrett, Pádraic Maher, P. Stapleton (0-1); B. Maher, **J. Barry**, K. Bergin; S. McGrath (0-2), J. Woodlock (0-1); G. Ryan (0-1), Patrick Maher (1-1), J. O'Dwyer 0-7 ; N. McGrath (0-4), S. Callanan (0-7), L. Corbett (0-2). Subs: M. Cahill (0-1) for Ryan; E. Kelly for Woodlock; J. Forde (0-1) for Shane McGrath; J. O'Brien for Callanan.

★ **KILKENNY:** E. Murphy; P. Murphy, JJ Delaney, J. Tyrrell; J. Holden, B. Hogan (0-1), C. Buckley; R. Hogan (0-6), C. Fogarty (0-1); M. Fennelly (0-1), C. Fennelly (0-1), TJ Reid (1-8); W. Walsh (0-1), R. Power (2-1), E. Larkin (0-2). Subs: A Fogarty for Walsh, P. Walsh for Holden, H. Shefflin for Fennelly, J. Power for R. Hogan.

THE ACTION

THIS WAS SENSATIONAL stuff from the throw in right until 'Hawk-Eye' signalled 'MISS' after John 'Bubbles' O'Dwyer's injury-time free from 97 metres to win the game tailed wide. All 82,179 spectators were glued to the action from the start and didn't take their eyes off the action until the decision was called on the late free. Some couldn't watch then. Millimetres decided the outcome. Amazingly, for the third year running, the All-Ireland finished in a draw

Having met yearly since 2009 in championship and league encounters both sides stormed into action with a ferocious intensity and true grit. Approaching the quarter mark the teams were tied on 0-6 apiece before Tipp pulled away. Seamus Callanan led the scoring before Patrick 'Bonnar' Maher caught a Darren Gleeson puck-out and headed for goal before managing to push the ball beyond Eoin Murphy.

Tipp were controlling the tempo with James Barry doing well on dangerman, TJ Reid while Cathal Barret also shone in defence. At the other end Callanan, who hit five from play marking JJ Delaney, missed a penalty. However Lar Corbett soon extended Tipp's lead to six points.

With Tipp surging ahead, Kilkenny fought back with Richie Power finding room to connect with the ball for a Kilkenny goal which started their revival. By the break everyone marvelled at the spectacle of poetry in motion and wondered how nerves could survive another half of fast and frantic hurling. It restarted at lightning speed. Kilkenny hit first with Reid cracking in a goal after good close control. Tipp responded. Corbett raced through and sent a bullet goal-bound but it just clipped the post and spun away on 41 minutes.

Eight minutes later Kilkenny attacked with speed as Fennelly off-loaded to Power, who raised another green flag to make it 3-16 to 1-18. Down the other end, Corbett was fouled but Tipp again missed the resultant penalty. 3-21 to 1-24 now as James Barry and Paddy Stapleton cleared ball at one end, with JJ Delaney and Paul Murphy sending it back as quickly.

To add to the drama, Shefflin arrived on the scene, but Bubbles levelled it on 68 minutes to a massive cheer. With time up, Brian Hogan fouled in possession of the ball and Bubbles stepped up to be the hero. A free from his own half to win it. As the fans cheered, it curled above the post. Barry Kelly consulted the modern technology, and Hawk-Eye signalled 'MISS'.

An unbelievable finish.

★★★★★

66

GROWING UP IN Drombane, hurling meant everything to me and above all, I always wanted to hurl in an All-Ireland final. I can clearly remember my father, Seamus who hurled with Tipp in the 1970s, training Sean Treacys and my first few days in a hurling field as a child were with the Treacys who wore blue and gold.

When I started playing the game my father rarely missed one of my training sessions, never mind a match! Be it with Tipp or in the black and amber of Upperchurch-Drombane or schools with Thurles CBS or Fitzgibbon cup with UCC.

He was there all the way through and thankfully all the training and games led to Croke Park. It was a dream come true when I finally got to play for Tipp on the first Sunday in September.

2014 was my first full year in the Tipp jersey and to play against Kilkenny was real 'Clash of the Titans' stuff. There were hurling legends like JJ Delaney, Tommy Walsh and Henry Shefflin still playing for them while we still had the likes of Lar Corbett, John O'Brien and Eoin Kelly.

Both teams knew each other inside out after meeting in the championship yearly since 2009, and on the sideline it was Eamon O'Shea against Brian Cody again.

Nothing really prepared me for that day, though.

It was manic.

With the noise, I couldn't hear Darren in the goals behind me. I couldn't hear Paidi 10 yards in front either. Over the years I became used to it and realised that's the atmosphere of Croke Park on All-Ireland final day.

You can't communicate by talking and no matter what training you do, nothing prepares you for it. But in 2014 I knew I was ready for it.

I'd never experienced the Artane Band before a final, and when I marched behind them I was thinking… *God, this is actually real.* All the weeks before the build-up were huge, especially in Tipp when it's against Kilkenny, but marching that day was the first time it really hit me.

I was looking around, thinking… *There's 82,000 people here… and it's real.*

With the emotion that runs through you during that parade, if you're not ready then, you'll never be. Obviously I tried to focus on the game but looking back, I can remember it clearly and those are special moments just marching behind the band.

All this, in my first full year with Tipp.

I was called in for the league final in 2013 against Kilkenny but then Tipp were beaten in the two championship games straight away so I didn't actually get any game until 2014. The first championship game in '14 against Limerick I was taken off with five minutes to go, and then against Galway in the qualifiers I was put in full-back in an accidental role as Jonathan Glynn was going to town; and I went back to do a job on him and keep the ball away from him. Eamon O'Shea didn't want to show his cards and moved me away from full-back for the Offaly game. My first game starting full-back was against Dublin in the quarter-final and then we beat Cork off the field in the semi-final.

We got through the year without having being tested in the full-back line.

We knew going into the final that the line was going to be targeted.

It was myself and Cathal Barrett's first year starting with Tipp, and Paddy Stapleton was in the other corner. We knew going into the game that we were going to be peppered with high ball.

Barrett was obviously small in the corner so Wally Walsh went in on him, and I was to mark TJ Reid. I didn't read much in the build-up but from talk we knew it would be an onslaught and that once the game started, ball after ball from the half-back line would rain in on top of us.

When it started, TJ didn't come in at all, so I went out.

Against Cork I was on Cadogan and he stayed in midfield so I went out and gave him a shot of a shoulder to settle down. He swung back the hurley, so I knew I had him unhinged and so I tried the same thing with Reid.

I went 40 or 50 yards and hit him a shot of a shoulder, and TJ just put out the hand to shake hands!

I realised immediately this was a different kettle of fish!

He was probably well used to this from Jackie Tyrell or Tommy Walsh at training, and had played in previous All-Ireland finals and while it didn't rock me, it had me thinking about it.

I was told, 'Stay on him all day… wherever he goes just follow'.

He had a habit of roving; if you got on top of him when he was full-forward he would go on the wing. Cathal Barrett marked Wally Walsh, but Paidi had licence to just hold the centre. That was the plan that day.

I didn't get a strike on the ball for a while, but I got a couple of collisions and blocks and tackles. There were only three wides in the entire game.

When I went into full-back, a lot of the ball was in the air and dropping, and everyone went for it. It was the last year of that style of play that started with Tipp and Kilkenny in 2009. It was a 'hit it and win it' kind of a game which wasn't the type of game we wanted to play but one we *had* to play.

When the ball came in, all big tackling forwards like TJ, Eoin Larkin, Walsh and Shefflin were there so we were under pressure, and had to lump it long to our forwards rather than placing the ball. A lot of the time you hit it in a second so they weren't on top of you hunting for a score, and it was the same the other end.

So it was relentless.

I watched it recently again and it was unbelievable to watch, probably one of the best finals in recent memory. Everyone on the field seemed to play well, the standard was so high. I felt I played well but so did TJ, then the other end of the field Seamie Callanan played well but so did JJ Delaney.

We should have pulled away after the start of the second-half. Lar hit the post and then two minutes later he came through and passed to Seamie, but Eoin Murphy came out and blocked him.

Bonnar and Noel missed chances, and we missed two penalties yet every chance they got down the other side, they punished us and then pushed ahead near the end. They brought Shefflin off the subs bench late on and I thought… *God, I can't be marking him when he wins his 10th medal and I'm still trying to win my first!*

It aggravated Tipp from a players' point of view; they were bringing him on to win his 10th. The ending of the game was more drama with 'Bubbles' taking the late free to win it. I was beside Darren Gleeson in the goals and didn't think it was over, and then with the wait for 'Hawkeye' everything stopped.

Bubbles had scored two frees from the backline in the first-half so the one person you'd fancy to put it over would have been him.

I wasn't sure after if that was the way every All-Ireland final was but talking to my father and others, the consensus was it was one of the best finals people ever saw. The ref, Barry Kelly let it flow and it was great as both teams wanted to play hurling.

Some games would be like that but the scoring percentages wouldn't be as high as they were that day. But it was a strange feeling after. Being a draw, it hadn't really ended.

Work was booked off but we had to get the suits and go to The Burlington, meet family and friends and we had a few pints, but it felt unfinished as we had to play again three weeks after.

There were mind-games coming up to the replay.

Talk was about how the teams would line up, who would adapt quicker?

Kilkenny changed styles the second day.

We didn't click and regretted not winning the first day even more. It was hard to take losing the replay but looking back, losing the semi-finals to Galway in 2015 and '17 were probably worse. Overall, I was extremely lucky though to play in the All-Ireland finals of '14, '16 and '19, and all against Kilkenny.

As games go, that 2014 draw stands out but there have been some great times hurling along the way. I remember watching my clubmates, David Carey and Pat Shortt playing schools hurling when I was young.

I wanted to emulate them.

I played Harty Cup with Thurles from junior cert year onward and started in the full-forward line with Timmy Hammersley and Pa Bourke. My dad was at all the training sessions in the Railway field or the Sarsfields field, and came in as an unofficial selector or consultant!

We finally won the Harty in 2009 after a gap of 53 years.

I recall the St Patrick's Day parade in Thurles and Jimmy Doyle, who played in 1956 which was the last time Thurles had won it, said a few words. And I said a few words as the 2009 captain too.

People always speak about St Kieran's as the nursery for hurling in Kilkenny and this century Thurles has been the equivalent for Tipp. When we won the All-Ireland in 2016 all the Tipp starting backs had gone to school in Thurles... Cathal Barrett, Paidi, Ronan, Mickey Cahill, Seamus Kennedy and myself all went there.

It was amazing to finally win the All-Ireland final in 2016. Immediately after the game I thought the top memory was holding the cup on the steps of the Hogan stand.

The best of all was walking the cup up through Upperchurch village behind a piper to a stage by the church on the Saturday after the game.

The cup doesn't generally go back straight away to a player's club but we had Mick Ryan there as manager and Michael Bourke as county chairperson at the time. It was incredible. That's one of the standout memories of my hurling career, to have that chance to walk from your primary school up through the village to the church, with people who supported you since you were five years of age. It was a special night.

The sport has been great to me, the friendships I've made with Tipp lads over the years have been the cornerstone. Meeting up five or six nights a week is what I miss most now that I have stepped aside.

It takes time to adjust.

I have great memories of Harty Cup days and my college years with UCC where we won two Fitzgibbon Cups and I'd still be a phone call away from lads I hurled with then, like Conor Lehane and Seamus Harnedy. The college years were very important for me as I didn't make the Tipp seniors straight from under-21. I always want to be a part of the GAA be it as a coach or in some other capacity.

It was good to add another All-Ireland in 2019 which helped cement this generation in the record books. It's something we spoke of; we wanted to be seen as a generation of great players, to stop people talking of the 1960s as the last golden generation of Tipperary hurlers.

In time, people are going to look back at 2010 to 2019 as a successful era for Tipperary hurling, and that final in 2014 will long be remembered as part of a golden era for hurling.

PADRAIC MAHER
(& SEAMUS CALLANAN)

TIPPERARY 2-29, KILKENNY 2-20
2016 All-Ireland SHC Final
Croke Park
SEPTEMBER 4, 2016

Padraic Maher was unbreakable against The Cats in 2016

★ **TIPPERARY:** D. Gleeson; C. Barrett, J. Barry, M. Cahill; S. Kennedy (0-1), R Maher, **P. Maher (0-1)**; B. Maher, M. Breen; D. McCormack (0-1), Patrick Maher (0-2), N. McGrath (0-1); J. McGrath (1-3), **S. Callanan (0-13)**, J. O'Dwyer (1-5). Subs: J. Forde (0-2) for Breen, N. O'Meara for McCormack, D. Maher for Cahill, K. Bergin for N. McGrath, T. Hamill for Kennedy.

★ **KILKENNY:** E. Murphy; S. Prendergast, J. Holden, P. Murphy; P. Walsh (0-2), K. Joyce, C. Buckley (0-1); TJ Reid (0-11), C. Fogarty; W. Walsh (0-1), R. Hogan (1-1), E. Larkin (0-2); K. Kelly (1-2), C. Fennelly, L. Blanchfield. Subs: R. Lennon for Joyce, L. Ryan for Larkin.

THE ACTION

A SUPERB SECOND-HALF performance from Tipperary steamrolled old rivals Kilkenny to claim the county's 27th senior hurling title, the first since 2010.

Premier talisman, Seamus Callanan put in a Man of the match performance and finished up with 13 points as Tipperary dominated the second-half and added the All-Ireland crown to the Munster title won earlier in the summer.

In the 20 previous finals between the old rivals, Tipp held a 10-8 advantage over Kilkenny, with the 2014 game between them ending in a draw. Tipp had lost seven of their previous nine championship encounters but in his first year managing his county, Michael Ryan reversed the trend.

Afterwards, Kilkenny manager, Brian Cody admitted his side were outplayed by the Premier County in every facet of play. 'It was comprehensive. We went in at half-time two points down, well in the game, and got a good start to the second-half and got the goal... they didn't blink, they came back at us and they got some terrific scores.'

Leaders shone for the champions all over the field with Callanan proving a constant thorn in the Kilkenny defence. He was ably assisted by Noel McGrath, John 'Bubbles' O'Dwyer and John McGrath. There were big displays too from Padraic Maher, who was outstanding in defence, as he had been all year.

Right from the off Callanan shone for Tipp. He led his marker, Joey Holden around Croke Park, scoring five first-half points, as Tipp led on a 0-14 to 0-12 scoreline at the interval.

The Cat's struck for a green flag as Kevin Kelly goaled for Kilkenny putting them 1-14 to 0-15 ahead seven minutes after the break. Rather than energise Kilkenny, the score just pushed Tipperary into top gear.

'Bubbles' released a rocket low to Eoin Murphy's right, as Callanan and Padraic Maher followed up with top quality points.

With Padraic and Ronan Maher dominant in defence and the trio of Bubbles, John McGrath and in particular Callanan scoring freely, there was only going to be one winner

'There's nothing revolutionary about forwards working hard... every team in the country sets out to do it, but we seemed to really get it right,' a delighted Michael Ryan said afterwards.

His side's second goal came with nine minutes left as Noel McGrath assisted his brother, John to seal Kilkenny's fate.

★★★★★

66

2016 WAS THE perfect year and the All-Ireland final was the perfect ending.

We steamrolled through Munster and then to meet Kilkenny and beat them capped a wonderful year. At that stage, we had been close for a number of years but we hadn't won an All-Ireland since 2010 and you'd be half wondering if we would ever win one again!

It was a sweet feeling.

Every All-Ireland I played in was against Kilkenny.

They have been part of the story. At the start of my career, they had the upper-hand on us but we have evened it out a bit more lately. For the players of my generation, our careers are defined by the games against Kilkenny.

We played them in 2009, '10, '11, '12, '13, '14 and we knew it was time to turn the tables. In 2014 we should have won the first day but Kilkenny were better than us in the replay. In 2015 we were beaten by a point by Galway in the semi-final, so to win the semi-final in 2016 by a point made it sweeter getting back to the final.

The Sunday before the game we had our last hard training session and played an internal game. That set the tone for the week ahead.

I was training in the Garda College at the time so my week was pretty busy from Monday to Friday. It was the normal 9am to 5pm at the time, so it kept my mind occupied on the week of the game. In the college in Templemore you are kind of locked away from the outside world.

Everything that was being said or written was happening elsewhere.

I kept away from it for the week and kept to my match routine. I called to our masseuse, Mick Clohessy to get my body right.

We trained Tuesday and Friday. The Friday night session is great as the crowd came to watch us, creating a buzz around it all. I remember leaving the field. The reception from the crowd was massive. Walking into the dressing-room afterwards gave me a great feeling.

It was a huge lift and I knew we were right for Sunday.

The day before I relaxed at home. Fuelled up on food. I had a good routine and stuck to it. Talk about other stuff. Rest. Prepare. It was all about being ready for the battle against Kilkenny.

Match day arrived and Mickey Cahill, my brother, Ronan and I drove to Portlaoise to meet the team bus that morning. We went to the Gibson Hotel before the game and had the whole top floor to ourselves.

At that stage we had an early dinner and spared the energy for the storm ahead. I walked around a bit. Other lads were resting up.

Some had music blaring.

There were massive bean bags on our floor in the hotel and some lads chilled out there. For an outsider walking into that room, they wouldn't have believed that we were going to face Kilkenny! Five minutes before we were due to leave the hotel, Mick Ryan brought us into a huddle and did what Mick does best.

He gave us a passionate talk, not building us up too much until it was time, but he spoke about all we had done to prepare and what the coming game and the coming hours meant to the people of Tipperary. It set the tone.

The bus journey to Croker is great. You can see the crowd out the window, the colour of the supporters, the buzz is building and then you see Croke Park in the distance. I will never tire of that. That gets me.

I fully tune in then. Some lads always like to get a feel for the ground and the conditions but I stay in the dressing-room until it's time to go out and hurl. That day the minors were in the final so a lot went out to see that game but there are televisions in the dressing-rooms so I sat back in the room by myself and watched it from there.

At the same time I was checking boots and tape.

Taking in the surroundings. The minors won and there was a good feeling before we ran out onto the field. Once we were on the field my focus in the warm-up was on getting the ball into my hand. During the parade, as always, I gather my thoughts.

If a helicopter landed beside me at that moment I wouldn't have paid any attention!

The game started in what felt like two seconds later.

It was hectic. And it flew by. The Kilkenny lads always keep you on your toes. They moved and switched as they often did, so you're looking at where the player you're marking is moving to.

TJ Reid and Richie Hogan switched around midfield and the half-forward line. Both could drift to their half-back line too. I was marking Walter Walsh so he was enough to keep me on my toes!

Seamie Callanan was on fire for us. He was causing them a lot of damage, firing over points whenever the ball came near. They had no answer to him. Keeping him supplied with ball was the key. Like all the other battles with Kilkenny there was no room but you have to fight for every ball.

Then you have to fight for room to clear it!

The second-half was ferocious. Kilkenny always just stay in the game waiting for half a chance. Players on both sides were mentally and physically tired. It was shot-for-shot until Bubbles scored a goal to lift the rafters. That lifted us up on a wave.

Games are often decided on big moments and that brought us dominance. It gave me a lift. I could sense the energy in our team and we drove it on from there. In the last five or 10 minutes we pulled away but we had so much heartbreak over the previous few years we never took the foot off the pedal.

We hurled as if we were chasing the game. Mick had driven into us the importance of tackling as well as hooking and blocking. Jason Forde came on and did well, and Seamie kept going with point after point.

When the final whistle went it was the sweetest moment. All the hurt and pain of other games just went away.

When you start the year as a county hurler your life is pretty much based around the next game, until you get to that moment.

What you eat.

When you sleep.

Where you go. It sinks in that you got there. Getting the cup is magnificent but I remember walking around the field feeling relieved. The supporters, family and friends were there to share it. It was so frantic after 2010 that it was good to have that moment in '16 to take it in and really experience the moment.

When we were back in the dressing-room we all had that feeling of achievement. We sang songs. The county secretary, Timmy Floyd led the chorus. It's pure satisfaction.

It was my brother, Ronan's first one. He played out of his skin. In the previous All-Ireland I won in 2010 he was only a young chap looking on and he had seen the heartbreak of other years. Being a sub in 2014 he worked his way onto the team.

By 2016 he was established. Afterwards, in the dressing-room he got sick. Our kitman, 'Hotpoint' Hayes, along with the doctor, had to put him into the back of the van and take him back to the hotel. With the heat and his energy used up he got a 24-hour migraine and it hit him hard.

His celebrations were cut short but he made up for it the following day alright!

You feel close to the history of the achievement on All-Ireland day. It's close to home. Both my parents and their extended families are both steeped in hurling.

John Maher of Killinan in Thurles was my father's uncle. He captained Tipp to an All-Ireland in 1945. There is a privilege in winning in that a lot of great hurlers never won medals. Great Tipperary teams in the 1970s and 80s went by without getting the opportunity to play in a final, never mind winning one.

So it's a privilege to play at a time when Tipp are strong.

A lot of people contributed to me getting to wear the jersey on All-Ireland final day. Hurling really mattered to me in school at Scoil Ailbe and Thurles CBS. Growing up, the highlight every week was going to Durlas Og every Saturday morning at ten o'clock for hurling training.

As I got older, Sarsfields grounds felt like home.

I know every inch of the place. Always hurling, there was no other sport. I can remember asking my father if I could go to a local soccer club in Thurles, Peake Villa to play and it was a firm 'No!' The way he looked at it was that it's okay if you want to play soccer and rugby and other sports as a young fella, but if you want to make it at hurling you just have to specialise in hurling. It was an easy decision from there!

The bar goes higher in hurling every year.

The standard across the country is incredibly high.

It was new territory when the lockdown for the coronavirus came and disrupted the 2020 championship but you deal with it as best you can.

Like everything, we take it one step at a time. Working as a community guard in Limerick is something I enjoy so my life experience is broader now than it was a few years ago. I was probably more in a bubble as an inter-county hurler a few years back but I relish the challenge as every year goes by.

I adapt as best I can because I want to win more medals with Tipperary.

To taste that victory in 2016 was class. That day went some way to healing some of the heartbreak we had suffered in the previous years.

We turned the tables on Kilkenny.

99

SEAMUS CALLANAN

Seamus Callanan savours victory after winning the All-Ireland title in 2016

❝

I JUST HAD one of those days in the 2016 All-Ireland final where everything worked out and thankfully we went on to win the game. It's one that will live long in my memory.

Of course, in 2019 as well it was wonderful to represent my club Drom Inch well by bringing the Liam MacCarthy cup to The Ragg as Tipperary captain, but from a personal point of view the game I had in 2016 was very special and I will probably never have a game like that again.

That day the ball bounced just right. It all seemed to click on the day with perfect ball coming to me. I had a great supply line of quality ball coming in. The lads out the field knew the runs I was going to make and supplied us in the full-forward line with the type of ball we wanted, and that only comes after years of hurling together.

The experience of big occasions really stands to you on a day like that.

There's always nerves before a game of that magnitude but to get your first point sets you off really. It's about staying in the process and hitting one ball, and then the next ball. Staying tuned into what's going on around you and right in front of you.

Every ball is different.

Some are coming at you fast, others are high, and it's about trusting yourself to make the right decision with the ball. It's one ball at a time.

While I got the scores, I missed an early free from about 25 yards when I hit it low and it was blocked down so it is really one moment at a time. Next ball.

Confidence and belief both play a big role in success.

It's funny. Some days the ball runs for you and other days I could go out and make those runs all day long and the ball might not come into my path or it might not bounce right. It's always hard to identify what it is. Sometimes I try and retrace previous steps in games and use it as preparation for the ball coming in, but it doesn't always work out like that.

You need a bit of luck to run with you.

Sometimes, if it's not going well, stuff can go through your head and it's important to stay positive and focus on the next ball. It's the same off the field. Being positive is very important. It's play by play.

I didn't realise what I had scored until someone told me after the match. The most memorable point I got was the last one from play.

It was a cross-field ball that Paidi Maher hit to the Hogan Stand side and I controlled it, came in on my left towards the middle and scored.

I knew at that stage the game was ours.

That was the icing on the cake for me on what had been a great day for Tipperary hurling. The difference that day in 2016 compared to before was that we had a maturity about us and the younger fellas that had come in, like Ronan Maher and Dan McCormack, all had a good head on their shoulders. We were confident but, of course, against Kilkenny we had to be alert because we knew what they could do if we weren't at full power at any stage.

We came across some unbelievable teams over the years and we were probably unlucky not to come away with another All-Ireland or two, but Kilkenny were a strong force all the time. It was a great decade for both counties really so for us to get three All-Irelands out of the decade has been a fair return.

There's never been much between the counties and that rivalry is as strong as ever now and will be for years to come.

The All-Ireland final day is massive for everyone who loves hurling.

I see how much it means to people. Hurling has that effect. I grew up opposite the school and beside the hurling field in The Ragg so it was on my doorstep.

Paudie Butler was the principal in our primary school so we had hurling at lunchtime! He coached us as juveniles and laid the foundations. A few of us around the same age would go to the field every day after school then. Hurling became a cornerstone.

We had lost a few county finals before we won the final in 2011. That was brilliant, because winning with the club is special.

Each win is unique.

The night I brought the cup back in 2019 and brought it to The Ragg as captain meant a lot to me and to our small community. The supporters were in the field, where I trained for years alone and with others. The wins are as much for the communities around the county and the supporters around the world as they are for the players.

The players now will be supporters looking in someday.

I never forget the privilege it is to play with Tipp and my time playing senior has been brilliant since I started in 2008. The preparation we do has changed a lot since then.

Now I stay fit over the winter and while I took a break when club action finished in 2019, I stayed in shape because a decent basic level of fitness is essential all year round. I have a programme to follow and now that I'm in my thirties I vary the training so I'd do a lot of bike work and things like that in winter.

I take every game as it comes.

I want to make the most of my time playing with Tipperary and it's always about the next ball and the next game. The ball doesn't always run for you as you'd like but it's important to trust your own decision making and maximising the ball that does come your way.

Contributing as best I can. That's important for me. If I score, then great. If I don't, then all that really matters is that Tipperary win.

Getting my work rate up was my goal in 2019. Hooks, blocks and tackles. If the forwards do that it puts the opposition backs under pressure. The goals flowed in 2019 but I worked hard in other years as well without getting the goals, so when we win and I make a worthwhile contribution, that's the main thing. It doesn't bother me who gets the goals or points once we win.

With experience, I found that if a game is getting away from me and I can't get to the pitch of it I need to focus. Maybe that's on a hook.

Or a block down.

Move the ball to a teammate.

Contribute. When I do that it can change how I see the game and that can get me into the game. I only judge myself on what I can contribute to the team.

It's great when it flows well but I'm playing long enough to know that it doesn't always flow or the spin on the ball takes the bounce a different direction so when it does come right in a big game it's brilliant. The final against Kilkenny in 2016 was one of the days the ball stuck to my hand like a magnet and I was in the game all the way through.

My game changed a lot across the years.

Just as Tipp can have highs and lows, a player's career is probably the same.

I had a dip for a year or two, but from 2014 on my game improved. Eamon O'Shea had an influence on me and developed my game. I grew in confidence and belief. By the time 2016 came around Mick Ryan was manager and the confidence was flowing through the team so we were playing well all year.

And when the All-Ireland final came around, we were at our peak and were after coming through a close semi-final with Galway. To put up the scoreline we did against Kilkenny and to be able to contribute to it was the standout highlight. We didn't dip much the following year and worked just as hard without the results at the end of the day.

It took Joe Canning scoring that late winner to put us away in the semi-final, so you need a little luck on your side. Galway beat us by a point and went on to win a close final after that. Again, we gave everything in 2018 but we had the league final, club games and a lot of championship games in quick succession.

That was tough as we were gone in early June.

I had returned after an ongoing back injury and it was hard believing the games were finished for the year because we were used to playing until much later in the summer. Liam Sheedy came back then in 2019 and, thankfully, we got it right but it is small margins all the time and you have to stay going and maximising your potential.

It was a seamless transition from Eamon to Mick, and then to Liam really, because they have all been hugely influential and made massive contributions to hurling in the county. They were there when I started playing senior as a teenager and are still having a big influence now.

Who knows what the 2020s will bring but the effort will be there from us to win every match. I want to keep going and see what else we can achieve, so a lot of reflecting will be left until I've finished playing but, for now, the goal remains the same and that's to do the best I can and give everything for the jersey.

NOEL MCGRATH

TIPPERARY 1-28, WEXFORD 3-20
All-Ireland SHC Semi-Final
Croke Park
JULY 28, 2019

Noel McGrath and manager, Liam Sheedy congratulate one another in 2019

★ **TIPPERARY:** B. Hogan; C. Barrett, S. Kennedy, B. Heffernan; B. Maher, Padraic Maher, R. Maher (0-2); **N. McGrath (0-4)**, M. Breen (0-1); D. McCormack, J. O'Dwyer (0-3), N. O'Meara; J. Forde (0-12), S. Callanan (1-2), J. McGrath. **Subs:** W. Connors (0-1) for McCormack; G. Browne (0-1) for Breen; M. Kehoe (0-1) for O'Meara; J. Morris (0-1) for O'Dwyer

★ **WEXFORD:** M. Fanning; D. Reck, L. Ryan (0-1), S. Donohoe; P. Foley (0-1), M. O'Hanlon, S. Murphy; K. Foley (0-1), D. O'Keeffe (0-2); L. Óg McGovern (0-1), C. McDonald (2-2), J. O'Connor (0-1); P. Morris (0-2), L. Chin (1-6) R. O'Connor (0-3). Subs: A. Nolan for Murphy; J. O'Connor for Reck; D. Dunne for J. O'Connor; C. Dunbar for O'Connor.

THE ACTION

THIS WAS A hurling cliff-hanger straight out of Hollywood. As classics go, a blockbuster.

With 10 minutes to play, Wexford were leading by three points, playing with an extra player and looked destined to reach their first All-Ireland final since 1996 but the character of this Tipperary team shone through.

Liam Sheedy's side will now face Kilkenny – for the sixth time in 11 years – after a dramatic comeback filled with controversy and brilliance. Hurling with 14 players after John McGrath got a second yellow card, Tipp dug deep. Most teams would be down and out but, despite three disallowed goals, Tipp roared defiantly, hitting seven of the last nine points. Four of the substitutes were on target to seal a memorable victory in front of 61,852, many of whom were hoarse from shouting by the end.

The heat of the day and the colour of the supporters brought a sense that these counties could produce a classic. Some recalled the 1968 All-Ireland or the titanic battles in 2001, and now a new generation got to experience the magic of Tipp against Wexford. From the start, Wexford's deep runners and quick offloads caused havoc in a bewildered Tipp defence. Referee Sean Cleere ruled out the first of three Tipp goals as Michael Breen kicked the ball to the net but the goal was harshly disallowed because of Jason Forde's collision with Matthew O'Hanlon in the build-up.

In the 10th minute, Tipp attacked again but Niall O'Meara overplayed his hand-pass to Seamus Callanan. The 'Goal King' swung on the hopping ball 14 metres to the right of the goal and sent it across Mark Fanning for the captain's seventh in seven games and his 34th overall in championship hurling.

Tipp drove on when Noel McGrath sent over the first of his fantastic long-range points but on 25 minutes Conor McDonald swivelled and rifled to the net. Then, approaching half-time, came a moment of bizarre drama. A Lee Chin free dropped by the crossbar before Brian Hogan caught it and pucked long, where Tipp won a free. Taken quickly, it sailed towards Bubbles, who deftly flicked it to John McGrath who batted to the net. As Tipp celebrated, the referee got the HawkEye nod that Lee Chin's shot had in fact gone over the bar when Hogan caught it, so Wexford got the point and the goal didn't count.

Davy Fitzgerald's model army were 1-14 to 1-12 up by half-time but with Noel McGrath in sensational form, Tipp prospered but then came a blow. John McGrath, who had been booked along with Damien Reck earlier, received a second yellow for a hurley flick. The Leinster winners hit 1-3 before Tipp dug deep and, with Noel McGrath putting in a Man of the Match performance, stayed the distance in the sapping closeness.

★★★★★

66

IT SENDS A shiver up my spine just thinking about the game.

It was a game for the ages. One of those days that are just on a knife-edge. The heat of the hot sun added to one of those true championship days that people will remember for years to come.

To have a part to play on a day like that means a lot. It's why I train year in-year out – be it in winter or summer. To come out of it on the right side is the extra bonus that makes it stand out in my mind, above all other games. That Wexford game will live with me for the rest of my sporting career and after that as well.

They had won an unbelievable Leinster championship and were coming in confident and as champions. They came at us hard but from our point of view we were prepared for the intensity. We had done well in the Munster championship and, while the Munster final didn't go as planned, we were still in a good place.

Prepared.

I always just follow the same routine, for all games. After that I can't really control anything else that happens. I'm not superstitious so I just go with the flow on match days. Whatever happens on the day is what happens.

Momentum is unbelievably important. Once we got that bit of road, we kept pegging back Wexford. Step by step, we got back level.

Conor McDonald got a goal which might have broken a lot of team's momentum but we kept going and going, first getting a point and then another score. We had put a lot of work into our fitness for 2019 and that stood to us.

I started at centre-forward for the first 20 or so minutes but hadn't been getting on much ball. The game was over and back, but I hadn't been involved a lot I felt before Tommy Dunne came in and told me to move to midfield.

Then I started to get on more ball.

Bubbles gave me a pass for a point. Barry Heffernan likewise and things started to move for me when I was in the middle of things. Everywhere I moved, the ball was there for me. It just fell the way I wanted it in the second-half.

I got two great passes for two points, one from Ronan Maher, who delivered a direct ball from our full-back line straight to my hand, then Seamus Kennedy gave me another nice one straight to my hand again. My job was to deliver ball to the forwards as best I could.

The last 20 minutes showed what we had in reserve.

We had to really dig and we found a new gear.

It showed what character we had within our group of players. On the pitch during a game you don't get to think about all the things that happen. So much was going on. The speed of the game stood out.

Hawkeye.

Disallowed goals.

A red card. There was a lot made afterwards of my brother, John being sent off and people said that we had been playing poorly up until then, but when he was sent off the scores were near level; it was close all through.

It wasn't as if we were lagging a lot behind at that time.

John wasn't the first and won't be the last sent off in a big game. That happens and has to be dealt with on the day, and it's just the consequence if you pick up yellow cards. We've all been in that situation and what it's like, so it was good for John, and for the group, that he got to make amends in the All-Ireland final.

Right after the Wexford game I didn't realise fully that we were denied three goals that seemed fairly legitimate because on the pitch you just have to get on with the job at hand.

With Wexford five points up in the second-half they could have gone to seven, eight or more ahead because it can happen so fast.

It could easily have got away from us.

It would have been easy for us to give in or give up but our character shone through. I think how we played showed the character of the group of players involved and it took us to a new place. It kept our season alive.

As a team, we had put a lot of work into 2019 overall so to get the reward was massive because it is fine margins in a game like that. Thinking back now there's a feeling of satisfaction from performing on the day and showing such character. I can still remember that winning feeling at the final whistle.

I think the Tipperary people that were supporting us were connected to the team that day. Those in Croke Park or listening on the radio around the world or watching on telly felt a sense of pride about how we performed. I got that sense from a lot of Tipp supporters afterwards.

We fed off the supporters responding to what they saw on the field. That connection with the supporters really matters to our team.

We all realised how much it meant, that despite all the obstacles that day we succeeded. Lads were on a high in the dressing-room. In fairness to the group it was actually the sixth All-Ireland semi-final that a lot of us had won, so we had the experience of knowing that while we had a great job done, we couldn't get carried away and think the job is done after a semi-final.

We had a few pints together afterwards to unwind.

Once you wake up on the Monday morning it's back on the throttle again with three weeks to an All-Ireland final which is just like a dream!

That Wexford game was probably similar to one of those classics that I grew up watching on the telly from the mid-90s between Kilkenny and Offaly or those games between Cork and Waterford from the early 2000s.

That 'glued to it' type of game.

One of my earliest memories is of being on the pitch after the All-Ireland final between Wexford and Limerick in 1996. The excitement, colour and celebrations were something I never forgot.

I was hooked and just wanted to be playing on big days after that.

Tipp were in the minor final the same day. I went to nearly every Tipp match with my mother and father after that, rarely missing a game from 1997 on.

All my life I've been involved in the game and can remember being very young over in Castleiney and watching the club seniors train. There'd always be a number of us younger lads playing on the smaller field on our own.

I was lucky enough to remember seeing my father, Pat playing senior hurling for Loughmore. I've always loved it and had a huge support network since my parents supported John, Brian, Patricia and me at sports. All the bonds you make in life matter, be it with teammates or those that help along the way.

Stephen Maher and Eamon Sweeney in Loughmore played a huge part when I was young, as did the staff in Our Lady's school in Templemore where we had some great days playing hurling with lads from other clubs. It all broadens your learning about the game.

On a day like that was against Wexford you're playing for all of them in some way.

There's serious enthusiasm and motivation within the Tipperary hurling unit, including both the players and the backroom team. That fed onto the training pitch every night in Dr. Morris Park, and from training it fed into every game we played and it was there in Croke Park that day too.

Nothing is left to chance.

We prepare in every way to be the best we can. I'd have my hurleys right well in advance of a game. The hurley making thing is strange because everyone has their own ideas and like different styles. A lot of the lads, if they picked up my hurleys inside at training they'd just throw them down… just wouldn't like the shape of them!

My teammate, Ronan Maher makes them for me.

A few others on the team get Ronan to make theirs as well. When I started playing minor for Tipp in 2006 and '07 it was Paddy Purcell from Upperchurch that made them and I used that style until 2013. After that I got a few from Ivan Canning up in Portumna in Galway. For the last few years, I've been getting them from Ronan.

It was great 2019 ended on a high. I really appreciate the happiness it brings because there's always ups and downs in sport and in life, and you have to deal with them as best you can. When I had a serious illness a few years ago my number one aim was to get back healthy first of all and then to get back playing sport.

If that was to be with Loughmore Castleiney and Tipperary I didn't know at the time, but I did know I wanted to get back. Having positive people around me helped on the road to recovery.

To have won two All-Irelands since then is unreal.

I'm working full-time with Chanelle veterinary as a key account manager but I have been in schools at different stages sharing with young people my experience of when I overcame a difficult time in my life. It is just sharing my experience of how I dealt with serious illness. Everyone has obstacles they have to overcome and I just share my experience of how I coped with adversity and built mental strength.

I'm thankful for every minute.

I enjoy every minute of every game. Sometimes the training at the early part of the year is tough going but it's the same for everybody so you put in the work and hopefully get the rewards at the end of it.

That third All-Ireland win put a nicer look on the decade.

It was Tipp's most successful decade in a long time so to be part of all three is special. There were some unbelievable games but of all the games across my years, that Wexford match is a day I will never forget.

That is the kind of day you play for and put the hard work in for. It stands out now as the greatest of them all. Sometimes you get the reward for all the effort. That day we did.

99

MORE
GREAT
SPORTS BOOKS
FROM
HEROBOOKS

www.**HERO**BOOKS.digital

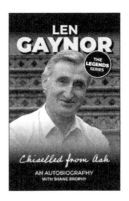

Chiselled from Ash
Len Gaynor: An Autobiography

CHISELLED FROM ASH is a story of love and honour.

It's the story of Len Gaynor's great love for the game of hurling, and how he has honoured the great game his whole life.

Len Gaynor won it all with Tipperary, finishing his career with three All-Ireland hurling titles, four Munster titles and two National League titles in the 1960s and 70s. But the flamboyant wing back also wanted to give back at the end of his career.

The Kilruane MacDonaghs clubman – and winner of three county titles - quickly proved himself to be one of the smartest and most ambitious coaches in the game.

At club level he strived to teach and help the next generation, and led his own Kilruane and neighbouring clubs to success – and at county level through the 1990s Len Gaynor managed Tipperary and Clare on the biggest stages in the game.

Chiselled from Ash is the story of one man's great love for a great game that has remained undimmed over seven decades.

Authors: Len Gaynor with Shane Brophy
Print Price: €20.00
Ebook: €10.00
ISBN: 9781910827208

Available on
Amazon
Apple Books
Kobo
And all good book shops

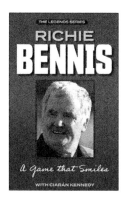

'A Game that Smiles'
The Richie Bennis Autobiography

RICHIE BENNIS IS one of the true legends remaining in the game of hurling. A towering figure in Limerick GAA, he played a central role as the county won the All-Ireland title in 1973 and then he strived as hard as anyone to see the Liam MacCarthy Cup return to the Treaty County.

It was a wait of 45 years – during which time Bennis worked at grassroots hurling in the famed Patrickswell club, where he hurled into his 40s and won 10 county titles. He also led Limerick as team manager to the 2007 All-Ireland final where they lost to Kilkenny.

In 2018, Limerick were crowned All-Ireland champions.

For Richie Bennis, a long agonising wait ended. His story is one of triumph, and heartache and personal tragedy, and a courage that was never dimmed.

Authors: Richie Bennis with Ciarán Kennedy
Print Price: €20.00
ISBN: 9781910827093

Available on
Amazon
Apple Books
Kobo
And all good book shops

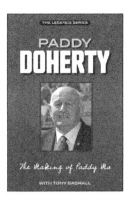

The Making of Paddy Mo
Paddy Doherty: An Autobiography

TO THIS DAY, Down's Paddy Doherty is still remembered as one of the most lethal finishers in the history of Gaelic football. The Ballykinlar clubman was fast, and breathtaking on the ball.

He led his county to a long awaited All-Ireland victory in 1960, and the following summer he captained the Mournemen and brought the Sam Maguire Cup back across the border a second time.

Doherty continued to rip apart defences throughout the decade and won a third All-Ireland crown with Down in 1968, when the Mournemen defeated Kerry in September for the second time, to add to seven Ulster titles and three National league titles.

The 1960s was a decade which is best remembered for the legend of Paddy Doherty.

And... The Making of Paddy Mo.

Authors: Paddy Doherty with Tony Bagnall
Print Price: €20.00
Ebook: €10.00
ISBN: 9781910827178

Available on
Amazon
Apple Books
Kobo
And all good book shops

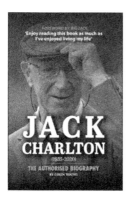

Jack Charlton
The Authorised Biography

AS ONE OF the true legends of Irish and English football, Jack Charlton was a man both loved and feared, but now the people who have lived with him all of his life introduce the real 'Big Jack' in this brilliant authorised biography which is presented in a foreword by Jack himself.

For the first time Jack's wife and family, his teammates as a World Cup winner with England in 1966, and his players during his management years with Middlesbrough, Sheffield Wednesday, Newcastle, and Ireland tell their stories of the man who dominated their lives.

Graeme Souness, Chris Waddle, and Peter Beardsley amongst others, are joined by Mick McCarthy, Niall Quinn and the greatest footballers who played under Big Jack for 10 years as Ireland team boss.

This is the most personable, inviting and intimate account of Jack Charlton's life, and the book contains photographs published for the first time from Jack and Pat Charlton's personal collection.

Jack Charlton: The Authorised Biography is written by former Daily Mail Northern Football Correspondent, Colin Young.

Author: Colin Young
Print Price: €20.00
Ebook: €10.00
ISBN: 9781910827017

Available on
Amazon
And all good book shops

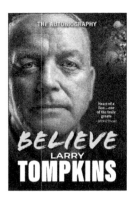

BELIEVE

Larry Tompkins: An Autobiography

HIS SELF-BELIEF WAS unbreakable.

His iron will inspirational.

Nothing could stop Larry Tompkins. No man, no team, as he made his football life the greatest story ever told in the long and brilliant history of the GAA.

Six years with his native Kildare left him empty-handed and heartbroken. He emigrated to New York to find a job and find a team he could lead to championship glory. In the United States, Tompkins' belief in himself never dimmed. He led Donegal to four New York championships in the Big Apple. He also found a new home for himself in Ireland and led Castlehaven to two Cork and Munster titles. In between, he also became the most valuable and feared footballer in Ireland.

BELIEVE is the story of a man who defied all the odds. In Cork's magnificent red shirt, he led his adopted county to two All-Ireland titles in 1989 and 90, one National League and six Munster titles, and he also was honoured with three Allstar awards.

Upon his retirement, Larry Tompkins continued to lead and inspire, and make others believe too. He managed Cork for seven years, winning Munster glory again, and drove Cork to the 1999 All-Ireland final where they agonisingly came up short.

BELIEVE is a story which proves to everyone, in every sport, that anything is possible and everything is there to be won!

Authors: Larry Tompkins with Denis Hurley
Print Price: €20.00
Ebook: €10.00
ISBN: 9781910827123

Available on
Amazon
Apple Books
Kobo
And all good book shops

Dark Arts
Mike Ross: An Autobiography

FOR THE FIRST time, Mike Ross brings sports fans into the dark heart of the professional game of rugby union. Ross is recognised as the greatest scrummager in Irish rugby history – and the man who was the foundation stone for the beginning of the Joe Schmidt era, which saw Leinster win back-to-back Heineken Cups and Ireland become the greatest team in Europe.

But Mike Ross might never have been a professional rugby player. He did not turn pro until he was 26 years of age. And he spent three years learning his trade at the toughest end of the game with Harlequins in England before coming home at 30, and chasing the dream of an Irish jersey.

Ross would play 61 times for Ireland, and over 150 times for Leinster. His story is one of big dreams and amazing courage, on and off the field.

He writes about the good times and the hardest times, facing the true beasts of the professional game every weekend. And he writes about his own life, and the suicide of his younger brother, Andrew at 16 years of age with an honesty and compassion that is rewarding for everyone who has experienced the sudden death of a loved one and has to rebuild their lives.

Authors: Mike Ross with Liam Hayes
Print Price: €20.00
Ebook: €10.00
ISBN: 9781910827048

Available on
Amazon
Apple Books
Kobo
And all good online stores

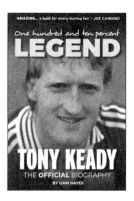

One Hundred and Ten Percent Legend
Tony Keady: The Official Biography

WHEN TONY KEADY died suddenly in August of 2017, at just 53 years of age, a whole county mourned and the rest of the country stopped in its tracks to say goodbye to a legend of the game of hurling.

Except Tony Keady was more than a legend.

In 1988, after leading Galway to a second All-Ireland title in succession, he was crowned the greatest hurler in Ireland. He was 25 years of age and there was nobody like him, nobody to touch him in the maroon No.6 shirt.

But, four years later, and still not 30, after being wrongly banned for 12 months by the GAA, he was also discarded by his own county and refused a maroon jersey the very last time he walked out onto Croke Park behind the Galway team.

A few months before his death, Tony Keady visited Liam Hayes and told him he wished to tell his own story. He felt it was time, but tragically time was not on Tony's side. One month after he died Galway won the All-Ireland title for the first time since 1988, and 80,000 people rose from their seats in the sixth minute of the game to applaud and remember a man who was more than a legend

Tony's wife, Margaret and his daughter, Shannon and his three boys, Anthony, Harry and Jake, decided to finish telling the story of a father and a hurler who always asked those around him for '110%'.

Author: Liam Hayes
Price: €20.00
ISBN: 9781910827048

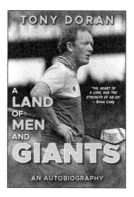

A Land of Men and Giants
The Tony Doran Autobiography

WEXFORD'S ALL-IRELAND winning hero Tony Doran was a giant in the game of hurling through the 1960s, 70s and 80s, at a time when full-forwards were ordered to plunder goals.

In his 19 years and 187 appearances as a Wexford hurler, Tony Doran successfully went for goal 131 times.

But Doran also played against giants from Kilkenny, Tipperary and Cork, and so many other counties, at a time when the game of hurling tested the wits and the courage of every man on the field.

Some of these men became giants.

A Land of Men and Giants is the story told by Tony Doran of a life spent living and competing against legendary men and true giants of the game.

A Land of Men and Giants: The Autobiography of Tony Doran is edited by award-winning writer and author Liam Hayes.

Authors: Tony Doran with Liam Hayes
Print Price: €20.00
ISBN: 9781910827031

Available on
Amazon

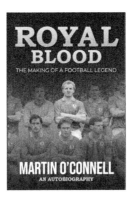

Royal Blood
Martin O'Connell: An Autobiography

THREE TIMES ALL-IRELAND winner, Martin O'Connell was crowned the prince of wing backs in 2000 when he was selected on the GAA's Team of the Millennium, and had a postage stamp issued in his honour.

This honour also stamped O'Connell's name down in Meath football history as the greatest of the greats.

As a Meath footballer, O'Connell truly had Royal Blood. He was a central player on Sean Boylan's 1987 and 88 All-Ireland winning teams, and then remained with Boylan to win a third All-Ireland in 1996 in an infamous replayed final against Mayo.

Now, O'Connell reveals the inside story of those battling years, and explains how it might never have happened after he quit the Meath team in the mid 80s. But his love of the game brought him back.

In addition to his three All-Irelands, Martin O'Connell won six Leinster titles and three National league titles and in 1996 was named Footballer of the Year. After retiring from the Meath team he continued playing football with St Michael's, his club and his first love in football, until he was 42 years old.

Authors: Martin O'Connell and David Sheehan
Print Price: €20.00
Ebook: €10.00
ISBN: 9781910827109

Available on
Amazon
Apple Books
Kobo
And all good online stores

Printed in Great Britain
by Amazon

72951824R00149